CALVIN'S OLD TESTAME

THE RUTHERFORD HOU

General Editor

D. F. WRIGHT

assisted by

D. F. KELLY

Consultant Editors

T. H. L. Parker, J. H. Leith, J. I. Packer, R. S. Wallace

Contributing Editors

R. C. Gamble, D. C. Lachman, A. N. S. Lane, J. G. McConville

CALVIN'S OLD TESTAMENT COMMENTARIES

Calvin's Old Testament Commentaries

Volume 20

DANIEL I

(Chapters 1-6)

Translated by

T. H. L. Parker

*John Calvin's Lectures
on the Book of
The Prophecies of Daniel*

*Taken down by the effort and industry of
Jean Budé and Charles Joinviller*

Geneva, MDLXI

WILLIAM B. EERDMANS PUBLISHING COMPANY, GRAND RAPIDS

THE PATERNOSTER PRESS, CARLISLE

Published 1993 jointly by Wm. B. Eerdmans Publishing Co. and
The Paternoster Press,
P.O. Box 300, Carlisle, Cumbria, CA3 0QS UK

Printed in the United States of America

Library of Congress Cataloging-in-Publication Data

Calvin, Jean, 1509-1564.
    [Praelectiones in librum prophetiarum Danielis. English]
    Daniel / translated by T. H. L. Parker.
       p.   cm.   — (Calvin's Old Testament commentaries; v. 20-)
    "John Calvin's lectures on the Book of the prophecies of Daniel.
Taken down by the effort and industry of Jean Budé and Charles Joinviller."
    Includes bibliographical references and indexes.
    Contents: 1. Chapters 1-6.
    ISBN 0-8028-2451-X (cloth) (v. 1)
    ISBN 0-8028-0750-X (paper) (v. 1)
    1. Bible. O. T. Daniel — Commentaries — Early works to 1800. 2. Bible. O. T.
Daniel — Prophecies. I. Parker, T. H. L. (Thomas Henry Louis) II. Budé, Jean,
1558-1610. III. Joan, Charles de, 16th cent. IV. Title. V. Series: Calvin, Jean,
1509-1564. Selections. English. 1993; v. 20-
BS1150.C35 1993 vol. 20, etc.
[BS1555]
221.7 s — dc20
[224'.507]   92-29588
                                               CIP

British Library Cataloguing in Publication Data

Calvin, Jean
    Daniel 1: Chapters 1-6. - Rev. ed. -
    (Calvin's Old Testament Commentaries Series; Vol. 20)
    I. Title II. Parker, T. H. L. III. Series
    224
    ISBN 0-85364-572-8 (cloth)
    ISBN 0-85364-573-6 (paper)

Contents

CONTENTS

General Preface

John Calvin is widely known as a man of one book — the author of the celebrated *Institutio* of the Christian religion. Yet for all the influence of that work, Calvin's most substantial legacy is his expositions of the Bible — the sermons, lectures, and commentaries on which he expended so much energy throughout his ministry at Geneva. Their qualities have often been praised. They remain more accessible and more instructive to the modern student of the Scriptures than any other corpus of biblical exposition from the sixteenth century.

English translations of Calvin's commentaries began to appear soon after they were first published. (As conventionally used, the category of commentaries encompasses both the lectures and the commentaries strictly so called; for the distinction see T. H. L. Parker, *Calvin's Old Testament Commentaries* [Edinburgh, 1986].) A complete version of both Old and New Testament commentaries was produced in the nineteenth century by the energies of the Calvin Translation Society. The New Testament ones were retranslated more recently under the editorship of D. W. Torrance and T. F. Torrance (Edinburgh, 1959-71). Given the distinctive place accorded to the Old Testament in the Reformed tradition of which Calvin was the most significant creator, it is only proper that his Old Testament commentaries be similarly set forth in a new translation.

The aim of the translation is simply stated — to let Calvin speak in his own words, as far as translation into another language allows. Annotation has been kept to a minimum, and the temptation to comment on Calvin's comments has been strictly eschewed. The translation has been done from the original sixteenth-century editions. The only feature of these editions not reproduced in this version is the text of the Hebrew Bible which some of them set alongside

Calvin's own Latin translation of it. In the course of his translation and commentary Calvin often cites Hebrew words. Where he does not provide a transliteration, one is given in square brackets, which are used to identify any such additions. For example, when Calvin includes words or phrases in Greek or French without translating them into Latin, an English translation is provided in square brackets. The sign 'Mg.' in the notes indicates that the following biblical reference is given in the margin of the sixteenth-century edition used.

In such an enterprise editors become debtors to many other labourers in the same field. We wish in particular to pay tribute to the encouragement, counsel, and critical reading of the Consultant Editors, and the participation of the Contributing Editors, of whom A. N. S. Lane painstakingly checked references and J. G. McConville the Hebrew, D. C. Lachman provided the bibliographical introduction, and R. C. Gamble assisted from the resources of the Meeter Center. And not least are thanks due to Dr. Nigel M. de S. Cameron, the first Warden of Rutherford House, for his energetic contribution to setting this translation project on course.

Our prayer is that these new translations will enable a new generation to appreciate the Old Testament expositions of one who was content to be known as the servant of the Word of God.

Rutherford House   The General Editors
17 Claremont Park
Edinburgh

Translator's Preface

The reader unacquainted with Calvin's Old Testament commentaries may be surprised on opening this book to find a set of lectures. In fact, from about 1555 all his Old Testament lectures were recorded verbatim by a team of three stenographers and printed as they stood (obvious slips were corrected when the lecture was read back to Calvin the next day). Consequently, all his 'commentaries' on the prophets, apart from Isaiah, consist of lectures to older schoolboys and students in training for 'missionary' work, principally in France. Besides these there were a number of older auditors — ministers from Geneva and the surrounding villages, for example, and better-educated refugees.

It will be helpful if we expand on this brief statement, so that the reader may know how he should approach the work.

In the first place, we have verbatim records of lectures, almost unedited (the 'almost' will be explained shortly), with many incidental asides, and familiarities, and repetitions. This means that we must read them with some degree of indulgence and also with the exercise of imagination.

With indulgence, in that we are not to expect the careful and precise style of the *Institutio*. Anyone lecturing extemporarily is bound, however powerful his intellect and whatever his command over words, to repeat himself and even now and then to commit himself to a form of words that he sees is going to land him into syntactical trouble before the end of the sentence. There is not a little repetition here and even the occasional obscurity of expression.

Imagination is also called for in the reading. Let the reader transport himself to a lecture room full, largely, of schoolboys in their teens. They will be busily taking notes of what Monsieur Calvin is saying. Sometimes, however, their raised faces register incomprehension. The lecturer notices it and repeats

ix

the point in other words. Now and then they seem to fail to understand the Latin and he repeats it in French.

An important aspect that must be noticed is that Calvin not only used no notes and did not dictate the lectures but also translated the biblical text extemporarily from the Hebrew (and Aramaic). This fact accounts for the varieties of renderings of the same word or phrase that we meet with. It also accounts for the frequent glosses on the text (which we place within brackets and print in roman characters to distinguish them from the biblical text in italics). In preparation for Calvin's expository lecture the boys had a Hebrew lesson on the passage from the Hebrew professor.

A further consequence in this respect is that when Calvin uses a Hebrew word we are given a valuable glimpse of his Hebrew pronunciation (and perhaps of that of the sixteenth century in general). Because these are verbatim records the Hebrew words are given as the scribes heard them pronounced by Calvin. The scribes recorded them not in their Hebrew characters but as transcripts or transliterations in the Latin alphabet. The Hebrew characters were added by the editor (and this is the qualification made earlier). It is for this reason that we have kept the transcripts as the scribes recorded them from Calvin's pronunciation and have avoided the unnecessary refinement of providing them also in modern form.

The substance of the lectures may be read in more than one way (and here no indulgence is needed!). We can study them as examples of sixteenth-century lecturing style and method. These on Daniel were from the first recognized as unusual; 'often more like history lectures than expositions of Scripture' was how one hearer described them, and the editors of *Corpus Reformatorum* in the nineteenth century even hesitated over including them because they did not conform to the modern conception of a commentary. Again, the historian of France will find them continually relevant to the beginnings of the French wars of religion. Yet again, the student of Calvin and his theology may read them for the light they throw on his life and thought.

But in the last resort, the lectures, for all their sixteenth-century dress, offer us a valid exposition of the prophet Daniel. Whatever may be said against the interpretation of individual places and the naivety of some of the judgments, the main drift is coherent and theologically firm. In place of the traditional referring of the prophecies to empires and persons and events in the post–New Testament era (Mohammed, the Pope, the Holy Roman Empire, Napoleon, Hitler, etc.), Calvin fixes a steadfast bound at 'Christ and his gospel'. All the prophecies relate, for Calvin, to the history of the period between the latter part of the Babylonian captivity and the preaching of the apostles. Christ is the end of classical history. If the lectures were history lessons, the message of Daniel was not relativized to classical history but classical history to Jesus Christ.

T. H. L. P.

Bibliographical Note

Calvin began his lectures on Daniel on 12th June 1559 and completed them in early April 1560. In his 14th September 1561 dedication 'to all sincere worshippers of God who desire the kingdom of Christ to be rightly constituted in France', he compared the situation of Daniel and his companions with that of the persecuted saints in France. Whether or not he undertook to lecture on Daniel with their plight in mind, he saw the opportunity afforded him by the publication of these lectures as providential, enabling him to illustrate to them how God proves the faith of his people by various trials.

The first edition, from which this translation is made, was published as:

> *Ionannis Calvini Praelectiones in librum prophetiarum Danielis,* Ioannis Budaei & Caroli Ionuillaei labore & industria exceptae . . . Genevae. M.D.LXI.

A French translation, almost certainly not by Calvin himself, was issued the following year:

> *Leçons de M. Iean Calvin sur le livre des propheties de Daniel,* Receuillies fidelement par Iean Budé et Charles de Ionuiller, ses auditeurs . . . Geneve: M.D.LXII.

The most accessible Latin edition is in:

> *Calvini Opera* 40-41 (*Corpus Reformatorum* 68-69; Braunschweig, 1889).

A somewhat abridged English translation by A. Gilby of the lectures on the first six chapters was published as:

BIBLIOGRAPHICAL NOTE

> *Commentaries of that divine Iohn Calvine upon the Prophet Daniell,*
> London: Iohn Daye, 1570.

The first and hitherto only complete English translation was that of the Calvin Translation Society by Thomas Myers, under the title:

> *Commentaries on the Book of the Prophet Daniel,* two volumes, Edinburgh: Calvin Translation Society, 1852-1853.

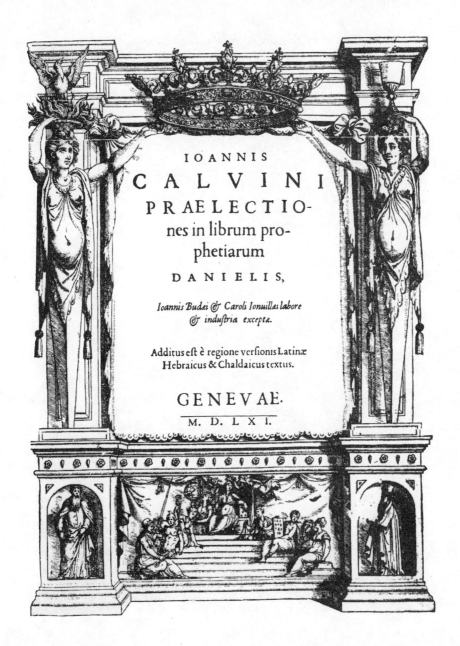

IOANNIS
CALVINI
PRAELECTIO-
nes in librum pro-
phetiarum
DANIELIS,

Ioannis Budæi & Caroli Ionuillæi labore
& industria excepta.

Additus est è regione versionis Latinæ
Hebraicus & Chaldaicus textus.

GENEVAE.
M. D. LXI.

John Calvin

*to all God's faithful servants who long for Christ's
kingdom to be well ordered in France,
Greetings!*

You and I have a homeland in common, a land whose loveliness attracts so many strangers from far shores. Yet for twenty-six years I have been absent from it without regret. For to live in a land from which God's truth, pure religion, and the preaching of eternal salvation have been banished, from which Christ's kingdom has been cast out, would not be at all pleasant or desirable; nor does a desire for it tempt me today. But it would be inhuman and wrong for me to forget the race from which I am descended, to cease to care for it. And I think that I have given clear proofs of how earnestly and warmly I desire to help our fellow-countrymen; it may be that my absence has actually been an advantage in that my studies have brought them richer fruits. The thought of such good not only wipes away all my sorrow but even makes my exile sweet and happy.

And so, since over all this time I have striven to help Frenchmen by my publications (nor have I ceased privately to arouse the slothful, to goad the laggards, to encourage the fearful, to exhort the hesitant or inconstant to perseverance), I must now take great care that my duty towards them does not cease at this time of crisis. An excellent opportunity has now been divinely given. For in publishing the lectures in which I interpreted the prophecies of Daniel it fell out most conveniently that I could show you, my heartily beloved brothers, as if in this mirror, that when God wished in this age to try the faith of his people by various assaults, in his wonderful wisdom he took care to support their minds on the old examples, so that they might never yield, never be broken by even the severest storms and tempests; or at the least, if they should ever waver, that they should not utterly fall. For although the race-

1

course set for God's servants is strewn with many obstacles, yet anyone who carefully considers this book will find that it contains everything useful for guiding a willing and energetic runner from starting point to finishing post. Good and active athletes will also acknowledge from experience that they have been well trained for the race.

First comes the sad but very useful story of how Daniel and his friends were carried into exile, while the kingdom and the priesthood were still standing. It was as if God had assigned the very flower of the chosen people through ignominy and shame to the depths of affliction. For at first sight what could be more shameful than that youths endowed with almost angelic virtues should fall prey as slaves to a haughty conqueror while the most wicked and abandoned despisers of God stayed safe at home? Is it a right reward for godliness and innocence that saints should suffer the punishment deserved by the ungodly — who all the while happily congratulate themselves that they have escaped scot-free? But here, lest we should find it hard that the irreligious quietly flourish while we are cast into the furnace of testing, we see as in a living image that while God spares the most wicked for a time, even shows them kindness, he tries his servants like gold and silver.

Second, there is an example of more than mature wisdom and remarkable temperance. These godly youths, still at a tender age, were being tempted by the enticements of the court. With a quite heroic nobleness of mind they were temperate and rose above the delights set before them. More, to extricate themselves from the snares of the devil, when they saw they were being cunningly entrapped to desert the sincere worship of God, they firmly and freely spurned the poison-tainted honour, even though in peril of instant death.

There follows a yet more ferocious and fearful context in a memorable example of incredible steadfastness. Daniel's friends were not moved by fierce threats to pollute themselves by worshipping the statue. In the end they were ready to vindicate the sincere worship of God not merely by their blood but even by the horrifying execution they were shown. The goodness of God which illumines the outcome of this drama [*tragoedia*] avails not a little to arm us with an invincible trust.

A somewhat similar contest and victory for Daniel himself is added. He preferred to encounter the fierce lions rather than to forgo for three days[a] an open confession of faith. Otherwise, by faithless pretence he might have exposed God's holy name to the mockeries of the ungodly. But, wonderfully rescued from the den as if from the grave, he triumphed over Satan and his party.

Here we do not encounter philosophers subtly and detachedly debating about virtues at their leisure, but the indefatigable constancy in godliness of holy

a. Text: *triduo* ('for three days'); cf. Dn. 6:7, etc. ('thirty days').

2

men challenges us with a clear voice to imitate them. Unless we are completely unteachable we ought to learn from these masters a wise caution, so as not to be ensnared if Satan tries to trap us with flattery; or if he attacks us with violence, to break down his assaults by intrepid contempt of death and all evils. Should anyone object that the examples of both the liberations we have recounted were rare, I freely confess that God does not always stretch forth his hand from heaven to rescue his people like that. But it should be enough for us that he solemnly and faithfully declares that he will be the guardian of our life whenever we are in danger. And if it seem good to him, he will check the fury and wild onslaughts of the ungodly when we are exposed to their passions. Yet we should not look only at the outcome but also at how courageously those holy men gave themselves up to death that they might maintain the glory of God. The fact that in God's kindness they were saved does not make their readiness any the less praiseworthy, for they had offered themselves in sacrifice.

It is important to consider how many were the disturbances that the prophet encountered during the seventy years of his exile. By none of the kings was he treated so humanely as by Nebuchadnezzar; and yet even him he found to be a wild beast. From the others greater cruelty; until on the sudden downfall of Belshazzar and the sack of the city, he was transferred to new rulers, the Medes and Persians. Their invasion filled everyone with fear and no doubt it daunted him as well. Although he was singled out in Darius's favour, so that his captivity was almost tolerable, yet the envy of the princes with their wicked conspiracy put him in extreme danger. But he had more care for the common safety of the Church than for his own quiet; how much sorrow must he not have felt, how much anxiety, when the state of affairs promised no end to the harsh and wretched oppression of his people! He believed in Jeremiah's prediction,[1] certainly. But it showed incomparable endurance that his hope did not fail when it was kept so long in suspense, when, tossed to and fro by tempestuous wave after wave, it was not drowned.

Now I come to the prophecies themselves. The earlier ones were intended for the Babylonians; partly because God wished to adorn his servant with definite insignia, which would compel that most proud, all-conquering nation to respect him, and partly because his name had to be thought worthy of respect among the heathen so that he might use this authority to exercise his prophetic office the more freely among his own people. After he had become famous among the Chaldaeans, God committed to him more important prophecies, peculiar to the elect people.

Moreover, God so accommodated the prophecies to the use of those people of olden times, softening sadness with timely remedies and upholding wavering minds until the advent of Christ, as to be no less relevant for our

1. Je. 25:12; 29:10.

age also. For what was foretold of the fluctuating and ephemeral splendour of the monarchies and of the perpetual state of Christ's kingdom is no less profitable to know nowadays than of old. For God shows that all earthly power which is not founded on Christ is perishing, and that speedy destruction is threatened to all kingdoms which over-exalt themselves and obscure the glory of Christ. Those kings who now rule over their wide dominions will, unless they willingly subject themselves to the rule of Christ, at last find by sad experience that that fearful judgment[2] refers to them also. What can be less endurable than that he, under whose protection their dignity remains safe, should be defrauded of his right? But we see how few of them admit the Son of God; they will leave no stone unturned, they will go to any lengths, to stop him crossing their borders. Many ministers of the crown also bestow all their care and industry on shutting the gates. They may claim to be Christian kings and boast that they are excellent 'Defenders of the Catholic Faith',[3] but such idle nothings are easily refuted if we hold a true and genuine definition of Christ's kingdom. For his throne or sceptre is nothing other than the teaching of the gospel. Only when all, from the highest to the lowest, hear his voice with quiet teachableness as his sheep and follow whithersoever he calls, does his majesty shine forth and his rule prevail.

In this teaching is contained a religion of certainty and the legitimate service of God. In it stand man's eternal salvation and true happiness. Yet they not only everywhere repudiate it but even drive it out with threats, terrors, steel and flame and use every violence to exterminate it. What blindness, what strange blindness, not to allow those whom the only-begotten Son of God gently invites to himself, to embrace him! Many in their pride think they would be degraded if they acknowledged their inferiority to the supreme King. Others refuse to have their passions bridled; and, since hypocrisy occupies the senses of all, they love the darkness and fear to be brought into the light. Yet there is no bane worse than Herod's fear[4] — as if he who offers the kingdom of heaven to the lowest and most contemptible of the common people would steal earthly empires from monarchs! Moreover, so long as some simply look to others, a mutual binding keeps them all in a deadly association under the yoke of ungodliness. For if they thought seriously about the true and right questions, if they merely opened their eyes, the knowledge would not be obscure.

But because it is quite usual for serious commotions to occur when Christ comes forth with his gospel, they think only of public order and have an honest excuse to reject the heavenly teaching. I agree that any change which gives

2. Dn. 5:26-28.
3. A title assumed by some European kings, but Calvin has particularly in mind the King of France.
4. Mt. 2:3, 16ff.

4

rise to disturbances can deservedly be seen as detestable. But it is a grave injury to God if he is not even granted the power to establish the kingdom of his Son when any tumults that may arise have been settled. Were heaven and earth to be turned upside down, the service of God is too precious for the least diminution of it to be weighed against any advantage. But those who pretend that the gospel is the source of disturbances lay an untrue infamy on it. Certainly it is true that God thunders in the gospel with a mighty voice that shakes heaven and earth. When the prophet gains acceptance for his preaching by this saying, it is a happy and desirable shaking.[5] And certainly, if God's glory is not pre-eminent until all flesh has been humbled, then human pride, which opposes that glory and never surrenders willingly to it, must be cast down by the strong and powerful hand of God himself. For if at the publishing of the Law the earth trembled,[6] it is not surprising that the force and efficacy of the gospel should appear more majestically. Therefore we should embrace with greater pleasure that teaching which rouses the dead out of hell and opens heaven for the unworthy on earth, which puts forth such extraordinary power that it is as if all the elements were in accord for our salvation.

But lo and behold! storms and tempests flow from another source. The nobles and great ones of the world will not freely submit to the yoke of Christ, and the ignorant masses reject everything that is for their salvation before they have even tried it. Some delight themselves in filthiness, like swine. Others riot and massacre as if they were stirred up by the Furies.[7] But some the devil completely enslaves and excites with especial fury to create every sort of riot. Hence the trumpetings, hence the conflicts and the battles when the Roman priest, that Heliogabalus,[8] at the head of his red and bloody cohort and his horned beasts, charges in reckless attack on Christ, reinforced by the filthy dregs of his clergy (from the same pot they all suck the gobbets with which they are fed, even if not with equal elegance). Many hungry offer themselves as mercenaries. A large part of the judges, so accustomed to stuff their bellies with sumptuous feasts, fight 'For kitchen and oven'.[9] But above all, out from the monkish cloisters and Sorbonnic[10] dens have come the rabble that kindle and fan the flames. I omit the secret scheming and wicked conspiracies — my best witnesses could be those

5. Hg. 2:7.

6. Mg., Ex. 19:18.

7. The Furies: the three daughters of Night and Acheron (see p. 6, n. 11).

8. Heliogabalus: the Roman Emperor Marcus Aurelius Antoninus (d. 222), infamous for his licentiousness (also, 'Elagabalus').

9. *pro culina et foco:* obviously a sardonic variant (by Calvin? or Erasmus?) of the common classical phrase *pugnare pro aris et focis,* 'to fight for hearth and home' (literally, 'for altars and hearths').

10. Sorbonnic: a reference to the rabidly anti-Reform Collège de la Sorbonne in Paris, the theological voice of the university.

who are the worst enemies of godliness. I name no one. It is enough to hint at some who are only too well known by you.

In this confused invasion of so many wild beasts it is not surprising if those who consider only the complex results of events are perplexed. But it is unjust and wicked of them to throw the blame of their lack of faith on the holy gospel of Christ. Grant that all Acheron[11] with its Furies engages in the battle. Does God sit idly in heaven, deserting and betraying his own cause? And when he has taken arms, will man's cleverness or craftiness or onslaughts hinder God's victory? The pope, they say, has the majority on his side — the just reward of unbelief, to start at the rustle of a falling leaf! You ministers of the crown, why are you so short-sighted? 'Let Christ depart, in case there should be disturbances.' Therefore you will soon feel how much better it would have been to have God on your side and to trust in his help and to despise all your fears, rather than to provoke him to open battle — merely lest you should anger the evil and the wicked.

Of course, when everything has been weighed up, the superstition hitherto prevalent among defenders of the pope is nothing but evil well presented; for they think it should not be removed for fear of the damage resulting. But those who have God's glory at heart and are endowed with sincere piety should have a very different object — so to devote all their activities to God as to commit all the results to his providence. If he had given us no promise, we should perhaps have just cause for fear and continual vacillation. But when he has so often declared that he will never withhold help when the kingdom of his Christ is being maintained, the only way to act aright is to rest on this trust.

Moreover, it is your task, my best of brethren, to take all prudent care that true religion may regain a sound position — that is, so far as each shall have the faculty and the calling. There is no need for me to say how greatly hitherto I have striven to remove any occasion for tumults. I call the angels and you all to bear witness before the supreme Judge that it is none of my doing that the progress of the kingdom of Christ has not been quiet and harmless. Indeed, I judge that it is due to my carefulness that private persons have not overstepped their bounds.

Now, although God has, by his wonderful power, advanced the restoration of his Church further than I would have dared to hope, yet we must still recall to mind what Christ commands his people — that they must possess their souls in patience.[12] The vision explained by Daniel[13] is relevant here: that stone which crushed all the kingdoms undertaking war against God was

11. Acheron: one of the rivers in hell.
12. Mg., Lk. 21:19.
13. Dn. 2:31-35.

not formed by men's hands; and rough and unpolished as it was, it increased to become a great mountain. I have urged you to be warned by this, so that you may wait quietly in the midst of the thunders and threats until at last those empty clouds will be dispersed by heavenly power and vanish away.

Yet I am well aware of how many indignities you have suffered in these last six months — let alone the innumerable fires throughout thirty years. I know that in many places you have often known the violence of rioting mobs, the bombarding with stones, the attacks with naked steel. I know how your enemies have watched and waited and then suddenly and unexpectedly broken up your peaceful meetings with violence. I know how some have been killed in their homes, some in the open streets; dead bodies dragged round for sport; women raped; many men beaten up; even a pregnant woman and her unborn baby pierced through; houses broken open and looted. But although far worse atrocities may still await you, you must show that you are Christ's disciples, well trained in his school; you must take care that no raging, intemperate actions of the ungodly shall shake you out of the moderation you have so far shown and which alone has overcome and broken all their assaults.

And if you should get worn down by the long struggle, remember this great prophecy which exactly depicts the state of the Church. At that time God showed his prophet what conflicts, anxieties, troubles, dangers the Jews would know from the end of the exile and their joyful return to their own land until the advent of Christ. But this contains a temporal analogy; these same things are true of us — indeed, they are to be adapted to our use. Daniel rejoiced for the wretched Church, so long submerged under a deep flood of evils, when he deduced from a reckoning up of the years that the day of liberation predicted by Jeremiah[14] was at hand. But he received the reply that the people's lot would be harder from the time they were set free, so that they would hardly recover from the continual succession of terrible calamities.

Their hope had been upheld for seventy years, but not without profound bitterness and sorrow and intense abhorrence. Now, however, God multiplied the time sevenfold and inflicted an almost mortal wound on their hearts. He declared that when the people had gathered strength after their return and had rebuilt the city and the temple, they would have to undergo fresh troubles. Not only that, but even in the midst of their first joy, when they had barely tasted the sweetness of his kindness, he assigned them to distress. What a catalogue of disasters soon followed! They are frightening even to listen to, and we can imagine how grievous and bitter they must have been to this ignorant people. To see the temple profaned by the audacity of a sacrilegious tyrant, the sacred things defiled and stained, all the books of the Law cast into the fire, and all religion abolished — what a horrifying sight! To see all who boldly and frankly

14. Mg., Je. 25:12; 29:10.

7

confessed that they stood firm in the worship of God thrown into the fire — what weak, feeble man could view it without profound dismay? But it was the tyrant's intention to drive the faint-hearted into apostasy by fierceness.

Under the Maccabees some relaxation seems to have been granted, but it was soon marred by savage massacres and it was never free from affliction and distress. For the enemy was far superior in men and munitions and there was nothing left for all who had taken arms in defence of the Church than to hide in the dens of wild beasts or to roam the woods in great need, completely destitute. Another sort of trial came when wicked and faithless men, boasting falsely of their zeal, as Daniel says, joined Judas [Maccabeus] and his brothers. This was an artifice of Satan, to spatter with infamy the band collected by Judas, as if they were bandits.

But the worst thing for the righteous was when some of the priests themselves became ambitious and betrayed the temple and worship of God by wicked pacts. For not only was the sacred office up for sale but it was purchased by murderous feuds, and even killing of fathers. So it happened that, although men of all ranks kept circumcision and sacrifices, they at last everywhere profaned them openly with corruptions, so that at the time that Christ appeared it was a rare miracle for anyone to be looking for the kingdom of God. Very few are praised for doing this.

Now, all through that shameful deformity of the Church, through the many scatterings abroad, among the dreadful terrors, the devastation of the countryside, the plundering of houses, the perils of death, Daniel's prediction upheld the minds of the godly. But that was when religion was still wrapped in obscure shadows and teaching was almost extinct and the very priests were degenerate and ruining everything that was sacred. How shameful, then, will be our weakness if the clear light of the gospel, in which God shows us his face as Father, does not lift us above all obstacles and strengthen us to inde-fatigable constancy! There is no doubt that in those days God's servants accommodated to their own age what the prophets had said about the Baby-lonian exile, so that they might soften unhappiness over contemporary troubles. In the same way we should fix our eyes on the miseries of those fathers and so not refuse to be gathered to that Church to which it was said, 'Poor little one, overwhelmed by tempest and comfortless! Lo, I will uphold you';[15] to that Church which elsewhere, after she had bemoaned that her back had been torn open by the ungodly like a field furrowed by the plough, went on rejoicing that their cords had been cut by the just Judge so that they did not prevail.[16]

The prophet did not encourage us to hope and patience simply by ex-amples from those days. He added an exhortation, dictated by the Spirit, which

15. Mg., Is. 54:11.
16. Mg., Ps. 129:1-4.

extends to the entire kingdom of Christ and belongs to us. Therefore, let it not be hard for us to be included in the number of those whom he declares will be tested by fire and made white;[17] for all the distresses of the cross are more than compensated for by the inestimable felicity and glory which it bears. Most find these things meaningless. Let us not be infected with their laziness and dullness but keep firmly in our hearts what the prophet soon after declares, that the ungodly will behave ungodly because they do not understand, but God's children will be endowed with understanding so that they may hold to the right course of the divine calling.[18]

It is also important to grasp what is the source of this common brutish blindness, so that we may delight in the heavenly teaching. The greater part despise Christ and his gospel because they please themselves quite fearlessly and with no sense of their ills; God's anger does not move them to horror and to desire earnestly and ardently the redemption that alone rescues us from the eternal abyss of destruction. They are captivated, or rather, bewitched, by pleasures and gratifications and other snares, and have no interest in a blessed eternity. There are numberless groups who contemptuously dismiss the teaching of the gospel; among some of them we chiefly see pride, among others weakness, among some a sort of intellectual drunkenness, among others a drowsy sluggishness. Yet we shall find that the contempt flows from a profane sense of security, in that none descends into himself to investigate his miseries and to seek a remedy for them. When God's curse falls upon us and his righteous vengeance presses upon us, it is monstrous insanity to cast off all care and go on pleasing ourselves as if we had nothing to fear. But it is an all too common fault that those who are a thousand times guilty and deserve a thousand eternal deaths cover up their drowsiness (or rather, laziness) with trifling ceremonies carelessly performed towards God.

Now, Paul declares that the gospel is a smell of death to all whose minds Satan has bewitched.[19] So if we are to taste its savour unto life, it is necessary for us to stand at God's judgment seat and there at once accuse our consciences, so that we may be wounded by a heartfelt dread and recognize the worth and value of the reconciliation that Christ has won for us by his precious blood. And so the angel,[b] to gain respect and authority for Christ's doctrine, preaches on the eternal righteousness which he sealed by the sacrifice of his death; and at the same time he expresses the manner and the purpose — that iniquity should be wiped out and expiated. Therefore, while the world goes on revelling

17. Dn. 11:35.
18. Dn. 12:10.
19. Mg., 2 Cor. 2:16.
b. If *Angelus* is the correct reading, the reference is to Dn. 9:20-27; if emended to *Apostolus,* the reference would be to 2 Cor. 2:16. Perhaps Calvin is unwittingly transferring Paul's words to the angel.

in licentiousness, let the knowledge of the condemnation we deserve terrify and humble us before God. While the irreligious give themselves up greedily to their earthly pleasures, let us no less eagerly embrace this incomparable treasure in which real blessedness is concealed. Let our enemies prate as much as they like that their one and only care is to have God propitious to them. While they think he can only be invoked in uncertainty they are certainly overthrowing the foundation of salvation. Let them attack our faith as irritably as they like, but let us be quite clear that only by his benefit can anyone receive the prerogative of freely and confidently calling upon God the Father in reliance on the patronage of Christ. But our minds are too attracted to the earth, and a zeal for godliness will never flourish in us as it should until we learn to raise them up and exercise them in the continual meditation and practice of the heavenly life. In this respect the incredible emptiness of the human race betrays itself. Although nearly all philosophers speak clearly of the brevity of this life, none aspires to that which is eternal. And so when Paul is commending faith and love to the Colossians he has good reason to say that they are animated by hope — which is laid up in heaven.[20] And elsewhere, speaking of the goal of the grace revealed to us in Christ, he says that, when we have renounced all ungodliness and worldly desires, it trains us to live soberly, righteously, and godly in this world, waiting for the blessed hope and advent of the glory of the great God and our Saviour Jesus Christ.[21] Let this expectation, then, destroy all obstacles and seize us for its own — and the more the world is filled with the plague of Epicureanism, the more earnestly we must strive to reach the goal, lest we, too, should be infected.

Moreover, although we must be sorry that such a great host should of their own will perish, yet they are rushing on to their destruction as if they had been assigned to it. We might well be upset by their mad fury if we did not remember that other admonition of Daniel, that sure salvation is laid up for all who are found written in the book.[22] And although election is hidden in the secret counsel of God (which is the first cause of our salvation), yet the adoption of all who are implanted in the body of Christ by the faith of the gospel is in no way doubtful.

Therefore, be content with this testimony and go energetically forward on the course on which you have made a good start. If you have to fight for a long time yet (and I warn you that there will be harder battles than you imagine) and if the fury of the ungodly boils over into every sort of violence and they stir up all hell, you must remember that the course has been marked out for you by the heavenly director of the contest, whose rules are to be

20. Mg., Col. 1:5.
21. Mg., Tit. 2:12-13.
22. Dn. 12:1.

obeyed the more readily because he will supply his own people with strength even to the end.

Since it is not right for me to leave the post in which God wishes me to remain, I dedicate to you this work of mine as a pledge of my solicitude to help you until my pilgrimage be done and the heavenly Father in his immense mercy gathers me together with you into his eternal inheritance.

May the Lord guide you by his Spirit, brethren heartily beloved! May he guard you by his protection against all the designs of our enemies and sustain you by his invincible power.

Geneva   August 19, 1561

The Printer

to the Godly Reader;
Greetings from the Lord!

Here, Christian reader, you have from the eminent John Calvin the lectures in which he interprets the prophecies of Daniel. They show the diligence and clarity and remarkable faithfulness which shine out of all his expositions on Holy Scripture. To explain again here the method by which our two brothers, Jean Budé and Charles Joinviller, recorded them would be superfluous, since it is clearly stated in the books which Jean Crespin published two years ago on the twelve so-called Minor Prophets.[1] In taking down these they followed the same course as in the earlier work. But just a word on why it seemed proper to add the original Hebrew to the Latin translation, which might seem strange to you. There were some studious and learned men who rightly wished to have the Hebrew in the aforementioned lectures — partly for other reasons, but especially because it is very pleasant for Hebrew scholars to have the original before their eyes (and that faithful interpreter drew the genuine sense of the prophet from the Hebrew). But even the less learned in that tongue will not be ungrateful to see Daniel speaking not only in a foreign but also in his own language, and so to understand what was said and how. This is why we did not want to omit the actual words of the holy man. It is also relevant that it is the custom of the learned interpreter, Calvin himself, first to recite each verse in Hebrew and then turn it into Latin. I wanted to make this short preface so that you should grasp the teaching method employed. But what copious and rich fruit all will receive from these lectures you may each judge better by reading them.

Farewell! If you receive any profit, give God alone the praise he merits, and pray always for the welfare of Calvin, his most faithful servant.

Geneva   August 27, 1561

1. See prefaces by Jean Budé and Jean Crespin to Calvin's *Lectures on Hosea.*

DANIEL 1–6

**The prayer which John Calvin used
at the beginning of his lectures:**

*May the Lord grant us so to be engaged in the heavenly
mysteries of his wisdom that we progress in true
godliness, to his glory and our own edification.
Amen.*

Lecture 1

The book of the prophet Daniel comes next. Its usefulness is too great to be easily expressed in a précis and will be better understood as it unfolds. Nevertheless, I will now give just a foretaste of it, to prepare us for reading and to stir our interest. But before I do that, let me briefly summarize the book. The division will help us in another respect too. We can divide the book into two parts.

Daniel relates how he acquired authority even among the unbelievers. For it was necessary that he should be raised to the prophetic office in a remarkable and unusual way. Matters were, as we well know, in such confusion among the Jews that it was hard for anyone to believe that there were any prophets at all. At the beginning, it is true, Jeremiah was still alive, and then Ezekiel as well. The Jews also had their prophets after the return. But Jeremiah and Ezekiel had almost finished their course when Daniel began to exercise his prophetic office. And others — Haggai, Malachi, and Zechariah — had been made prophets to exhort God's people, as we have seen. Thus, their office was, so to say, restricted. As for Daniel, he would hardly have been reckoned as a prophet had God not raised him up in a wonderful way, as has been said. Therefore we shall see, up to the end of chapter 6, how he was divinely adorned with outstanding insignia, so that the Jews might be quite assured (unless they wanted to be wicked and ungrateful to God) that they had been given a prophet. Among the Babylonians he was well known and revered. If the Jews despised one who was admired even by the heathen, would it not be like deliberately stifling and treading under foot the grace of God? Daniel, therefore, had sure and conspicuous insignia by which he could be recognized as the prophet of God and which placed his calling beyond doubt.

Then comes the second part, in which God foretells through him what was awaiting the chosen people. Therefore, from chapter 7 to the end of the book we have visions relating particularly to the Church of God. There God predicts the future. And this forewarning was more than necessary. It had been a hard enough temptation for the Jews to bear seventy years of exile. But after they had returned to their own land, God protracted the full liberation from seventy years to seventy 'weeks', so increasing the delay sevenfold.[1] The minds of them all could well have been broken and dismayed a thousand times, for the prophets had spoken so magnificently about the redemption that the Jews might have expected a happy and completely blessed state as soon as they were freed from the Babylonian captivity. But when they were oppressed by so many afflictions (and that not for a little while, but for more than four hundred years, whereas they had been exiles for only seventy years) redemption might have seemed a fairy-tale. There is no doubt that Satan tempted many to fall away — had God been having a game with them when he took them out of Chaldaea and led them back to their homeland? This is why God showed his servant by a vision how many and grave afflictions awaited the chosen people.

Moreover, Daniel predicts in such a way that he describes almost historically things that were still hidden. And this also was necessary; for in such turbulences the people would never have had any idea that these had been divinely revealed to Daniel unless the heavenly testimony had been proved by the actual event. Therefore the holy man had to speak and prophesy about future things as if he were narrating what had already happened. But we shall see all these things in their order.

I return to where we began — that we should now see briefly how useful this book is to the Church of Christ. First, the subject matter itself shows that Daniel did not speak out of his own ideas but that whatever he proclaimed had been dictated by the Holy Spirit. For, if he had been endowed only with human wisdom, how could he have conjectured the things we shall see afterwards? For example, that other monarchies would arise which would destroy the Babylonian Empire, at that time the supreme power in the world? Again, whence did he divine the coming of Alexander the Great? or of his successors? A long time before Alexander was born Daniel predicted what he would do. Then he shows that Alexander's kingdom would not last; for it is at once divided into four 'horns'. Other things which he mentions demonstrate assuredly that he spoke at the dictation of the Holy Spirit.

An even more certain trust in this fact can be gained from other narratives — when he warns how many miseries the Church would face from two cruel enemies, the King of Syria and the King of Egypt. He recites their pacts; he relates the enemies' attacks on two fronts; then the many changes. All this that he clearly points to was so realized that it is obvious God was speaking by his

1. A reference to Dn. 9:24. See Calvin's comments on that verse (Calvin Translation Society II, pp. 195-202).

mouth. It is, therefore, a great thing and very profitable for us to learn for sure that Daniel was only an instrument of the Holy Spirit and that he proclaimed nothing from his own fancy.

Now, the fact that authority was given him to establish the credibility of his teaching more firmly among the Jews applies also to us. How shameful and wicked is our ingratitude if we do not accept God's prophet, whom even the Chaldaeans were compelled to honour — the Chaldaeans whom we know to have been superstitious and full of pride and arrogance. These two nations, the Egyptians and the Chaldaeans, were self-satisfied above all others. The Chaldaeans thought that wisdom dwelt with them alone and were not at all disposed to receive Daniel unless they were actually forced to, or to confess that he was a true prophet of God unless it was wrung from them.

Now that Daniel's authority has been established, we must say something about the matters he treated. First, on the interpretation of dreams. Nebuchadnezzar's first dream was concerned, as we shall see, with the most important matter of all — that whatever is splendid and powerful in the world passes away, while the kingdom of Christ alone remains stable, alone is perpetual. In the second dream of Nebuchadnezzar, Daniel's wonderful constancy is apparent; for it was very offensive to humiliate the highest monarch in the world as he did: 'You exempt yourself from the rank of humanity and want to be worshipped as God. Hereafter you shall be a mere animal.' No one today would dare to prophesy like that before monarchs, would even dare to give them a polite warning if they sinned. When therefore Daniel boldly told King Nebuchadnezzar of the disgrace which was awaiting him, he gave a memorable and rare proof of his constancy. This also sealed his calling, showing that his fortitude was from the Spirit of God.

We must pay especial heed to the second part, where we see how God takes care of his Church. The providence of God extends, of course, to the whole world. If a sparrow does not fall to the ground without his permission, he undoubtedly looks after the human race.[2] Therefore nothing happens to us by chance. But in this book God kindles a light for us, that we may learn that he so governs the Church as to make it his special care.

If things ever were in confusion in the world, so that it might be thought that God was asleep in heaven and had forgotten the human race, it was in the great change of those days — no, changes many and multiple and various. The stoutest heart might have fainted, since there was no end to the wars. Now Egypt was dominant; now there were tumults in Syria. When everything was being turned upside down, what could one say but that the world had been neglected by God and that the unhappy Jews were deceived in their hope that God, their liberator in the past, would be the guardian of their safety for ever? For although all the nations were together involved in these many disasters, yet the result of

2. Mg., Mt. 10; Lk. 12; i.e., Mt. 10:29-31; Lk. 12:6-7.

17

the Syrians overcoming the Egyptians was that they abused their power by turning against the Jews, and Jerusalem was laid open to plunder as if it were the reward of victory. If the other side was victorious, they avenged their injury on the Jews or sought compensation from them. So on every side these unhappy people were pillaged; even after they had returned to their own land they were far worse off than they had ever been as exiles, or tenants, in far lands. But to be forewarned that these things would come was the best of all supports to lean on.

We today must apply the same doctrine to our own use. We see, as in a mirror or a picture, God showing solicitude for his Church, even when he seemed to have cast off care. We see that it was according to his purpose that the Jews were exposed to the outrages of their enemies. But on the other side, we should realize that they were wonderfully preserved; indeed, by a greater and more wonderful power of God than if they had lived quietly, without molestation. These things therefore we must learn from chapters 7 to 9.

Now, when Daniel numbers the years right up to the advent of Christ, what a clear and firm testimony we have to oppose to Satan and all the sneers of the ungodly! For it is certain that the book of Daniel was extant and read before all this happened. He enumerates seventy 'weeks' and says that then Christ will come. So let all those foolish, ungodly men come and push themselves forward and assert their impudence as loudly as they like! In the end they will be overthrown, convinced that Christ is the true Redeemer promised by God from the beginning of the world. For God did not wish him to be revealed without sure demonstration, surpassing all the proofs of mathematicians. It is, therefore, especially noteworthy that, after Daniel had spoken of the various distresses of the Church, he foretold the time when God wished to reveal his only-begotten Son to the world.

What he also asserts of the office of Christ is one of the chief principles of our faith. For he spoke not only of his advent but foretold that then the shadows of the Law would be abolished because Christ would bring its fulfilment with himself. And when he foretold the death of Christ, he also told of the purpose of his death — to blot out sin by the sacrifice of himself and to give eternal righteousness.

Finally, we must also observe that even as he trained the people of old to bear the cross, so he also warns us that the state of the Church will not be tranquil after Christ has been revealed, but that the children of God will have to battle to the very end and not hope for the fruit of victory until the dead arise and Christ himself gathers us into his heavenly kingdom.

We now have comprehended in brief, or at least have had a foretaste of, how useful and fruitful this book is for us.

Now I come to the words themselves, because, as I said, I wanted only to touch on a few things; and in any case, reading it will show better what fruit we shall receive in each of the chapters.

CHAPTER 1

1 *In the third year of the reign of Jehoiakim, king of Judah, came Nebuchadnezzar, king of Babylon, to Jerusalem, and besieged it.*
2 *And God delivered Jehoiakim, king of Judah, into his hands, and part of the vessels of the house of God,* and he took the things away [or, 'the men'; it can be read either way, for Hebrew does not use the neuter. Yet I prefer to translate it as neuter, because it at once goes on: he took them away] *into the land of Shinar into the house of his god.* [This would fit neither the king nor the captives; therefore the prophet seems to be speaking of the vessels. Then follows a repetition of this statement, namely] *He placed the vessels in the treasure house of his god.* [This is not saying two differing things; the prophet is confirming the same statement by explaining it in different words. He says that the vessels which Nebuchadnezzar had taken away into the land of Shinar were placed in the treasure house. Hebrew, as we know, uses 'house' generally for any sort of place, like calling the temple 'the house of God'. We must notice also that 'the land of Shinar' is a plain close to Babylon, and that the famous temple of Bel was there, which the prophet was probably speaking of in this verse.]

Daniel dates his being led away into captivity with his companions — *in the third year of Jehoiakim.* Here a difficult question arises. Nebuchadnezzar began to reign in the fourth year of Jehoiakim. How then could he attack Jerusalem in his third year and carry off captives at will? Some interpreters solve this problem with what seems to me a trifling conjecture — that 'fourth year' should be referred to its beginning, and so that time could be comprehended under 'third year'. But in chapter 2 we shall see Daniel being brought before the king in the second year of his reign. They escape from this new problem with another solution. They say that the years were not numbered from the beginning of the reign but that this was the second year from the defeat of the Jews and the capture of Jerusalem. But this is artificial and forced.

A more probable conjecture seems to me that the prophet was speaking of Nebuchadnezzar the First or, at least, to be placing the reign of Nebuchadnezzar the Second during his father's lifetime. We know that there were two kings of this name, a father and a son; but because the son performed many famous and memorable deeds, he was called 'the Great'. Hence, whatever we shall have hereafter on Nebuchadnezzar can only be understood of the second, that is, the son. Josephus[3] says that this son was sent by his father against the Egyptians and the Jews. The cause of the war was that the Egyptians were frequently urging the Jews to rebel and enticing them to throw off the yoke.

---

3. Josephus, *Antiquities of the Jews* 10:6; 10:11:1.

Therefore, Nebuchadnezzar the Second was waging war in Egypt when his father died and he went home with all speed lest he should be ousted by a coup. Josephus reckons that he left the expedition and came home to make sure things were stable. And there is nothing absurd, in fact it is very common, to call him a king who nevertheless holds the kingdom in common with his father. So I interpret it like this: 'In the third year of the reign of Jehoiakim came Nebuchadnezzar, by the orders and under the command of his father' — or, if anyone prefers it, the elder Nebuchadnezzar came. For neither view is absurd, whether we take it of the father or of the son.

Therefore *came Nebuchadnezzar, king of Babylon, to Jerusalem;* that is, by the hand of his son he besieged Jerusalem; or, if the other exposition is preferred, he himself was present — or, that he was present to wage war is also possible. But this was done in the third year of the reign of Jehoiakim.

Interpreters are deceived here too. Josephus says it happened in the eighth year.[4] But he had never read the book of Daniel. He was an unlearned man, with little knowledge of Scripture. I think he had never read three verses of Daniel. It was a horrifying judgment of God that a priest could be such a stupid man as Josephus. But in the other place I have referred to he seems to have followed Metasthenes.[5] He cites others also when he speaks of the downfall of that monarchy. But these things are quite consistent — that the city was first taken in the third year of the reign of Jehoiakim, and some nobles of the royal line (among them Daniel and his friends) were led away as a sort of token of triumph. Later, when Jehoiakim had rebelled, he was treated far more harshly, as Jeremiah had foretold.[6] Hence, Daniel had already been taken while Jehoiakim still held the kingdom, even if it was as a vassal of King Nebuchadnezzar.

Jeremiah's prediction was fulfilled, that the early figs were the better. Those who were taken into captivity last thought they were better off than the others. But the prophet soon disabuses them of this empty boast and shows that the first captives were treated more gently than the rest of the people who had stayed unharmed at home. Hence I take it that Daniel was one of the first captives. And from this we can perceive how incomprehensible are the judgments of God. If anyone in all the nation was irreproachable at that time it was certainly Daniel. Ezekiel numbers him among the three righteous men by whom God might be appeased.[7] There was such outstanding virtue in Daniel that he was like a heavenly angel among mortals. Yet he was taken away into

4. Josephus, *Antiquities* 10:6:1.

5. I.e., Megasthenes, a Greek historian contemporary with Alexander. See Josephus, *Antiquities* 10:11:1.

6. Mg., Je. 24, i.e., 24:1-10.

7. Mg., Ezk. 14, i.e., 14:12-20.

exile and lived as the slave of the king of Babylon, while others, who had provoked the wrath of God against them in so many ways, dwelt quietly in their nests. The Lord did not deprive them of fatherland or cut them off from their inheritance, the sign and pledge of their adoption. Anyone who tries to work out why Daniel in particular was among the first exiles merely betrays his insanity.

Let us learn to admire the judgments of God, which surpass all our thoughts, and let us also remember the saying of Christ, 'If these things are done in a green tree, what shall be done in the dry?'[8] As I have said already, there was an angelic holiness in Daniel, and yet he was dragged off ignominiously into exile and was brought up among the king's eunuchs. If this happened to such a holy man, who from boyhood had devoted himself entirely to piety, what indulgence it is that God should spare us! For what have we deserved? Who would dare compare himself to Daniel? We are unworthy even to untie the laces of the shoes on his feet, as the old proverb says.

And there is no doubt that Daniel wanted to show even by the time of its happening that it was a singular and extraordinary gift of God that this trial did not overpower him nor was able to turn him from the true path of godliness. When Daniel saw that he was, so to say, set up as an example of disgrace, he still did not cease to worship God purely. But when he says that King Jehoiakim had been divinely delivered into the hand of King Nebuchadnezzar, his expression removed any offence from the minds of the godly. For had Nebuchadnezzar been the superior, God himself could seem to have yielded, and thus his glory to have been outdone. But Daniel here expressly states that King Nebuchadnezzar took Jerusalem and conquered the people not by his own power or strategy, nor by fortune and chance, but because God wished to humble his people. Hence Daniel puts forward God's providence and judgment, lest we should think that the capture of Jerusalem meant that God was not standing by his covenant that he made with Abraham and his seed.

He speaks especially of the temple vessels. For the notion could seem quite absurd and shake the minds of believers: Why does God want this? The temple of God to be despoiled by a wicked and ungodly man! Did not God swear that his resting place should be there? — 'Here shall be my resting place for ever; here will I dwell, because I have chosen her.'[9] If any place on earth ought to have the distinction of being unconquerable, sound, and intact, it should be the temple of God. But when it was sacked, when its sacred vessels were profaned, nay more, when a heathen king carried off to the temple of his god what had once for all been consecrated to the living God, could not (as I have said) this trial have shaken the minds even of the saints? Certainly none

8. Mg., Lk. 23, i.e., 23:31.
9. Mg., Ps. 132, i.e., 132:13-14.

wa3 3o otrong ao not to be suddenly attacked by this temptation: 'Where is God? Why is he not defending his temple? Although he does not dwell in the world and is not enclosed in walls of wood or stone, yet he chose this to be his house, and the prophets have often asserted that he is seated among the cherubim.[10] So what does he mean by it?' As I have said, Daniel recalls us here to the judgment of God and tells us succinctly that it ought not to seem strange to us that God visits ungodly and wicked apostates with such severe punishment. For under the word 'God' is a tacit antithesis.[11] The Lord did not deliver Jehoiakim into the hand of Babylon without good cause. God therefore made him a prey, that he might inflict punishment for the rebellion of the wicked people.

Now he goes on:

3 *And the king commanded* [or, 'gave an edict to'] *Ashpenaz* [or, 'said to Ashpenaz', as some translate, keeping the Hebrew phrase], *the chief of the eunuchs, to bring some of the children of Israel and of the royal line and of the princes* [or, 'nobles'].

Here Daniel carries on his story and shows why he and his comrades had been taken away. The king had ordered that there should be brought to him, not some of the common folk, but youths from the chief aristocracy, to stand before him, that is, to minister to him. From this we gather that Daniel and his comrades were youths of distinction and superiority, that they were of royal birth, or at least had very high-born parents. The king did this to emphasize that he was in charge. It may also be that he had the more subtle plan of using them as hostages. He hoped (as we shall see) that if he brought them up in his court they would defect and become enemies to the Jews and that so he could make use of them. Again, he hoped that, because they were of high birth, the Jews would be more subdued for fear of creating dangers for these unhappy exiles, the relatives of the king and of nobles.

As for the words: he calls Ashpenaz 'the chief of the eunuchs'. By this last word he means boys who were brought up in the king's court as in a sort of school for nobles. For it is hardly likely that this Ashpenaz was superintendent over other governors. We infer from this passage that the boys whom the king prized and held in honour were under his care.

'Eunuchs' in Hebrew is *sarisim*. But this word refers to any overseers. Potiphar was called by this name,[12] yet he had a wife. The name is used

10. Mg., Pss. 80, 99; Is. 37, etc.; i.e., Pss. 80:1; 99:1; Is. 37:16.
11. Here 'a tacit antithesis' means 'an implied consequence'. *Because* God is God, *therefore* he punishes Jehoiakim.
12. Mg., Gn. 37, 40; i.e., 37:36; 40:3, 4.

everywhere in Scripture for the satraps of a king; but because satraps were chosen from the sons of the nobility, it is not probable that they were castrated and so called eunuchs (for Josephus ignorantly says these Jewish boys had been castrated).[13] But since the eunuchs were favourites among the oriental kings, boys were (as I have already said) commonly called by this name whom the king brought up in a sort of school for nobles, so that in time he might make them governors of his various provinces.

Therefore, *the king ordered some of the children of Israel, from the royal line and from the nobility, to be brought.* This is how the sentence should be understood. He did not order them to be brought from the common people but from the royal line, so that he might make it clear that he was the victor and could do what he liked with them. By 'nobles' he means those who enjoyed influence with the king of Judah. And Daniel belonged to that tribe, as we shall see later.

Some think that פרתמים, *partemim,* is derived from *Perah,* that is, the Euphrates. And by 'governors' they understand those to whom the provinces on the banks of the Euphrates were entrusted. But this does not square with the present passage, which relates to the Jews. Hence we see that the word is used in a general sense and ought to comprehend all nobles.

The rest tomorrow.

Grant, almighty God, whenever you show us such a bright mirror of your wonderful providence and your judgments among the people of old, that we may have assurance that we too are under your hand and protection. With this support, may we hope, whatever befalls us, that you will be our guardian and never abandon our safety; so that we can quietly and confidently call upon you and boldly await any danger amid the changes of this world. May we stand fast in your unfailing Word and rest upon your promises, not doubting that the Christ to whom you have committed us and who by your will is the Shepherd of all your flock, will so care for us that he will lead us through the course of our warfare, however grievous and turbulent it may be, until we arrive at that heavenly rest which he has won for us by his blood. Amen.

13. Josephus, *Antiquities* 10:10:1.

Lecture 2

There follows the fourth verse:

4 *Boys in whom there was no blemish* [for I omit the Hebraism, which has already been explained to you] *and fair in appearance* [or, 'in face'], *and understanding in all prudence* [that is, 'skilled in all prudence'], *and understanding scholarship and clearly expressing knowledge, and in whom is strength; so that they might stand in the king's palace, and them to be taught* [that is, 'that they may be taught'] *the erudition and language of the Chaldaeans.*

In yesterday's lecture we saw that the prefect, or master of the eunuchs, had been ordered to collect some noble youths from the royal line or from princely houses. Daniel now describes the qualities which Nebuchadnezzar demanded. They were to be *boys* (not seven- or eight-year-olds, but adolescents) *in whom was no blemish,* that is, in whom there was nothing faulty but who were physically sound; and who were *fair in appearance,* that is, manly and open in appearance. After that, he adds, *skilled in all prudence and understanding scholarship* and, finally, *expressing knowledge* (those who take this participle actively seem to me to be right; for otherwise it would be a weak and inept repetition. Hence I consider that here the eloquent are meant, those that do more than understand — for many are aware in their own minds of what something means but cannot express it to others. Skill in self-expression is not given to all.) Therefore Daniel puts both here — that they are to have understanding and also be able to express their thoughts.

And in whom is strength: for כֹּחַ, *coah,* is nearly always used for strength, as in Isaiah 40: 'They who fear the Lord shall change strength',[1] that is, 'shall be renewed in their vigour.' Again: 'My strength fails' (Psalm 22),[2] that is, 'my vigour fails'. Therefore to understanding, learning, and eloquence he joins strength, or vigour — or physical activeness, which is the same thing.

That they might stand in the king's palace and be taught the erudition — I cannot translate the term ספר, *sepher,* in any other way. Literally, it is 'a letter'; but it means 'teaching' or 'instruction' — *and the language of the Chaldaeans.*

We now see that the king ordered noble youths of royal or princely blood to be brought to him not only on account of their high descent but also because his intention was to select as servants those who were talented, who were well born, as they say, good speakers, and capable of producing the best that could be expected of them, and also who had excellent physical health. And without doubt he wished to keep them in his favour so as to entice some other Jews. Then after they had been given authority, they could (if the situation demanded) be appointed governors in Judaea and rule over their own nation, remaining nevertheless as servants of the Babylonian Empire.

This was the king's purpose. We have therefore no cause to praise him for generosity. That he was looking to his own benefit is clear enough. All the same, we can see that the good and liberal humanities were not so despised then as they are today and during the last few centuries. For so much barbarism has prevailed in the world that it has been almost a disgrace for noblemen to be reckoned among the learned and cultured. The highest decoration for nobles has been to be completely uneducated. They have boasted that they were no clerks (to use the common word). And if any nobles have been trained as scholars, it was for no other end than to gain bishoprics and abbacies. So, as I said, they were almost ashamed to acquire learning. But we see that the age of which Daniel was speaking was not so barbarous. For the king gave orders that the boys he wanted among his princes should be taught. True, it was strictly from utilitarian motives (as was said); but nevertheless, we should note that this was the custom.

That he requires in them scholarship and experience might seem absurd, in that they were too young to be taught so much wisdom, so much scholarship or expertise. But we know that the wishes of kings are quite immoderate. When they command this or that to be done for them, they always soar up above the clouds. Thus spake Nebuchadnezzar! And Daniel in relating his commands gives them a regal cast: the king commanded that there should be selected some outstanding youths, in each of whom should appear something wonderful. There is therefore no need for us here to discuss carefully the meaning of 'learning, knowledge, and prudence'. The king simply wanted boys to be

1. Is. 40:31.
2. Ps. 22:15.

25

brought, adolescents, clever and of such a bent that they would be apt and ready to learn, naturally good speakers, and of robust physique.

For it at once goes on *that they might learn* (or, 'might be taught') *the erudition and language of the Chaldaeans.* We therefore see that King Nebuchadnezzar was not demanding full-fledged doctors but boys of good breeding (as we have already said), that is, with rare inborn qualities and of whom great things might be hoped. If he intended them to be liberally instructed in the learning of the Chaldaeans, it implies that he did not want them to be already intellectually perfect and cultivated. Rather he was looking at their natures. His purpose in wanting them to learn the Chaldaean language[3] was that they might gradually fall away from their own nation and forget that they were Jews, even become accustomed to the Chaldaean way of life, for language is the special bond of communication.

As to the 'erudition' itself, it may be asked whether it was lawful for Daniel and his companions to learn those arts filled with deceptions. For we know what the learning of the Chaldaeans was like. They professed that they knew the destiny of every man — just as today there are still many impostors in the world, who call themselves genethliacs.[4] Once upon a time they misused an honourable name and called themselves *mathematici* — as if there were no mathematics without those deceptions and illusions of the devil! It was because they used that name that the Caesars in their laws joined 'Chaldaeans' with 'mathematicians'; in my view the two terms are synonymous. But the solution is easy. The Chaldaeans not only pursued the astrology which is called 'judiciary,' but were also skilful in true and genuine astronomy. For the old writers say that the course of the stars was observed by the Chaldaeans, because no region in the world was so flat and gave an open view towards every horizon. Therefore the Chaldaeans were in a favourable position to study the heavens laid so open to human view, and they were the more disposed to study astronomy. But as the spirits of men are also diverted into empty and foolish curiosities, they were not content with that legitimate science but slipped off into foolish and perverse imaginations. For what these genethliacs teach about the fate of individuals is mere madness.

Daniel, therefore, had the possibility of learning those arts, that is, astronomy and other liberal scienes — just as Moses is said to have been learned in all Egyptian sciences;[5] and we know that the Egyptians were infected with similar aberrations. But both of Moses and of our prophet it can be said that they were taught astronomy and other liberal sciences. It is, however,

3. Calvin uses the term 'Chaldaean language' for what is now called 'Imperial Aramaic'.
4. Genethliacs: those who compute nativities. Calvin confesses that he has no precise knowledge of the different kinds of Babylonian magicians and I have therefore used the literal translation of *genethliaci.*
5. Mg., Acts 7, i.e., 7:22.

uncertain whether the king commanded that they should go into the subjects more deeply. But we must hold that Daniel had not been seduced to implicate himself completely in those impostures of Satan, for, as we shall soon see, he abstained from the royal food and drink. My opinion is, therefore, that whatever the king may have commanded, Daniel was content with the pure and genuine science of natural things. The king's aim was (as has already been said) merely selfish; he wanted Daniel and his comrades to change their nationality and defect from their own people, as if they were native Chaldaeans.

Now he goes on:

5 *And the king appointed them an allowance* [*debar*, 'thing'] *of the day in its day* [that is, 'for each day'] *from the bit* [literally; but here it means 'the portion'; 'from the portion of'] *the king's food and from the wine of his drink. And that they might be educated for three years; and from the end of them* [some translate it 'and from the part of them'; that is, as a certain part of the youths. But there is no doubt that here the prophet means a space of time, as we shall see later. That therefore from the end of the time] *they might stand before the king.*

In this verse also Daniel shows that the king ordered that those who had been brought from Judaea should be so fed that he might make them drunk with pleasures and so forget their own race. For we know that if anywhere there is cunning in the world, it reigns in kings' palaces. Therefore, when Nebuchadnezzar saw that he was dealing with a relentless and unyielding people (and we know that the Jews were tough and almost untameable in spirit), he determined to get servants who would be voluntarily submissive. Hence his endeavours to soften them with allurements. This was why he ordered for them *an allowance of the portion of his food and drink.* Just as today it is the highest honour in the halls of princes *d'estre servi de la bouche* ['to be served from the (king's) table'], as they say. Nebuchadnezzar wanted Daniel and his friends to be maintained not merely splendidly but even royally, as if they were members of the royal family. Yet they were captives and exiles; for he had carried them off violently from their native land as spoils of war (as we said yesterday). And so he did not act like this out of liberality, to be thought virtuous in feeding those unhappy exiles on his own food and drink. But (as we said) he cunningly tried to win the boys over, so that they might prefer to be thought Chaldaeans rather than Jews, and so deny their own people. This was the king's purpose. But we shall see that God governed Daniel and his comrades by his Spirit, so that they should beware of these snares of the devil and also abstain from the royal food and drink for fear of being polluted. But these things will be said later on in their own place. At present we are concerned only with the king's cunning. So he orders that they should be given every day some of his drink and his food. It was not from parsimony that a portion was doled out daily but because the king wanted the food to be prepared for them just as for himself and the other princes.

He adds *that they might be educated for three years,* that is, until they were quite trained in the Chaldaean sciences; and also, until they were fluent in the language. Three years was enough for them in both respects, because he had selected clever boys, who learned languages and sciences easily. They were endowed with such natural ability that there is nothing surprising in the three years ordered by the king.

Lastly, he says *that from the end of them* — that is, 'of the three years'. We have said that this should not be referred to the boys, as if the king later chose out only some of them. For we shall see in its place that a certain time was fixed. There is therefore no need of a long refutation. For it is certain that the prophet was speaking of the end of three years. It had been said a little before *that they might remain in the palace;* but this ought also to be understood of the time, which we have just been mentioning. Therefore they did not at once appear before the king; this was simply what they were intended for. When he says the king had ordered them to be maintained, so that he might afterwards use them in his service, Daniel is saying the same thing twice — they had received a splendid education because the king wanted them as his servants at his table and in other duties.

Now he goes on:

●

6 *And there were among them of the sons of Judah, Daniel, Hananiah, Mishael, and Azariah.*
7 *And the chief of the eunuchs* [that is, the master of the eunuchs] *gave them names. He named, I say, Daniel Belteshazzar, and Hananiah Shadrach, and Mishael Meshach, and Azariah Abednego.*

Now the prophet comes to what is strictly relevant to his purpose. He is not intending to narrate a history, but briefly to give the necessary facts, so that we may know how God prepared him for himself and afterwards laid on him the prophetical office. Therefore, after he had related that youths were brought from the royal line and from noble families, who had good natural parts, and were clever, and could speak well, and were physically strong, he now adds that he and his comrades were among that number. He omits the others, because there was nothing worthy of mention about them. And (as I have already said) what he has related hitherto has been, as it were, incidental. Now, therefore, we must observe the prophet's purpose — that he and his three comrades had been carried into exile and given a royal and excellent education in the palace of King Nebuchadnezzar, in order that afterwards he might become a ruler himself — and his friends also in the same rank. He does not say that he was of the royal house, but only of the tribe of Judah. But it is probable that he was of an illustrious and not a common family: for kings prefer to take those who are to rule a whole people from their own kindred rather than from that of others. Besides, the kingdom had been cut off from Israel, and it may be that out of modesty Daniel did not praise his own race or openly say that he was born of a noble and renowned family. He was content with the brief statement that he and his comrades were of the tribe of Judah and had been brought up among the children of nobles.

He says *their names were changed* — that the king might erase from their hearts the memory of their own nation and make them defect from their origins. As for the interpretations, I think that what you have already been told will be sufficient.[6] I am certainly not inquisitive about obscure names, especially the Chaldaean. Of the Hebrew names we know that that given to Daniel meant either 'God's judge' or 'God's judgment'. Therefore, whether his parents gave him this name by the secret prompting of God, or from common usage, Daniel was called by this name that he might be God's judge. So also with the others. The interpretation of Hananiah is certain: that he received 'mercy from the Lord'. Mishael means 'sought (or asked for) from God'. Azariah, again, is 'the help of God', or 'one whom God helps'. But all these things have already been explained better to you. I have just mentioned them, because the change was not uniform. For our purpose it is enough to know that the names were changed in order to abolish the memory of the kingdom of Judah from their hearts. Some of the Hebrews say that these were the names of wise men.

However that may be, the king's purpose was to seduce these boys' minds so that they should no longer have anything in common with the elect people but should degenerate into the ways of Chaldaea. Daniel could not help the chief, or master, of the eunuchs changing his name; it was not in his power to stop him — and the same must be said of his friends. It was enough for them to retain the memory of their nation, which Satan sought to blot out entirely by this artifice. And yet the stain of servitude was a grave temptation to them. For when their names were changed, the king, or Ashpenaz the prefect, wanted to force them into submission, so that, whenever they heard the new name, it was as if a badge[a] of their slavery were set before their eyes. We see, then, the purpose of this change of names — that those wretched exiles should be acutely aware that they were not free but cut off from the nation of Israel; and that by this mark or symbol they were bound in servitude to the king of Babylon and his court. This was a severe trial. But it did not matter that God's servants were insulted before men so long as no corruption infected them. For it follows that they were divinely governed and remained pure and sound; for Daniel afterwards says:

6. That is, by the professor of Hebrew. See pp. 34, 46, 101.
a. Reading *indicium* ('token', 'mark') for *iudicium* ('judgment').

8 *And Daniel placed upon his heart* [or, 'in his heart'; that is, 'decided, determined, with himself'] *that he should not be polluted by the portion of the king's food and in the wine that he drank; and he sought from the master* [that is, 'he asked the master'] *of the eunuchs that he might not be polluted.*

Here Daniel shows that he put up with what he could neither refuse nor escape; but yet that he took care not to fall away from the fear of God nor to forsake his own people, but always to keep the memory of his nation, and that he remained unharmed and blameless and a sincere servant of God.

He says, then, *that he determined in his heart not to pollute himself with the food and drink of the king, and that he asked the governor* under whose care he lived not to be forced into this situation. Here it is asked whether food and drink were so important that Daniel needed to shrink from them. For this seems a kind of superstition; or at least, Daniel seems hypercritical in rejecting the king's food and drink. We are aware that to the pure all things are pure — a rule valid in every age. We read nothing like this about Joseph, and it is likely that Daniel afterwards used foods indifferently, when he enjoyed great honour from the king. Hence, this was not his usual behaviour. Therefore, it might well seem thoughtless zeal and be ascribed (as was said) to a hypercritical spirit. 'If Daniel rejected the king's food only temporarily, it was fickle and inconstant of him to permit himself liberty later on where previously he had abstained. But if he was acting sensibly and rationally, why did he not continue in his purpose?' I reply: Daniel abstained from courtly splendours in the beginning from fear of being entangled. It was lawful both for him and for his comrades to take any sort of food or drink. But he saw what the king was after. We know how easily we can be trapped and deceived, especially when we are treated with distinction; and experience shows how hard it is to keep our heads in affluence, for excess follows hard on the heels of plenty. That is too common, and the virtue of temperance in the midst of abundance of food and drink is very rare.

Yet this was not Daniel's whole reason. Here we do not have simply a praising of his sobriety and continence (many twist this passage into a praise of fasting and say that the highest virtue in Daniel was that he preferred herbs to courtly delights). Daniel wished to guard against excesses in food and drink, not only because he saw the certain danger of his being ensnared by them, but he determined in his heart not to taste the food of the court so that even at that table he might continually recall the memory of his people. He wished therefore so to live in Chaldaea that he might recollect that he was an exile and a captive, yet sprung from the holy race of Abraham.

Now we see Daniel's purpose. He was not merely aiming at temperance in food or in pleasures, but he wanted to avoid the snares of Satan which he saw around him. There is no doubt that he was aware of his own weakness, and it is very praiseworthy that he distrusted himself and wished to flee far from all snares and traps. For what the king had in mind was assuredly a devilish net to catch a bird, as I have said. Daniel refused the trap — doubtless God enlightened the mind of his spirit that he should beware in good time. Therefore, not wishing to fall into the meshes of the devil, he freely abstained from the king's food and drink. This is the sum of the passage.

It can be asked why Daniel claims this praise for himself when his comrades behaved in the same way; for he was not the only one to reject the king's food and drink. But for his teaching to have greater weight and authority his hearers had to know that from his childhood he had been governed by the Spirit of God. Therefore he says that he in particular spoke, not by way of boasting, but to gain credit for his teaching and to show that God had for a long time formed and polished him for the prophetic office. Yet we should also note that Daniel was the leader among his comrades. For this would not have entered their heads, and they might have been corrupted, had Daniel not warned them. God therefore wished Daniel to be the leader and master of his companions in bringing them to this abstinence.

Hence also we infer that whoever among us is endowed with a richer grace of the Spirit has an obligation to teach others. For it is not enough for someone to be temperate and, taught by God's Spirit, to keep to his duty, unless he also stretches out his hand to others and tries to unite them with himself in the fellowship of piety and the fear and worship of God.

Such an example is here set before us in Daniel, who not only rejected the pleasures of the court, which might have made him drunk — rather have been like poison to him — but also admonished and persuaded his comrades to do the same. This is why he calls it a 'pollution', or abomination, to taste the king's food. Of itself, as I said, this was not abominable. Daniel was free to eat and drink at the king's table. But it was an abomination because of its consequence. Before that time, while they were already in Chaldaea, the four had without doubt eaten the food like anyone else and had allowed themselves to eat whatever was set before them. They did not ask for vegetables when they stayed at an inn on their journey, but they began to ask for them when the king tried to infect them with his delicacies and to seduce them into preferring their new situation to returning to their own people. When they perceived the snares laid for them, it became a pollution, or abomination, for them to enjoy the feasts and to eat from the king's table. We must therefore note the reason why Daniel thought himself polluted if he lived sumptuously and ate and drank what was provided by the king — because (as I have already said) he was conscious of his own weakness and wanted to beware in good time lest he should be taken in the snares and fall away from godliness and the worship of God and degenerate into Chaldaean customs, as if he had been brought up there and was merely one among their princes.

I will leave the rest until tomorrow.

31

LECTURE 2

Grant, almighty God, that so long as we shall be pilgrims in this world, we may so take food and drink for the infirmity of our flesh as never to be corrupted, never to be led astray from sobriety; that we may remember so to use abundance as to be abstinent even when we have everything. Grant also that we may patiently bear poverty and hunger and so freely eat and drink that always we may set the glory of your name before our eyes, and that our frugality may lead us to aspire to that fulness by which we shall be fully refreshed, when the glory of your face appears to us in heaven, through Jesus Christ our Lord. Amen.

Lecture 3

9 *And God had given Daniel* ['had placed Daniel'] *into kindness and mercy before the prefect of the eunuchs.*

Yesterday Daniel recounted what he had asked of the master into whose care he had been entrusted. Now he inserts this sentence to tell us that his request had not been in vain; the prefect of the eunuchs had treated him kindly. For the request would have been regarded as a capital crime had he betrayed Daniel to the king. It is improbable that he used the word 'pollute' or openly and bluntly called the king's food 'filth'. Yet what he now relates could still be easily inferred from his words — that he asked the prefect to be allowed to eat vegetables because he did not think it lawful for him to eat the king's food. We mentioned the reason yesterday; but the King of Babylon might quickly have flared up if he had learned it: 'What! I give honour to these captives. I could treat them like slaves, but I feed them delicately as if they were my own sons. Yet they despise my food as if I were myself polluted.'

This, then, is why Daniel here related that he was in the prefect's good graces. For (as we shall see in the next verse) the prefect merely refused his request. Where was his favour? Although he would not give Daniel what he asked, he showed uncommon kindness in not reporting him to the king (favour-seeking courtiers have a way of being quick to bring accusations!). On the other hand, it could be that the prefect knew that this had been already granted to Daniel by his servant. If there had been any connivance by the prefect, this would be the favour and mercy of which Daniel now speaks. Daniel's intention is not doubtful; he did not hesitate to choose a path which would keep him pure and sound; nor would he defile himself with the pleasures of the Baby-

33

lonian court. He explains how he escaped the danger, with the prefect treating him kindly when he could straightway have delivered him over to death.

The form of words should be noticed: *God placed him into grace and mercy before the prefect.* He could have used the ordinary expression and said that he was in favour; but he ascribes it to the beneficence of God that he had found a heathen man so kind and well disposed. The phrase, as was explained to you,[1] is common in Hebrew. For example, Psalm 106 says 'God placed the Jews into the mercies of the gentiles when they led them captive';[2] that is, he caused it that the victors should not treat them so cruelly as they had done at first. For we know how harshly and roughly and even often contemptuously the Jews were treated. When the inhumanity was softened, the prophet attributes it to God, who gave his people 'into mercies'. The sum of it is that Daniel turned towards mercy and kindness the heart of a man in other respects not very kind.

He relates this so that we may be the more ready to do our duty if ever we encounter some hazard when God calls us. It may often happen that we cannot obey God's orders and demands without physical danger. Laziness and softness creep over us and we shun the cross. Daniel, therefore, to encourage us in obeying God and his commands, here says that he was in favour with the prefect because God brought it about that his servant should find favour while faithful to his duty. And so we learn to cast our cares upon God when terror threatens us from the world or when men would menace and prevent us from living by God's standards. We know that it is in the hands of God to turn the hearts of those who rage against us, and to deliver us from every peril. This, then, is Daniel's intention in saying that the prefect was kind to him.

We also gather a general doctrine from this verse — that the hearts of men are governed by God. He softens hard iron and makes wolves into lambs, as it seems good to him. For when he redeemed his people out of Egypt he also gave them favour with the Egyptians, so that they carried out many precious vessels with them.[3] It is certain that the Egyptians had been hostile to the Israelites. Why, then, did they give them whatever personal possessions they held dear and precious? Because the Lord put a new feeling into their hearts. Or again, the Lord can irritate those who had been our friends so that they become hostile to us. Let us know, therefore, that both things are in the power of God — to turn men's hearts to kindness, and again, to harden hearts which had previously been kindly. It is true, of course, that everyone has his own disposition from the womb. Some are fierce, savage, and bloodthirsty; others are friendly, kind, and gentle. This variety is from the secret ordination

---

1. See p. 29, n. 6.
2. Ps. 106:46.
3. Ex. 3:21-22.

of God. But God not only forms each disposition from the womb, but on particular days, even at particular moments, he changes the feelings of a person according to his own goodwill; in the same way that sometimes he blinds men's minds or awakens them from stupor. For we see the dullest of men possessing acuteness or having some remarkable plan in what they do; whereas others who have excellent perspicacity become stupid when they most need judgment and discretion.

Therefore, we must remember that the minds and hearts of men are so governed by the secret instigation of God that he changes their feelings as seems good to him. So there is no reason why we should be so frightened of our enemies. Although they roar and foam out their rage and are filled with savagery, they can yet be turned by the Lord. And so let us learn by Daniel's example to keep steadfastly on our course and not to turn aside even if the whole world opposes us: for it is very easy for God to remove all the opposition. We shall find those kind who were most cruel, when the Lord wishes to spare us. Let us bear in mind both the sense of the words and also the purpose of the prophet in this verse.

He goes on:

10 *And the prefect of the eunuchs said to Daniel, 'I fear my lord the king, who has appointed* [for *minnah,* "to narrate", signifies "to ordain" or "appoint": therefore, "who has appointed"] *your food and your drink; wherefore shall he see your faces sad* [or, "thin", or "gloomy", or "severe". It comes from the word זעף, *zaaph,* which means "to become angry", but colloquially it is used of thin, or gloomy, or severe, faces] *more than the boys who are like you?* [Others translate "your equals" as "those who are after your likeness". This could be the sense: "Those who today are like you will later be sleek and fat while you will be thin. This change will create danger for me"] *and you will make my head answerable to the king* [for חוב, *hob,* is "debtor" in Hebrew. From it is derived this verb, which means "to make answerable."]'

Daniel suffers a rebuff from the prefect. And certainly (as I have earlier mentioned) the man's kindness was praised, not because he agreed to Daniel's wish and entreaties, but because he kept secret something that could have brought Daniel into great danger. The words themselves betray his humanity, because, although he denies the petition, he excuses it in a friendly way and with gentle words, as if he said that he would gladly do it did he not fear the king's anger. This, then, is the sum of it. The prefect dared not gratify Daniel's wish but he acted kindly towards him and his comrades so as not to put them in mortal danger.

He says that *he feared the king who appointed the food.* Here he is not to be blamed for fearing mortal man more than the living God, for he could have no knowledge of God. Although perhaps he thought that Daniel's request sprang from sincere religious motives, he did not imagine that it had anything to do with him. He thought the Jews had their own particular cult, but the Babylonian religion held the first place for him. Many common people think that we are acting quite rightly in rejecting superstitions, but they slumber on in the error that for them it is right to live in the old way that they were brought up in and which was handed down to them by their elders. So they use rites which they are willing for us to reject. Thus this prefect could have a right opinion of Daniel and his comrades without being touched by any desire to learn in what way the one religion differed from the other. He simply makes the excuse that he was not free to allow Daniel's petition because the king would treat it as a capital offence.

Now he goes on.

11   *And Daniel said to Melzar, whom the prefect of the eunuchs had set over Daniel, Hananiah, Mishael, and Azariah,*
12   *'Prove* [or, "test"] *your servants ten days, and let these be served to us from the vegetables* [simply, "vegetables"], *and we will eat* ["which we may eat"], *and water, which we may drink.*
13   *And let our countenances be looked upon before your face and the countenances of the boys who eat the portion* ["bit", as we said] *of the food of the king; and as you shall see, so do with your servants.'*

When Daniel had learned from the prefect's reply that he could not accept his request, he applied to the servant. For the prefect had many servants under him, as we know is usual with great governors. For it is probable that the office of prefect was equivalent to *le Grand Écuyer*[4] at the present day in France. This was therefore one of the servants in charge of Daniel and his companions. Daniel had recourse to this remedy and obtained his wishes — yet not without some ingenuity, as we shall see. But this shows Daniel's uncommon constancy. When he had tried unsuccessfully he did not give up. And it is the true and real test of faith that we do not grow weary if we meet with rebuffs and we do not think our way is barred. Then if we do not straightway turn back but instead try other paths, we really show that godliness is rooted in our hearts.

It could have seemed excusable if Daniel had been resigned after his rebuff. For who would not say that he had done what he could? But he surmounted the obstacle, and when he got nothing out of the chief governor he comes to his servant. And it was an uncommonly clever way of trying. For the servant could not make the same objection that we have just heard from the prefect. No doubt he knew something about Daniel's requests and the repulse and denial. So Daniel forestalled the servant's objection and showed

---

4. *magni Scutarii:* in French *le Grand Écuyer,* the royal equerry. Here obviously is intended the *Écuyer de bouche,* the functionary who supervised the catering.

how he could agree without danger. It was as if he said, 'We have not been successful with the prefect, because he was afraid for his head. But now I have thought out a new way, by which you may gratify our wishes without incriminating yourself. The affair will be entirely secret. *Test your servants for ten days and try us out; let us be given only vegetables and let us be given water to drink.* Now, if after that time our faces are comely and healthy, nothing will be suspected, no one will imagine but that you have been feeding us well, as the king commanded. The test will be safe for you and you will have as little cause for concern as we; so there is no reason why you should reject our requests.' There is no doubt that when Daniel proposed this, the Spirit of God was directing his wisdom and moving him to ask as he did. It was a singular gift of the Spirit that Daniel found a way to sway the mind of the servant who had charge of him. But again, we must remember that he spoke like this, not rashly or on his own initiative,[a] but by the moving of the Holy Spirit. For it would not have been clever but rash if Daniel had invented this plan by himself without being assured by the Lord of a happy outcome. There is therefore no doubt that he knew from a secret revelation that it would turn out well and according to his intention if the servant allowed him and his friends to eat vegetables. And that is why I said that he spoke only with the Spirit as his leader and master.

It is also very useful to note that we often let ourselves embark on ventures only to be at the last disappointed because we are carried away by our own carnal sense and do not consider what will be pleasing to God. It is not surprising, when men conceive this and that hope, if they find themselves deceived at last; for there is no-one who does not impose on himself by his foolish hopes, no one who does not disappoint himself. It is not for us to promise ourselves whatever we want. Therefore, let us take good heed of Daniel; he did not undertake or attempt the things we have seen out of foolish enthusiasm, nor did he speak thoughtlessly, but he was assured by the Spirit of God of what would come to pass.

And he says, *'Let vegetables be served us which we may eat and water which we may drink.'* We see that the four youths did not abstain from the king's food from fear of touching what was unclean. For the Law never prohibited the drinking of wine, except to Nazarites,[5] and it allowed the eating of flesh, of which there was plenty at the royal table. Why, then, were they so scrupulous? Because, as we said yesterday, Daniel did not wish to become addicted to the pleasures of court, which would quickly have made him lose his nationality. So he wished to eat not only frugally but even poorly, and never pleased himself in that way. Although he was raised to the highest honours,

a. Reading *motu* ('movement') for *metu* ('fear').
5. Mg., Nu. 6, i.e., 6:1-4.

he was always, so to say, at one with the wretchedness of the captives. We need seek no other motives for Daniel's abstinence. He could have eaten only bread and other plain foods, but he was content with vegetables, that he might lament and feed his mind with the memory of his fatherland — which would soon have been forgotten if he had been submerged in the splendours of the court.

He goes on:

14 *And he heard them in this word and proved them for ten days.*
15 *And at the end of ten days their countenance was seen to be comely* [or, 'healthy'; and they themselves] *fatter in flesh than all the boys* [namely, 'the rest'] *who ate the portion of the king's food.*

The result was a miracle. Daniel did not become emaciated and weak from the poor food but his appearance was as healthy as if he had fared sumptuously. From this we should gather what I have already said. It was by a divine moving that he persisted steadfastly in his intention of not being polluted by the king's food. By what happened God confirmed that he was the author of the solemn request and plan of Daniel and his comrades. It is, of course, certain that bread in itself does not have the power of sustaining us. We are nourished by the secret blessing of God, as he said in Moses, 'Man does not live by bread alone':[6] that is, bread does not supply strength to man. Bread in itself has no life. How, then, can it bring life to us? Therefore, bread has no virtue of itself, but we are nourished by the Word of God — that is, because God so appoints it that our life is sustained by foods. Hence he inspires bread with potency. But we ought to realize that our life is not sustained by bread or by other foods but by the secret blessing of God. Moses was not speaking here about teaching or about the spiritual life; but he says that our corporeal life is nourished by the grace of God, who imparts their own particular service to bread and other foods. It is therefore true in general that whatever food we eat, we are nourished and sustained by the gratuitous power of God.

But the example which Daniel here relates is unique. God showed by the event (as I have said already) that Daniel and his friends remained pure and sound only by being content with vegetables and water. Now, here we should note first of all that we must be very careful not to become slaves to our gullets and so be seduced both from our duty and from the obedience and fear of God, when we ought to be living frugally and abstaining from feastings. Today we see many who think this is their worst cross — I mean, if they do not get sumptuous meals of all sorts of food. Others have become so hardened in splendour that they cannot do without it and be satisfied with moderation.

6. Mg., Dt. 8, i.e., 8:3.

So they are always befouled in their own filth; they cannot give up the pleasures of the table. But Daniel shows us quite clearly how on occasion God not only reduces men to poverty but also how sometimes it is necessary to renounce all pleasures. Daniel (as we saw yesterday) did not place virtue in the abstaining from this or that food. All he had so far related was simply to let us know that he was forewarned of the danger of defecting to the customs of a foreign race and becoming so involved in the Babylonian way of life as to forget he was a son of Abraham. Yet it was necessary to renounce the courtly pleasures. Although luxurious foods were available, he freely rejected them as a deadly pollution — not (as we saw before) in themselves but on account of the consequences.

Thus, when Moses fled from Egypt he passed over into a new life, very different from the former. For he had lived elegantly and sumptuously in the king's court, as if he were the king's grandson. But afterwards, in the desert, he lived frugally and even had much ado to get any food at all. He esteemed the riches of Egypt, says the apostle,[7] less than the cross of Christ. Why? Because he could not both be regarded as an Egyptian and also keep the grace which had been promised to the children of Abraham. It was a sort of denial to remain for ever in the king's court.

Therefore, we should know it is a true test of our frugality and temperance if we can be hungry when God drives us into want and necessity — more, if we can voluntarily give up pleasures which are at our disposal and yet are harmful. To subsist now on vegetables and water would be very silly — there can sometimes be greater intemperance in vegetables than in the best and grandest foods! If anyone in poor health desires vegetables and such like foods which are not good for him, he will certainly be condemned as intemperate. But if he eats food that is good and rich (as they say) and so nourishes himself, he will be praised as frugal. To have a passion for water and go on swilling it down, while refusing wine, is not at all praiseworthy, as we know.

Therefore, if we are to realize how great Daniel's virtue was, we should not linger on the sort of food involved, but direct our thoughts to his purpose. He wanted to live, so far as he could, under the rule of the king of Babylon without separating himself from the customs of his race or forgetting that he was an Israelite. And without making such a distinction Daniel could not sufficiently spur himself on and shake off his torpor or awaken himself from it. (Just as, if decent food is available, we are not easily kept in our duties.) It was necessary for Daniel to practise before them some act of plain and re-markable distinction, showing himself separate from the Chaldaeans; hence it was that he asked for vegetables and water.

Finally, this place teaches us that even if we had only roots or the leaves of

7. Mg., Heb. 11, i.e., 11:26.

39

trees, if the earth did not yield us even the smallest seed, yet God could bless us with no less physical strength and energy than those have who enjoy unlimited plenty. The liberality of God in supplying us with bread and wine and other foods is, of course, not to be despised. For Paul makes both things a cause for praise — that he knows how to abound and how to suffer want.[8] When the Lord gives us food and drink bountifully we are able soberly and frugally to drink wine and eat pleasant food. But when God takes bread and water away from us and we have to fast, let us know that his blessing is sufficient for us in the place of any sustenance. For we see that Daniel and his friends were healthy and flourishing, even plump of flesh, when they had eaten only vegetables. Why was this, except because the Lord, who could nourish his people in the desert with manna alone when there were no other foods,[9] today turns into manna for us foods which would otherwise be poisonous? For if anyone asks physicians whether vegetables and that sort of stuff are fit to eat, they will say that all such things are very harmful. And they speak the truth.

Nevertheless, when we have no wide choice of foods, to get what best suits our weakness, if we are content with herbs and roots, the Lord will (as I have said) be able to nourish us as richly as if he furnished a table well filled with all delicacies. For just as temperance is not in the food but in the palate (for if luxury entices us to desire poor food we are nonetheless still intemperate, and if we eat the best of foods it is no set-back to our temperance), so we must hold the same thing about the property of foods — that it is not the quality of this or that food *per se* which sustains us, but the blessing of God, as it seems good to him. For we shall sometimes see the childen of the wealthy thin and weakly, even when they have been taken great care of. We shall see country children looking lovely, full in face and plump in body; and yet they eat what they can get — sometimes even very harmful things. Because they lack fine foods, the Lord by his blessing makes basic fruits, pork, and bacon, and such like, and even kitchen herbs, which seem to be worse, do them much more good than all the delicacies of the wealthy. This, then, is also to be noted in Daniel's words.

He goes on:

16 *And it came to pass that Melzar took for himself the portion of their food and the wine of their drinking* [that is, the wine that the king had apportioned for their drinking] *and gave them vegetables.*

When Melzar had seen that he could humour Daniel and his friends without danger (in fact, that he could make something out of it), he became good-natured and kind. No need now for him to argue about it! For any

8. Mg., Phil. 4, i.e., 4:12.
9. Mg., Ex. 16, i.e., 16:4-36.

opposition will often put us off when we are hoping to gain something; or we give up if what we desire demands too great effort. But when the prize is in our hand and there are no dangers, we are all for it. So we see what Daniel meant in this verse: that Melzar saw it would be useful to him and that he could make a profit out of the food which the king had appointed for the youths if he gave them vegetables instead.

But we must also observe what is in Daniel's mind. He wants to show here that the favour which kept him and his friends healthy and sound should not be ascribed to men. In what sense? Because he would never have made the request to the man Melzar unless he had seen that it could be safely granted. From the way that Melzar consulted his own welfare and personal advantage and wanted to avoid all argument and trouble, we easily gather that the favour can not be ascribed to him that Daniel and his friends received what they asked. The whole thing was so governed by God's providence that the man became kind. And God plainly shows that the whole praise is due to himself, so that he might exercise the gratitude of Daniel and his friends.

Grant, almighty God, that we today, who live among so many enemies, with the devil never ceasing to stir up new troubles and with the whole world against us, may know that you have bridled the devil and that all the ungodly are subject to you and you turn them in whatever direction you desire, and that you direct their hearts. Let us learn from experience that we shall always be safe and sure under the protection of your hand, just as you have promised, and may go on in the path of our calling until we arrive at last at the blessed rest which is laid up for us in heaven through Christ our Lord. Amen.

Lecture 4

17 *And to these four boys God gave* [I say] *to them knowledge and learning in all erudition and wisdom; and Daniel had understanding in all visions and dreams.*

Here the prophet shows what we have already touched on — the reason why he gained authority was that he might carry out the duties of a prophet more fruitfully. He had to be stamped with clear marks, so that first the Jews, and afterwards foreigners, should be aware that he was endowed with the prophetic spirit. Part of this grace was bestowed on his three friends. But he surpassed them all, since God had fitted him for a unique service. We should note this purpose, for it would be weak to say this was a reward paid to them by God for their frugal, even mean, eating and their voluntary abstinence from courtly pleasures. God's purpose was quite different. He wished, as I have said, to exalt Daniel in order that he might show effectively that the God of Israel was the only God. Because he also intended Daniel's friends for high positions at some time in political government, he gave them also a portion of the Spirit. But it is important for us to keep our eyes on Daniel; for, as I have said, God had before determined him to be a prophet and wished, so to say, to decorate him with his insignia of office, so that his teaching should meet an already prepared reception. He says, therefore, *to these four boys* (that is, 'youths') *was given knowledge and learning in all erudition and wisdom;* but Daniel was endowed with the unique gift of interpreting dreams and understanding visions.

When Daniel here speaks of 'erudition', he without doubt means simply the liberal arts and not at all those magical arts which, if they were not practised then, later flourished among the Chaldaeans. But we know that among those unbelievers there was no sincerity. I have already suggested that Daniel had not been tainted by the superstitions which were then highly prized by that nation. They corrupted astronomy, not content with the genuine science. But Daniel and his friends were trained among the Chaldaeans in such a way that they did not engage in those pseudo-exercises or rather corruptions, which must always be distinguished from true science. It would also be absurd to say that God approves the magical arts, when, as we all know, they were strictly prohibited and condemned by the Law in Deuteronomy 18.[1] Since then, God abominated magical superstitions as tricks of the devil, it could not have been consistent for Daniel and his friends to have been divinely endowed with the gift of progressing excellently in all the erudition of Chaldaea. This should therefore be restricted to true and natural science.

As for Daniel himself, he says that *he also understood visions and dreams.* We know from Numbers 12 the two ways in which the prophets understood what was God's will.[2] There God, reproving Aaron and Miriam, says that ordinarily whenever he wished to reveal his purpose to the prophets he would speak with them 'by visions and by dreams'. Moses, however, was exempted from this common order; he spoke with him face-to-face, mouth-to-mouth. Therefore, whenever he wished to make use of prophets, it was by visions or by dreams that God revealed to the prophets what he wanted to be passed on to the people. So that, when it is here said that *Daniel understood dreams and visions* it is equivalent to saying that he had been given the prophetic spirit. His friends were excellent doctors and masters in all learning, but he alone was a prophet of God.

This is the better confirmed by what has already been said: Daniel had already been decorated with the insignia of God in order that he might afterwards undertake the prophetic office with the more confidence and that his teaching might meet with the more credit. God could, of course, have formed him in a single moment. He could have struck everyone with such terror or reverence that they at once embraced his teaching. But he wished to exalt his servant gradually, so that he might come forward at the right time with sufficient experience. All would know that these marks had for many years been stamped upon him, distinguishing him from the common and ordinary rank of men.

Afterwards he goes on:

18 *And at the end of the days on which the king had decreed that they should be brought in, the chief* [or, 'prefect'] *of the eunuchs brought them before Nebuchadnezzar.*
19 *And the king spoke with them; and of them all there were not found any like Daniel, Hananiah, Mishael, and Azariah; and they stood before the king.*

1. Dt. 18:10-12.
2. Nu. 12:6.

LECTURE 4

20 *And* [In] *every word, wisdom, and understanding, which the king enquired of them, he found them tenfold above all the genethliacs and astrologers* [that is, more excellent than the genethliacs and astrologers] *who* [were] *in all his kingdom.*

Now Daniel relates how he and his friends were brought in at the appointed time. The king had fixed three years for them to be trained in all the Chaldaean learning. So the chief of the eunuchs brought them in. Daniel says that he and his friends were approved by the king as being superior to all the others. By these words he confirms what I have already said — that the Lord had over a long period of time adorned them with such grace that they stood out in the king's court. The king himself recognized that there was something quite unusual in them. Therefore both the king and all his courtiers could not help viewing these four youths with respect. Thus God wished to magnify his own glory: for without doubt the king was forced to admire the one who had made them superior to all the Chaldaeans. For the king had spared no expense and no trouble in educating his own people. When he saw these foreigners, these captives, so excel them, he would feel a stab of envy. But, as I have already said, God wished to exalt himself in this way in the person of his servants so that the king might be forced to acknowledge there was something divine about the youths.

Then where did their excellence come from? The Chaldaeans boasted that they themselves were wise by nature and all other nations mere barbarians. Therefore when the Jews were so pre-eminent, it follows that the God whom they worshipped was the one who distributes to each, as he wishes, shrewdness and insight. For none possesses a good intelligence by nature; it is a grace given from heaven. Therefore God had to be glorified when Daniel and his friends far surpassed all the Chaldaeans. It is God's custom to throw his enemies into amazement at his power, even when they do their utmost to flee from the light. For what was King Nebuchadnezzar's aim except to blot out any remembrance of God? That he might have about him Jews from noble families who would attack the religion in which they were born? This was Nebuchadnezzar's plan. But God frustrated the tyrant's purpose and made his own name to shine the brighter.

Now he goes on:

21 *And Daniel was until the first year of King Cyrus.*

Interpreters make heavy work of this verse; for we will later see that Daniel was shown a vision in the third year of King Cyrus. Some put forward the rather weak solution that Daniel would 'be' until that time, but yet that he did not die at once in the first year of King Cyrus. Others explain the word היה, *haiah,* as 'to be subdued'. But this is quite inconsistent with the story.

44

Therefore, the opinion of those is right who say that Daniel 'was until the first year of King Cyrus' in that he executed his office as a prophet — although they do not put it so plainly. But I prefer to explain more clearly what they say obscurely. For they say that the change can be noted after he set out for Media. But we can take the words in a better sense, that Daniel had a great reputation among the Chaldaeans and Assyrians and was acknowledged as an outstanding prophet. We also know that he interpreted the vision of King Belshazzar in the very night he was killed.

The word *fuit, he was,* is simple and absolute, but it depends on what has gone before — that he always obtained credit and authority as a prophet among the kings of Babylon. This is therefore the sum of the verse.

Now, in chapter 2 Daniel relates how God brought him on to the stage, to begin the prophetic office for which he was destined. Of course, God had, as we have said, already stamped on him sure marks by which he could be recognized as a prophet. But at this point God intended to prove by the event the power of the grace he had conferred on Daniel. First he simply narrates the story and then comes to the interpretation of the dream.

This, then, is the beginning of the chapter:

CHAPTER 2

1 *And in the second year of the reign of Nebuchadnezzar, Nebuchadnezzar dreamed dreams; and his spirit was worn down and his sleep was interrupted in him* [as they translate; or, 'departed from him'; or, 'was upon him'].

Here Daniel says that King Nebuchadnezzar dreamed in the second year of his reign. This seems to conflict with what we saw in chapter 1. For if Nebuchadnezzar captured Jerusalem in the first year of his reign, how could Daniel have already been classed among the wise men, among the astrologers? At that time he would only have been a student. It is also easy to gather from the context that he and his friends had been promoted then to minister before the king. These things therefore seem to be inconsistent — that Daniel and his friends were committed for training in the first year of Nebuchadnezzar but that in the second he was already in peril of death as belonging to the number of the magi. Some (as we have mentioned elsewhere) date the second year from the capture and fall of the city. They say that Nebuchadnezzar was called king from the time he obtained the settled monarchy. Before he had destroyed the city and temple, and the people too, he could not be reckoned a firmly established monarch. Hence they refer this dating to the capture of the city, as I have said.

45

But I incline rather to the other and more probable opinion that he had reigned in association with his father. And I have explained that his campaign against Jerusalem in the time of Jehoiakim was a commission from his father, and that he returned to Chaldaea from the Egyptian expedition for fear anyone should attempt a coup. He wanted to forestall any uprisings. Therefore there is nothing absurd in saying that Nebuchadnezzar reigned before his father was dead, since he had already been called to share the throne; afterwards he reigned alone; and in the second year of his reign the event now related took place. There is nothing forced in this explanation; it is consistent with the story. Hence I prefer this opinion.

He says that *he dreamed dreams,* and yet he relates only one dream. But it is not surprising that it is put in the plural, for so many things were involved in this dream.

He now adds that *his spirit was worn down,* to make us realize that the dream was out of the ordinary. For this was not the first dream Nebuchadnezzar had ever had, nor was he so terrified every night that he called for all his magi. Therefore, there was in this dream something extraordinary, which Daniel wanted to express in these words. I do not know whether the usual translation at the end of the verse, *his sleep was interrupted,* really fits; and the other exposition, which our brother Dominus Antony[3] told you, squares best — that 'his sleep was upon him', that is, he began to sleep again. So the genuine and simple sense of the words seems to me to be that *his spirit was confused,* that is, extreme terror overpowered him and he realized that the dream came from God. Then, as if thunderstruck, he fell asleep again, as if he were dead. While he was worrying and worrying about the interpretation of the dream he at last became quite stupefied and fell asleep. This also is why he forgot the dream, as we shall see.

He goes on:

2 *And the king ordered that there should be called* [I do not know what words to use for translating these Hebrew words: I will just give the substance of it. So, 'that there should be called'] *the astrologers, and soothsayers, and diviners, and Chaldaeans, to tell the king his dreams* [that is, 'to explain his dreams to the king']; *and they came and stood in the sight of the king.*

This verse demonstrates more clearly what I have just said. The dream was such that the king felt that it came from God. What made him call the magi was not primarily his dream but his terror. He could get no rest, even when he went to sleep. It felt like a red-hot iron in his brain. The Lord would

---

3. That is, Antoine Chevalier, professor of Hebrew in the Academy of Geneva, formerly French tutor to the future Queen Elizabeth I of England.

not allow him to rest but intended his mind to be in a turmoil until the interpretation of the dream had been given.

Profane authors are not amiss in classifying dreams among divinations. They speak in varying ways, of course, because there is no certainty or solidity among them. Yet they have a firmly rooted conviction that dreams have something to do with divination. It would be silly and childish to extend this to all dreams whatsoever, in the way that some leave no dream without interpretation, and so make themselves ridiculous. For we know that dreams occur for different reasons; for example, from our thoughts during the day. If I have been thinking over something in the day, it comes back to my mind in the night, because my mind is not so wrapped in slumber as not to retain some seed of understanding, although, granted, it is smothered. Experience teaches us clearly enough that our daytime thoughts run on in our sleep. Again, many dreams are begotten of various states of the mind or body. If someone takes sadness to bed with him — perhaps from the death of a friend or from some loss, or an injury he has sustained, or any sort of trouble — the mental preparation will conceive conformable dreams. The body itself generates dreams. We see those who are feverish now imagining fountains for their thirst, now fires, now conceiving all sorts of imaginations. We see also that intemperance disturbs men in their sleep. Drunken men are carried away into a frenzy of dreams. Thus there appear many natural causes so far as dreams themselves are concerned. Hence, to want to seek divination or sure reasons in them all is too silly for words.

But on the other hand, it is certain that some dreams have a quality of divination. I omit what the old histories relate. But certainly the dream of Calpurnia, Julius Caesar's wife, could not be fictitious, because, before he was killed, it was widely said, 'Caesar has been killed', as she had dreamed.[4] The same can be said of the physician of Augustus. On the day of the battle of Pharsalus he told him to leave his tent; and yet there was no reason why the physician should order him to be carried on his litter out of the tent except because he had dreamed it was necessary. Wherein lay the necessity? It was beyond human conjecture. Augustus's camp was captured at that moment.[5] No doubt many such stories are fables, but I have been selective. And I have not yet touched on the dreams mentioned in God's Word. For I am saying what even the heathen will be forced to admit.

Aristotle had pleasure in rejecting any feeling for a divinity (for he was bigoted in this matter, and wanted to compress the nature of God into the scope of man's understanding and grasp everything with his own discernment). Yet he made the confession that dreams did not always come by chance but that there

4. Plutarch, *Lives: Caesar* 63.
5. Dio Cassius, *Roman History* 47:41 (Calvin confuses the battles of Pharsalus and Philippi).

LECTURE 4

was a μαντική [*mantikē*], that is, a quality of divination, in some. He disputes on the origin of dreams, to which part of the mind they belong, whether they were 'intellective' or 'sensitive', and comes down at last on the side of the latter, but only in so far as it is 'imaginative'. Afterwards, when he asks 'Are dreams causes or something similar?' he inclines to the view that they are rather symptoms of incidentals [*accidentia*] which come to pass by chance. He cannot allow that dreams are divinely sent, and in explanation says that many stupid men dream and have the same sort of dreams as the wisest. Then he turns to the brute beasts. For some of them, like elephants, dream. Since, therefore, dreams are common among brute beasts, and since the wise dream more rarely than the crassest idiots, it seems improbable to Aristotle that dreams are divinely sent. Therefore he denies that they are θεόπεμπτα [*theopempta,* 'sent from God'] or θεῖα [*theia,* 'divine'], but says they are δαιμόνια [*daimonia,* 'demon-sent']; that is, he invents a certain medium between the divine and the demonic. And we know in what sense philosophers take 'demonic', which in Scripture has a bad sense. Aristotle says, therefore, that dreams are sent by aery inspirations, and not from God. Because, he says, the nature of man is not divine but inferior; and yet it is superior to the earth, that is, so to say, angelic.[6]

Cicero disputes on this at great length in book 1 of *On Divination*[7] (although he recants in book 2 some of the things he had earlier said when he was an Academic).[8] Among other arguments to prove that there are gods, he adds dreams: 'If there is any divination in dreams, it follows that there is a certain divinity in heaven. Not, however, that man's mind cannot conceive any dream without heavenly inspiration.' Cicero's reasoning is valid: 'if there is any divination in dreams, there is a certain divinity'.[9]

Notice also the distinction that Macrobius makes — although he clumsily confuses *genera* and *species*[10] (for he was not a man of good judgment, but a rhapsodist who heaped together without order and without method things he had read): Now, let this be taken as settled, that the opinion that there is some sort of divination connected with dreams is with good reason fixed in the hearts of all.

Hence also that saying of Homer's, ἐκ διός ἐστιν ὄναρ [*ek dios estin onar,* 'a dream comes from Zeus'].[11] He does not understand this generally or promiscuously of any sorts of dreams, but when he introduces his characters, the heroes, he also says that they had been divinely warned in their dream.

6. Aristotle, *On Divination through Dreams.*

7. Cicero, *On Divination* 1:20:39–1:30:65, presenting a Stoic view.

8. Academic = sceptical Platonist. In *On Divination* 2 Cicero refutes the arguments of book 1.

9. Cf. Cicero, *On Divination* 1:5:9–1:6:10 (refuted by Cicero, 2:60:124, etc.).

10. Macrobius, *Commentary* on Cicero's *Dream of Scipio,* analyzes different kinds of dreams (3:1-11).

11. Homer, *Iliad* 1:63.

Now I come to the dream of Nebuchadnezzar.

In this dream two things are to be noted. First, that all memory of it was lost and blotted out. Second, that it had no interpretation. Elsewhere we see a dream remembered and yet with its interpretation unknown. But here Nebuchadnezzar was not only perplexed about the interpretation of the dream but, because the vision itself had vanished, he had a double perplexity or anxiety. Now, as for the first point, that Daniel was able to provide the interpretation, there is nothing new in this. It happens occasionally, if rarely, that someone may dream without a myth [*figura*] or riddle [*aenigma*]; that is, he recognizes the substance of the dream and has no need of a diviner [*coniector*] (for they call interpreters of dreams *coniectores*). This, as I said, does happen, but only rarely. But it is very common in dreams for God to speak allegorically or enigmatically. And this is known not only among the heathen but also among the servants of God themselves. When Joseph dreamed he was worshipped by the sun and moon, he did not know what it meant. When his sheaf was worshipped by the sheaves of his brothers, he did not grasp the meaning of it. He tells his brothers about it quite openly.[12] God therefore spoke to him through dreams almost enigmatically until the interpretation came to pass.

The dream of King Nebuchadnezzar was similar. We see that God also reveals his will to unbelievers, but not clearly; for seeing, they do not see, and it is just as if someone offered them a closed book or sealed up letters.[13] As it is said in Isaiah, God speaks with a lisping and stammering tongue to unbelievers.[14] The will of God was revealed to King Nebuchadnezzar in such a way that he was still perplexed, even lay stupefied. Hence the dream could be of no use to him until Daniel was brought in as interpreter, as we shall see. God did not so much want to keep the king in suspense; but he blotted out the memory of the dream in order to goad him the more. Because some neglect those dreams which they do not remember, God fixed such a red-hot iron, as I have said, deep in the mind of this unbeliever that he could get no mental rest, but went on dreaming even when he was awake. God was drawing him to himself by secret cords. This, then, was the reason why God did not at once give an interpretation of the dream and even wiped out the memory of it from his heart until he should receive both from Daniel.

We will leave the rest until tomorrow.

Grant, almighty God, from whom every perfect gift proceeds —
and although some men excel others in intelligence and clearness
of mind, yet none has aught of his own but you distribute to each

12. Mg., Gn. 37, i.e., 37:5-10.
13. Mg., Is. 29, i.e., 29:10-12.
14. Mg., Is. 28, i.e., 28:11.

according to the measure of your free liberality   grant that whatever understanding you give us we may use to the true glory of your name. Grant also that whatever has been given us we may with humility and modesty acknowledge to be from you and may take good care to keep ourselves in soberness, not desiring too much or corrupting the true and genuine knowledge of things, but remaining in the simplicity to which you call us. Grant also that we may not linger on in earthly things but may learn rather to raise our minds to the true wisdom of knowing you to be the true God, and give ourselves up in obedience to your righteousness, and be content with this one thing only, to obey you and consecrate ourselves entirely to you, that your name may be glorified in our whole lives, through Jesus Christ our Lord. Amen.

Lecture 5

Yesterday we saw that the magi were, by the king's command, summoned not merely to explain his dream but even to tell him what he had dreamed, because he had forgotten it.

He mentions four sorts [*species*] of magi, or at least three with a subspecies [*genus*] added as a fourth: so I will briefly touch on how they seem to me. Several expound חרטומים, *hartummim,* as genethliacs; while אשפים, *assaphim,* they think were physicians. As to the first, I would not wish to argue very strongly. But I see no justification for the second. They say these were physicians who from the pulse of a vein or artery could diagnose a man's health. But this is baseless and I subscribe rather to the view of those who think that astrologers were called by this name. In the third place are put מכשפים, *mecasphim,* whom they call 'conjurors'. Others, however, change the meaning and say that these were the astrologers who judge of things future or foretell unknown things from the position of the stars. But I can offer nothing more than that we cannot establish with certainty what the words mean in Hebrew. For when a thing is dead and buried, who shall distinguish between the terms of the unknown art? כשדים, *casdim,* I do not doubt was put as a class [*genus*]. Although it is a national name, the magi adopted it as their own for its excellence, as if they possessed the nobility and superiority of the whole race. And we know that the name was common throughout Greece and Italy. Anyone who claimed he could predict the hidden future from the stars or from other modes of divination was called a 'Chaldaean'.

As for the other three words, I have no doubt they were terms of honour. This is why they called themselves 'mathematicians', as if there were no learning in the world outside themselves. But although they had sound foun-

51

dations, it is certain they were full of superstitions. There were the arioles[1] and diviners; and we know that their particular line was to supply auguries. Therefore, although they were highly prized among their own countrymen, they are condemned by the Law of God. Whatever learning they claimed was mere imposture. They were called magi as a general name and were also called 'Chaldaeans' (a little later, when Daniel repeats that they spoke before the king, he does not enumerate the three sorts but says only 'Chaldaeans').

It is surprising that Daniel and his friends were not summoned among them. For he ought to have been called among the first; for the king had, as was said, found them to excel tenfold the magi and all the arioles who were in all his kingdom. Since their ability was known to the king, how was it that he overlooked them when all the magi appear, called to such a hard task? It could be that the king omitted them because he had more faith in his own countrymen, or because he regarded them as suspect and did not want to divulge his secret to captives of whose trustworthiness and loyalty he was not yet sure. That might certainly be the case. But we must consider God's purpose more closely. And so I do not doubt that the king's forgetfulness proceeded from God's providence, in that he did not wish his servant Daniel and the others to be involved at the outset with the magi and arioles. Hence Daniel was not summoned with the rest, in order that his subsequent prophecy should be the more wonderful.

Now he goes on:

3 *And the king said to them, 'I have dreamed a dream and my spirit is worn out in trying to know* [or, "to understand"] *the dream.'*

I will join on the next verse:

4 *And the Chaldaeans said to the king in Syriac, 'O King, live for ever. Tell your dream to your servants and we will give the explanation.'*

Daniel first relates the overweening confidence of the Chaldaeans in daring to promise an interpretation for a dream still unknown to them. The king says that he had been disturbed in trying to understand his dream — by which he intimates that some kind of enigma had been divinely set before him. Therefore he is here confessing his ignorance; and the importance of the matter can be inferred from his words. When the king declared that he wanted to enquire about something obscure and profound, which was beyond his grasp, when, above all, he confessed that he was worn out in spirit, the Chaldaeans ought to have been touched by anxiety or some solicitude. But they just boldly advertised themselves as the best interpreters of the dream as soon as they should have understood it.

1. Ariole: one who divines from omens. As with genethliacs, I have preserved the literal translation of *arioli*.

52

When they say, *'O King, live for ever'*, it is not a simple or bare prayer. They are bidding the king to be of a good and cheerful mind because they can free him from all care and trouble by their speedy explanation of the dream. We know how free impostors are with words — hence the saying of the old poet 'They enrich the ears and empty the purses.'[2] And certainly the inquisitive who feed on the wind and are taken by such snares deserve to get the wind in their ears. But down the ages it has been well known that there is no being more confident than an astrologer — a man not content with true science but making divinations about life or death and forecasting all events. They claim that nothing is hid from them. In general we must hold that it was foolish and rash to make an art out of divining dreams. For although there is some (indeed, a sure) interpretation of dreams, as was said yesterday, yet, as we shall see later, this should not be regarded as a proper science but as a special gift of God. Just as a prophet will not deduce from assured reasons what he will say but will explain the oracles of God, so also those who want to interpret dreams will not have sure rules to follow; but if God reveals what he means by the dream then the one endowed with that gift may assume the role of interpreter. Properly speaking these are antitheses and inconsistent: general, perpetual science, and special revelation. When God claims for himself the revelation of what he has already impressed on someone's mind by a dream, it follows that this cannot be framed as an art and science, but men must wait for revelation by the Spirit. That, therefore, the Chaldaeans so brazenly advertised themselves as good interpreters of the dream not only betrays their rashness but shows them up as mere charlatans who feigned to possess a science which was no science, as if by their divinations they could predict what the king's dream meant.

Now he goes on:

5 *The king replied and said to the Chaldaeans, 'The word has gone out* [or, "gone away"] *from me. If you will not declare to me the dream and its interpretation, you will be made into pieces* [others translate it "blood", הדמין, *haddamin*, but the other explanation is the more usual. I will not labour the point, for there is little difference between them] *and your houses will be set a dunghill* [that is, "will be reduced to a dunghill"].'

Here the king demands of the Chaldaeans more than their profession can bear. For although, as I said, their obtuse boasting promised an interpretation of the dream, whatever it was, yet they had never claimed that they could tell anyone what he had dreamed. So we see that the king acted unfairly in not considering what they had professed and what were the limits of the art and science (if there was any science in it!).

When he says that the thing or word had gone away from him, it will

2. Cf. Aulus Gellius, *Attic Nights* 14:1:34.

admit of two senses. For מלתה, *millethah,* can be taken for 'edict', as we shall see later. Thus, it may be read as (the edict) 'flowed'. But because a little later he repeats the same phrase when he seems to have understood the dream (in verse 8, in fact), the explanation fits quite well that the king says that his dream had vanished. I leave this undecided.

Observe carefully once again what we mentioned yesterday. Terror was so deeply engraven into the king that he could have no inward peace. Yet he had not learned enough for the least taste of the revelation to remain. He was like a bull stung by a gad-fly rushing about everywhere and rolling around. Such was the madness of this unhappy king because God harassed him with these fearful tortures. And yet the memory of the dream was entirely blotted out of his mind. Nevertheless, he confessed that the dream had happened; and because the magi, while emphasizing the limits of their science, boasted that they were the interpreters of the gods, the king did not doubt to get from them what they had never claimed. Arrogance gets its just reward when men, swollen with their perverse confidence, assume in regard to others more than they are equal to, and, all thought of modesty flown, want to be regarded as angelic spirits. Without doubt the Lord wanted to make a laughingstock of the foolish boasting so common among the Chaldaeans when the king curtly demanded that they tell him the dream before they offer their explanation.

Afterwards he adds threats, now openly tyrannical. Unless they expound the dream it is the end for them. His threat is not of an ordinary execution; he says he will annihilate them, if we take the statement as *haddamin,* meaning 'pieces'. If we take it simply as 'blood', it will be a threat of death. However that may be, the king was obviously furiously angry; in this Nebuchadnezzar was worse than any wild beast. For how could the Chaldaeans be blamed for not knowing the king's dream? They had never made such a claim, as we shall see later; no king ever demanded what is above human capacity. Therefore we see that there was a feral raging in the king when he threatened the magi and arioles with death, more, with a cruel execution. Tyrants often give a loose rein to their passion, for they think anything is lawful for them. Hence the saying in the tragic poets 'Because he wants it, it is lawful.'[3] And Sophocles has good reasons for saying that anyone who crosses the threshold of a tyrant throws away his liberty.[4] But if we collected all the examples of this we should hardly find one like Nebuchadnezzar. Therefore it follows that the king's mind was impelled by such devilish fury that he wanted to exact punishment on the Chaldaeans, who yet were innocent in this respect. We know that they were impostors; we know that the world was deceived by their impostures; we know

---

3. *Quod libet, licet;* cf. Seneca, *Trojans* 336-37, and often in other writers.
4. Fragment 788 in A. Nauck, ed., *Tragicorum Graecorum Fragmenta* (Leipzig, 1856), p. 253.

they deserved death (for it was a capital crime according to the law to claim the power of forecasting by magic arts);[5] but in regard to the king, no crime could be laid at their door. Why then threaten them with death? Because the Lord in this way intended a miracle, as we shall see later. For if the king had let the Chaldaeans go, he could have at once repressed the anxiety which had worried and tormented him. The affair would also have been less known among the people. God therefore keeps on torturing the king's mind, so that he rushes headlong into a fury, as we have said. The fierce and savage threat was enough to excite everybody. For there is no doubt that high and low trembled when they heard of the king's blazing wrath. This, then, is the sum of it, and we should note the purpose of God's providence, why he so wished the king to flame up without moderation.

He goes on:

6 *'And if you will show the dream and its interpretation, a gift and a present and great honour* [or, "reward"] *you will receive from my face* [that is, "from me"]. *Therefore show me the dream and its interpretation.'*

Here the king changes his tune. He tries to entice them with a hope of gain to give their minds to telling his dream. So on the one hand he terrifies them, to drag the account of the dream and its interpretation out of them unwillingly if need be. But in case they might be won by fair words, he takes that line, and promises them *'a gift and a present and honour'*. That is, he provides a liberal reward if they will tell his dream and interpret it faithfully.

From this we infer the same thing that all the histories declare — that the magi made a good living out of their predictions and conjectures. The Indian sages, however, were men of frugal and austere life, and not greedy for gain. We know that they lived the sort of life in which neither money nor goods nor anything else was necessary. They were content to eat roots, had no need of clothing, and slept on the ground. And so avarice was unknown among them. But as for the Chaldaeans, we know that they used to be gadding about everywhere making the simple and credulous pay through the nose. The king was therefore following the usual custom when he promised a reward, a big reward at that.

But here we must notice that the Chaldaeans broadcast their prophecies just from desire for gain. When science becomes venal it cannot help being adulterated with many vices. Thus, when Paul speaks of the corrupters of the gospel, he calls them 'merchants'.[6] For once gain becomes the object it cannot fail immediately (as has been said) to degrade even otherwise good teachers

5. Mg., Lv. 20, i.e., 20:27.
6. Mg., 2 Cor. 2, i.e., 2:17.

and to pervert all sincerity into falsehood. When avarice reigns, there you will find flattery, there servile compliance, there craftiness. In short, truth is completely smothered. Wherefore it is not surprising that the Chaldaeans were so abandoned to deceit when their only aim was what they could make out of it and how much cash they could rake in. Of course, it is perfectly right for honest teachers to receive their upkeep from public funds. But if anyone be motivated by avarice (as has been said) all the purity of his teaching must necessarily be perverted and debased.

From this passage we again infer how anxious the king was; for he would spare no expense to get the interpretation of his dream out of the Chaldaeans. On the other hand, he was furiously angry with them, as if they were not supplying what the offered reward deserved.

Now he goes on:

7 *They replied a second time and said, 'Let the king expound* [or, "relate"] *his dream to his servants and we will show the interpretation.'*
8 *The king replied and said, 'Truly* ["in truth"] *I have known* ["already I am aware"] *that you are gaining time, because you know that the word has gone forth from me* [that is, "that the dream has gone from my mind"; or, "the verdict has proceeded from my mouth"].'

Let us add the next sentence:
9 *'Moreover, if you will not show me the dream, there* [is] *but one verdict for you. And a lying* [or, "false"] *and corrupt word you have prepared to say before me until the time changes* [that is, "passes away"]. *Therefore tell me the dream and I will know that you will show me* [that is, "you are able to explain to me"] *the interpretation.'*

Here he relates the magi's excuse. They say, quite truly, that their art is capable of doing nothing more than to give the interpretation of a dream. But the king wants to be told what his dream was. From this again it is clear that he was seized by a sort of monstrous fury and was quite unyielding. Kings sometimes boil over with rage, but one cautionary word will quieten them. The saying is very true: 'Wrath is broken by a soft word.'[7] But since this perfectly fair response of the magi does not lessen the king's anger it follows that he was completely carried away by some devilish fury. But all this was, as I said, governed by the secret purpose of God, to make Daniel's explanation the more wonderful.

So they ask that *'the king will relate his dream'* and again promise that they will be ready with the interpretation. But this was altogether too arrogant, as was said. At such a perilous moment they ought at least to have amended

7. Pr. 15:1.

their pride and foolish boasting somewhat. Their persistence in such foolish boasting and deception shows that they had been blinded by the devil. Those who are so involved in their superstitious arts will presumptuously maintain their madness. The magi give a clear example of this in the way they keep on falling back on their knowledge in the interpretation of dreams.

Now there follows the king's protest. *'I know'*, he says, *'that you are gaining time, because you know that the thing has gone from me'*, or, 'the word has been declared', if we take the former meaning. The king here accuses them of worse duplicity: the magi do not possess what they claim; they want to slip out of it because they know the king has completely forgotten his dream. So it is just as if he said, 'You promise that you will tell me a sure interpretation of the dream; but this is false. Were I to relate the dream it would be easy to detect your arrogance, because you would not be able to explain the mystery [*aenigma*]. But although you know that I have forgotten the dream you want me to tell it to you.' But *'this is just gaining time'*, he says. 'So you cover over your ignorance and still cherish the opinion that you are learned. If my dream had stuck in my memory, I could easily detect your ignorance, for you cannot perform what you are claiming.'

So we see the king accusing the magi of another fault — that they are impostors, deluding the people with false pretences. He tells them they deserve to die if they will not tell him his dream. This is a bad and faulty argument. Yet it is not surprising if tyrants can always find excuses for their barbarity. Nevertheless, we must bear in mind what I have said, that the magi deserved the rebukes, for they were empty wind-bags, making false promises that they could conjecture the future from dreams and auguries and the like. But as for the king, there was nothing more unfair than to attach such a crime to the magi. For although they deceived others, they also deceived themselves, being blinded, even bewitched, by their foolish belief in this pseudo-wisdom. Nor did they mean to deceive the king. For they thought that something would at once occur to them and they could set him free from all anxiety. But the king attacks them all the time in a blind rush of savagery. So we must observe the primary cause — he is being tortured by God and cannot have a moment's peace until he has got the explanation of his dream.

Afterwards he adds: *'If you do not explain the dream to me, this one verdict stands'*, he says; that is, 'what is already decreed about you all. I shall not ask who is individually guilty or who wants to deceive me, but I shall cut off completely the whole line of the magi. In short, none will escape execution unless you tell me both the dream and its interpretation.'

Afterwards he adds, *'You have prepared a lying and corrupt word, that you might say here before me — and this takes away your excuse.'* Again the king protests against the deceit and malice of which they were not even aware. It is as if he said that they were deliberately seeking specious pretexts for deceiving him. But he says *'a lying'*, or 'deceitful', *'and corrupt word';* that is, 'your excuse is disgusting', or as we say colloquially, 'it stinks'. 'If there were any excuse, I could accept what you say, but I see there is nothing but deceit in your words, deceit that smacks of rottenness.' So now we see that the king was not only angry that the magi refused to tell him his dream but also that he accused them of the graver fault of uttering something disgusting and deliberately wanting to make fun of him.

Afterwards he adds, *'Tell me the dream and then I will know',* or 'by which I will then know', 'that you are able to interpret its substance faithfully.' Here the king takes up another argument to convict the magi of cunning: 'You have boasted that the interpretation of my dream is not difficult for you. On what grounds? For you still do not know the dream itself. If I tell it to you, you will be able to say whatever occurs to you. But I am asking about a dream which is hidden both from you and from me; and all you can say is, "when I tell you the dream, the rest will be easy". I shall only know that you are good and skilful interpreters of dreams when you can tell me this dream. The one depends on the other. And you are too presumptuous about what is still unknown to you. When, then, you rush in so rashly and want to persuade me that you know the interpretation, you are deceiving me in this way as well. Both your rashness and your deceit are uncovered by the game you are playing with me.' This is the sum.

The rest tomorrow.

Grant, almighty God, inasmuch as in our earthly pilgrimage we daily need the teaching and governance of your Spirit, that we may with true modesty depend both on your Word and on his secret inspiration, lest we take too much upon ourselves. Let us be conscious of our own ignorance and blindness and stupidity and always flee to you and not be drawn hither and thither by the cunning of Satan and the ungodly, but remain so fixed in your truth that we never swerve from it, while you direct us through all the course of our vocation and we arrive at the heavenly glory of your kingdom which is won for us by the blood of your only-begotten Son. Amen.

Lecture 6

10 *The Chaldaeans answered before the king and said, 'There is not a man on earth who can explain the word* [or, "matter" *(rem)*] *of the king. And therefore no king or prince or governor has sought a like thing from any magus or astrologer or Chaldaean.'*

The Chaldaeans again apologize for not being able to tell the king his dream. In effect they are saying that this is no part of their art or science and that there is no precedent for interrogating the learned in this way — that they should reply both *de facto* and *de jure*, as they say. They certainly claimed to be interpreters of dreams; but their conjectures could not embrace the dreams themselves but only covered the interpretation. This was obviously a fair excuse. But the king did not admit it. He was moved with fury (as was said yesterday), and that not without the secret impulse of God, that he might unmask the magi and arioles and astrologers as mere impostors who deceived the people. And we must continually keep our eye on the purpose, that God wished to exalt his servant Daniel and exempt him from the common rank. They add also that no kings or princes ever acted like this towards the magi and the learned.

Afterward he goes on:

11 *'And the word about which the king asks is precious* [or, "rare"]; *and there is none who can explain it before the king, except the gods, whose habitation is not with flesh.'* [Many of the words are superfluous, as that language permits.]

They add that what the king seeks exceeds human grasp. Doubtless this was an unwilling confession; for, as was said previously, they had acquired such fame for their wisdom that the common people thought nothing was hid from them, nothing unknown. By confessing their ignorance in this matter they were no doubt seeking safety in flight. In their extreme peril they were forced to have recourse even to this subterfuge.

It may be doubted why they say here that the word which the king asks about is 'precious'. For they do not know what the king had dreamed. Whence then the preciousness? But it is not surprising for those who are anxious and smitten with extreme fear to babble senselessly. They say that *'the thing is precious'* — they put some flattery in with their other excuses to soften the king's anger and so escape the imminent death that he threatens them with. *'The word which the king asks about is precious'* — and yet this could also probably mean that this was no common thing, that the king's dream had been divinely sent and was afterwards buried in sudden oblivion. Therefore there must be a certain mystery here, and it is not without reason that the Chaldaeans say that this business, or 'thing', was too great and high for the common capacity of the human mind.

So they add, *'there can be no other interpreters than the gods* (or, "angels")'. Some refer this to angels. But we know that among the magi a multiplicity of gods was worshipped. It is therefore simpler to expound it of their crowd of imaginary gods. They had, of course, lesser gods. For all nations always nursed the opinion that there was one supreme god, who alone ruled. And under him they invented lesser gods. And each fabricated a god for himself after his own wishes. Here then they call them 'gods' in the common parlance and opinion. Yet it can be referred to the *genii* or gods of the air. For we know that all unbelievers were imbued with the opinion that there were intermediary gods. The apostles fought strenuously against that ancient error. And we know the Platonist books are stuffed full with the doctrine that between the heavenly *numen* ('divinity') and human beings there are demons or *genii* as mediators. Therefore, these words are easily understood when we remember that the Chaldaeans thought that angels alone were interpreters, not because they held a genuine or clear scriptural view of angels, but because there flourished among them the Platonic doctrine, or superstition, about *genii* who both live in heaven and have commerce with the highest god and are at the same time 'familiars' to mortals. Because humans are clothed with flesh they cannot raise themselves to heaven so as to perceive all its secrets. Hence it follows that the king acted unfairly in demanding an angelic or divine office of them. This excuse was also credible. But the king's ears were deaf and he was carried away by his fury. God was driving him with the Furies, so that he could not be at rest.

Hence, therefore, his violence, which Daniel adds:

12 *Therefore the king in his great wrath and anger commanded that all the*
wise men of Babylon should be killed.

The threat that we saw earlier was horrifying, but now Nebuchadnezzar
goes even further. He does not simply menace the Chaldaeans with death but
actually orders them to be killed. Another such example will hardly be found in
all history. But we must always note the cause: he was in this turbulence of mind
because God wished to bring his servant Daniel into the open, to be a spectacle
to all. And all this was a preparation for his being known by everyone. It was
done openly so that the wise men of Babylon might be found to be empty,
promising more than they could perform. Had they been endowed with the
utmost learning they would still have lacked the gift of revelation which Daniel
possessed. Hence the king gave his command and sentenced them all to death. It
may also be that he then realized something he had never thought of before —
that there was a great deal of emptiness in their claims and in all their art many
conjuring tricks. When their superstitious practice failed to succeed, his rage at
once surfaced. (We see those who are thought, in common parlance, very devout,
break out into what I have called a rage, when they understand that their fictitious
worship profits nothing, and curse their idols and hate what hitherto they had
followed.) So it may be that Nebuchadnezzar now smelt out their impostures in
this vital matter, whereas previously no such idea had crossed his mind. He sees
he has been deceived and is at the same time in this perplexing affair and in such
anxiety left without advice from those from whom he had hoped everything, and
he is a hundred times more mad than if he had started off calmly.

Afterwards he goes on:

13 *And the decree went out; and the wise men were being put to death. And*
they sought Daniel and his friends to put them to death.
14 *And then Daniel sought to learn* [about] *the purpose and decree from*
Arioch the chief of the king's body-guard who had gone out to put to death
the wise men of Babylon.
15 *He replied and said to Arioch the king's commander* [it is the same word
'prefect' that we saw a little before], *'Why does the decree hasten from the*
presence of the king?' *Then Arioch opened the affair* [or, 'word'] *to Daniel.*

From the words it appears that some of the wise men had already been
killed. For Daniel was not sought out for death among the first. When the magi
and Chaldaeans were indiscriminately haled off to execution, Daniel and his
friends were in the same danger. And he expressly says *the edict went out,* that
is, 'was made public' (this phrase occurs in Latin, too, sometimes), *and the*
wise men were being put to death. Daniel was then also sought out. The king
never allowed his decree to be treated lightly when once it had been pro-

olaimcd. If he had publicly commanded this and no executions had followed, would it not have been ridiculous? We therefore gather by probable inference that many of the magi and Chaldaeans had already been killed.

Now, although the king's cause was not lawful, they were given a just punishment. For (as was said yesterday) they deserved to be exterminated. The pest should be removed, so far as possible. Had Nebuchadnezzar been like David or Hezekiah or Josiah, he could with good right have killed them all and purged the earth of such a pollution. But he transgressed in that he had only been carried away by his blazing anger. Yet God took just punishment on the Chaldaeans. And this warning ought to have profited the whole people, but they were hardened in their error and were without doubt made the more inexcusable in being blind to such a judgment of God.

That Daniel was also destined for execution when he had not even been summoned by the king shows how unfair are the edicts of those kings who fail to make due enquiries into the cases they judge. Nebuchadnezzar had very often heard Daniel and had been forced to admire his skilfulness and his singular gift of wisdom. How, then, did he come to forget him when he needed the advice he alone could give? Therefore, we see that, although the king inquired carefully about the dream, he had not taken really serious action. For the thought would without doubt come into his mind, 'Look! you have already noticed the incredible gift of heavenly wisdom in the captive Jews. Summon them first of all.' Hence the king's negligence in not summoning Daniel at least along with the others is uncovered. We said that this had been governed by the secret providence of God, who did not wish his servant to get mixed up with those ministers of Satan whose science consisted of nothing but tricks and delusions. And as for the king, we see that he neglected the gift of God and, so to say, stifled the light set before him.

Now he drags Daniel away to death. I said that tyrants are commonly unjust and practise terrible violence because they cannot take the trouble and labour to investigate a case. Yet we see how God wonderfully rescues his own out of the jaws of death, as happens with Daniel. For it ought to seem a wonder to us that Arioch spared his life when he was killing the rest — and they natives. How then did it happen that Daniel met with more kindness than the Chaldaeans, when he was a foreigner and a captive? Because his life was in the hand and protection of God, who restrained the commander's mind and hand so that he did not at once butcher him. And it is said that *Daniel asked about the purpose and decree*. Some translate it, 'prudently and shrewdly'; and עֵטָה, *etah,* means 'prudence', as also טְעֵם, *teem,* is metaphorically taken for 'understanding', when it signifies 'taste'. But afterwards we shall see *teem* taken for 'decree'; and since this meaning seems to fit better here, I accept it. Daniel was asking the commander what the king's decree and purpose was. Arioch is also called the 'commander of the body-guard'. Some render it, 'of the executioners', others, 'of the cooks'. For *tabah*, טבח, means 'to slay'; but the title derived from it signifies 'a cook'. This is what Potiphar was called in Genesis 39[1] — the man to whom Joseph was sold. To me there seems some absurdity in saying that Potiphar was the commander of the executioners. But if we say that Arioch was commander of the cooks, it hardly seems to square with his office that he was sent to kill the Chaldaeans. Therefore I prefer to interpret it more temperately, that he was the commander of the body-guard. For, as I said, Potiphar was called רב טבחים, *rab tabbahim,* and here only the pronunciation is changed.

It goes on: *Daniel also said, 'Why does the decree hasten from the sight of the king?'* By these words it seems that Daniel was indirectly blaming the king's anger and also his ingratitude; his anger because he did not investigate carefully enough before he burst out with the cruel penalty, and his ingratitude because he now drags off to death one who, despite the king's knowledge of his capabilities, had not been consulted. When then he says 'hasten', I have no doubt he was finding fault with the king because he had not been summoned or heard and yet was being slaughtered along with the rest, as if he were equally to blame (that is, if the 'Chaldaeans' had been guilty in this respect). The sum of it is that there was no reason why the king should be in such a hurry; if he enquired more carefully he might perhaps find what he wanted.

Afterwards he adds that *Arioch explained the matter to Daniel.* From this it appears that Daniel had been ignorant of the whole affair so far. So we may guess how frightened he was. He had been in complete ignorance, and now suddenly and incredibly he was being dragged off to execution. He needed to be strengthened by God to compose himself and beg for time from the commander and from the king, so that he could tell the king his dream and give its interpretation. That Daniel could be so composed was a remarkable blessing from God; otherwise his mind would have been stupefied by terror. And we know how in sudden crises we lose our composure and our hearts fail us. When, therefore, nothing like this appears in Daniel, it is certain that his mind was being governed by the Spirit of God.

Afterwards he adds:

16 *And Daniel went in and asked from the king that he should be given time, and might bring the explanation* ['interpretation'] *to the king.*

This verse contains nothing new, except that we must note something that has not been expressed. The commander granted Daniel's request and took him to the king, though with some apprehension, for he knew how furious the king was. To fail to carry out his decree at once was offensive. But, as already said,

---

1. Gn. 39:1.

because God had taken Daniel under his protection, he turned the commander's mind to such kindness that he did not hesitate to bring Daniel to the king.

Something else can be gathered from the context — that Daniel obtained what he asked. For it says that *he returned to his house;* without any doubt because he had obtained one day from the king, so as to make good his promise on the morrow. Yet it is surprising that this was granted, for the king wanted to be told his dream without delay. Daniel does not expressly state the reasons he laid before the king, but probably he confessed what we shall see in its due place — that he was not endowed with such discernment that he could explain dreams, but that he hoped by the blessing of God he would return on the morrow with a new revelation. The king would never have given permission if Daniel had seemed doubtful or had not declared that he hoped for a secret revelation from God. He would have been rejected out of hand and would have provoked the king's anger even worse. (And it is common for Hebrew to omit something from its proper place and then take it up in a later context.) But when he modestly confesses the truth, that he could not gratify the king until he had received from the Lord what he would faithfully hand on to him, the king grants him the time. And we shall see this more clearly later.

He goes on:

17   *Then Daniel came* [went away] *to his house and opened the word* [or, 'affair'] *to his friends Hananiah, Mishael, and Azariah.*
18   *And to plead for mercies* [literally; that is, 'that they should plead for mercy'] *from the face of the God of heaven about this secret, so that Daniel and his friends might not be killed with the residue of the wise men of Babylon* [that is, with the remaining wise men of Babylon].

We see for what purpose and with what confidence Daniel asked for time. His purpose was to implore the grace of God. And he was confident because he knew that he was in danger of a double punishment if the king should be balked of his hope. If on the morrow he should return empty-handed, the king would not be content with meting out a quick and straightforward death but would show Daniel terrible cruelty, as if he had been mocking him. Without doubt, then, Daniel hoped for what he in fact obtained — that the king's dream should be revealed to him.

So he proposes to his friends that they should beg mercy from God at the same time as himself. Daniel already had the powerful and remarkable gift of being an interpreter of dreams; moreover, he alone was God's prophet, as we saw. For God used to reveal his purpose to the prophets either by dreams or through visions.[2] Daniel had obtained both. From Mishael, Hananiah, and Azariah

2. Mg., Nu. 12, i.e., 12:6.

associating themselves with him in prayer, we infer that they had no motive of ambition or self-seeking. For if they had been jealous of Daniel, they could not have prayed with one consent. For they did not individually make up their own prayers; they only prayed that the interpretation of the dream might be revealed to Daniel. Hence we see that they sincerely agreed in their prayers and that all pride and ambition and self-seeking were far from them.

Moreover, it is worth noticing that they are said *to beg mercy from God.* For although they are not entering the presence of God as being guilty, yet because they hoped to be given freely what they asked, the word 'mercy' is used. So often as we flee to God for help in our needs, our eyes and thoughts must always be turned on his mercy. For it is his free generosity alone that makes him kind to us.

What is said at the end of the verse, *lest they should perish with those that were left of the wise men of Babylon,* some expound as if the four friends were worried about the lives of the magi and wanted to save them from death. But although they desired the welfare of all men, there is no doubt that they are here separating themselves from the magi and Chaldaeans, as they had a completely different outlook from them.

Now he goes on:

19   *Then the secret was revealed to Daniel in a vision of the night: then Daniel blessed the God of heaven.*

Here it can be inferred that Daniel did not vacillate or pray with his friends doubtfully. For we ought to remember that saying of James: 'Those who doubt and fear and pray to God diffidently are unworthy to be heard. Let not such a man think', says James, 'that he will obtain anything from the Lord if he is tossed about like the waves of the sea.'[3] So, by God showing that he is propitious to the prayers it is clear that Daniel prayed with complete confidence, convinced that his life was in God's care. He also felt that God had not harassed King Nebuchadnezzar's mind for nothing but had prepared some remarkable and memorable judgment. Convinced of this, he conceives a firm faith and prays to God as if he had already received. And on the other hand we see that God never shuts his ears when he is called upon rightly and sincerely — as also it is said in the Psalm, 'He is near to all who call on him — but in truth.'[4] But there can be no truth where faith is lacking. Because Daniel brought faith and sincerity to his prayer, he was straightway heard and the secret of the dream was revealed to him in a vision of the night.

I cannot go on any more now.

3. Mg., Jas. 1, i.e., 1:6-8.
4. Mg., Ps. 145, i.e., 145:18.

LECTURE 6

Grant, O almighty God — for we stand in danger every day and every moment, not only from the savagery of a single tyrant but the whole world is incited by the devil against us and the princes of this world are armed and driven on to destroy us — grant, I say, that we may feel and that you may show by experience itself that our life is in your hand and that you will be a faithful custodian and will not suffer one hair of our head to fall; but that you will so keep us that the ungodly also may know that today we do not glory in your name in vain, call upon you in vain. And when we shall have experienced your fatherly care in the whole course of our life, grant that we may at last attain to that blessed immortality which you have promised us and which is laid up for us in heaven through Jesus Christ our Lord. Amen.

Lecture 7

20 *Daniel spoke* [literally, 'replied'] *and said, 'Blessed be the name of God for ever and ever; his is wisdom, and power is his'* [there are three superfluous particles. But the meaning is clear.]

Here Daniel proceeds with his narration. He thanked God after the dream of King Nebuchadnezzar had been revealed to him. He summarizes the words he had used: *'Blessed be the name of God'*, he says, *'for ever and ever.'* This is something we should ask for daily; when we pray that God's name be hallowed, a perpetuity is indicated under that form of prayer. But here Daniel breaks out in praises of God with great fervour, acknowledging his singular blessing in snatching him and his friends from death, against all hope. And when God confers some wonderful blessing on his servants, they are the more stirred up to praise him; as David said, 'You have put a new song in my mouth.'[1] And twice Isaiah uses the word, 'That God has given cause for a new and fresh song, for he has dealt marvellously with his Church.'[2] Thus there is no doubt that Daniel wished to praise God in an unusual way because he had experienced this exceptional grace of being rescued from imminent death.

Afterwards he adds, *'of whom'*. Here the relative is taken for a causal particle, so that it should be rendered, *'because his are wisdom and power'*. The added particles can be confirmatory and can be taken for an exclusive particle, as if he were saying that there is one God to whom is due the praise both of wisdom and power. For apart from him either would be sought in vain.

But it seems that this thanksgiving does not fit the present occasion.

1. Mg., Ps. 40, i.e., 40:3.
2. Mg., Is. 42, i.e., 42:9-10.

For Daniel ought to have celebrated the praises of God for revealing the vision to him and should have been content with this alone. But here he proclaims God's glory on account of both his power and his wisdom. When Scripture wants to distinguish the true God from all invented gods, it uses these two principles — that God governs all things by his hand and keeps them under his rule; and then, that nothing is hid from him. These two things cannot be separated when the majesty of God is being considered. We see that men fabricate things for themselves and so come to have an innumerable medley of gods, ascribing to each its particular office. This is because they cannot be content with a simple unity where God is concerned. Others invent a sort of half-god. Such are all those that prate about 'the naked foreknowledge'. They confess that nothing is hidden from God but that he foreknows all things; and to this they refer all the predictions that are made in the Scriptures. What they say is true. But yet they diminish God's glory — no, they completely tear him asunder; for they make him like the Apollo whose office of old time was to foretell the future (as unbelievers used to think). So when they sought a forecast of the future, the Apollo had the power to reveal this or that. There are many today who think God is like that, foreseeing all things; yet he either keeps his secrets or else deliberately withdraws from governing the world. In short, their 'foreknowledge of God' is frigid and an idle speculation. As I said, they rob God of one part of his glory, and, so far as in them lies, tear him apart. But when Scripture wishes to assert what is proper to God, it joins these two things inseparably: that God foresees all things because there is nothing hid from his eyes; and then, that he himself determines what is to come, governs the world by his will; nothing happens by chance but only by his government. And so Daniel now takes this principle, or these two principles, that the God of Israel alone deserves the name of God because to him belong wisdom and power. Let us therefore remember that God is defrauded of his just praise when these two are not kept whole — that he foresees all things, and that he governs the world so that nothing happens except by his will.

But because that would still be frigid (that wisdom and power are God's alone and in himself alone) unless the wisdom were to shine in the world and the power also were able to be known, he goes on at once to say:

21 *'And himself* [or, "himself is he who"] *changes times and divisions of times; he sets up kings and deposes kings. He gives wisdom to the wise and learning to those who know learning* [that is, "to those who are strong in learning"].'

In these words Daniel explains more clearly what might be obscure. He teaches that God is the fountain of wisdom and power in such a way that he does not confine within himself what belongs to him alone but sheds it through heaven and earth. And we must notice this carefully. For it seems that the saying was not really very sublime when Paul affirmed that God alone is wise.[3] But when we reckon that the wisdom of God is set before our eyes on all sides in the heavens and on earth we shall better realize how and in what sense Paul pronounced that God alone is wise. God therefore, as I have already said, does not keep wisdom enclosed within himself but makes it flow throughout the whole world.

The sum of this verse is that all the power and wisdom which are in the world are a witness to the power and wisdom of God. It is men's ingratitude that, when they find something praiseworthy in themselves or in others, they at once appropriate it as their own. Thus God's glory is diminished, but it is by their perversity in the face of his self-revelation. But here we are taught that, so far from derogating from God's wisdom and power, all the wisdom and power to be seen in the world rather enhance them the more. So we grasp the prophet's intention — God sets these testimonies of his power and wisdom before our eyes like mirrors, when things change in the world, when men are powerful in wisdom, when some are raised on high and others cast down. Experience teaches us that these things are not due to human contrivance or to any balancing of nature. Supreme kings fall and others gain their high honours. Daniel therefore tells us that we are not to look to heaven alone for God's wisdom and power, because it is manifest to us on earth, and daily examples of both offer themselves to our eyes. Now we see how these two verses hang together. He had said that wisdom was of God alone; now he shows that God does not conceal it within himself but reveals it to us, so that now we may know from ordinary experience that whatever wisdom there is flows from him and that he is its unique source. We must think just the same of his power.

Therefore, 'he it is who changes times and divisions of times'. We know that it is all ascribed to fortune that the world goes through uncertain changes, so that every day something will be changed. And the irreligious infer from this that all things are turned around by a blind impulse. Others say that the human race is the play-thing of God and that men are tossed about like balls. But, as I have already said, there is nothing surprising in those of a perverse and corrupt mind viewing all God's works in the worst light. As for us, let us hold to what the prophet teaches here, that all the changes [revolutiones], as they are called, are testimonies to the power of God and indicate that human affairs are divinely governed. For it is necessary to hold either the one or the other, either that nature rules in human affairs or that fortune switches hither and thither things which ought to go smoothly forward. As far as nature is concerned, its system would be equable if God, in his singular purpose, as it

3. Mg., Rom. 17, i.e., 16:27.

seems good to him, did not make changes in the conditions of the times. The philosophers who give nature the supreme rule are much saner than the rest, who set fortune in the highest place. For if we admit what these latter mean, that human affairs are turned about by the impulse of accidental fortune, where does this fortune come from? If we ask them for a definition, what do they reply? They are, of course, compelled to allow that the name 'fortune' is an empty concept. But neither God nor nature will have any place in the empty and so to say changeable government of the world where all things without any order rush into their earthly form. If this be granted, the doctrine of Epicurus will certainly find a place; for if God resigns supreme control of the world and all things come about by accident, then God has ceased to be. But in these changes he is stretching out his hand to claim the rule of the world for himself.

Therefore, let us remember in all the changes which continually come upon us and in which the appearance of the world is, in a sense, renewed, that the providence of God shines and things do not flow on in an even current; for what is proper to God alone cannot then be ascribed to probability. God, I say, so changes empires and the alternation of times that we may learn to look to him. If the sun rose and set equally, or at least if there were an assured yearly symmetry without adventitious change, we should not have shorter days in winter and longer in summer. Then we would be able to infer that there was a sure order in nature; and in this way God would be, as it were, deposed from his rule. But when winter days are different from summer; when spring does not always have the same weather — sometimes it is stormy or snowy, sometimes it gives us summer warmth; again, when summers are so variable that no two years are the same; when the weather will change within hours or minutes and the heavens put on a new face — when we see all these things, God is as it were waking us up so that we may not lie stupidly in our own gross ideas and imagine that nature is some divinity, thus depriving God himself of his legitimate honour and transferring to our own conceptions what he claims for himself alone. If in these common things men are forced to acknowledge God's providence, if any very important change occurs (as when God transfers empires and as it were transfigures the world) should we not then be the more affected — unless we are quite stupid?

Therefore Daniel with good reason here corrects the perverted opinion which controls nearly everyone's mind, that either the world is changed by chance or that nature is the supreme divinity. For he asserts that it is God who changes times and brings about vicissitudes. But strictly he is speaking of empires, as the context shows, that he sets up and deposes kings. We find it hard to believe that it is by God that kings are set on their thrones and then cast down again. For we think that an empire is gained by industry or by hereditary right, or just by fortune. God is overlooked when human industry,

70

or power, or good fortune, or the like, is elevated like this. So it is said in the Psalm, 'Neither from the east, nor from the west; but God is judge alone.'[4] The prophet there laughs at the discourse (as they call it) of the wise, who gather together all the arguments to show that empires come to men either by their own planning and power or by good fortune or by other human and inferior means. 'Look around wherever you will', he says, 'but from the rising of the sun to its setting you will not find a reason why one rather than another is in power. The Lord therefore is judge alone' — that is, government remains in the power of God alone. So also in this passage the Lord is said to appoint kings and to remove them when it seems good to him.

This fine argument could be treated more fully; but because the same occasion will occur in many other passages, I am now briefly touching only on what the verse contains. For the estate of kingdoms and their ruin and changes will be frequently spoken of. I therefore do not want to load you with everything that I have in hand. It will be enough to show Daniel's intention.

Afterwards he adds *'he gives wisdom to the wise and learning to those who are endowed with learning'*. In this second clause the prophet confirms what we have already said: God's wisdom is not hidden in darkness but is revealed to us. For God daily gives us sure and clear evidences of it. He also here corrects men's ingratitude; by taking the praise away from God's excellence and giving it to themselves, they are always close to being sacrilegious. Daniel therefore declares that there is no wisdom in men save from God. Some, of course, are wise; they may be highly intelligent. But the question is, does it come from themselves? Daniel shows that men are ill-natured and envious when they claim anything for themselves, even if all are ravished with admiration of them; for they have nothing of their own. Who will boast that he is wise by his own strength? that he begat the wisdom with which he is endued? Since, then, God is the sole author of both wisdom and learning, gifts with which he adorns men, these do not obscure his glory but rather should enhance it.

22 *'He reveals deep and hidden things; he knows what* [lies] *in darkness, and light dwells with him* [or, "in his power"].*'*

He pursues and confirms the same line of thought: that it is from the Spirit of God that all mortal men draw all the understanding and light that they have. Yet he goes further in this verse than before. For he had said in general that men are wise and understand by the blessing of God. But now he takes up one particular — that where there is rare and unusual intelligence, the gift of God is shining more clearly there. As if he were saying that it is according

4. Mg., Ps. 75, i.e., 75:6-7.

to the measure of his liberality that God distributes to individual mortals whatever shrewdness and intelligence they may possess, but that he adorns some with such understanding that they appear to be interpreters of himself. Therefore he is speaking here properly of the prophetic gift — as if he were saying that the goodness of God is seen not only in the common prudence of men (because none is so backward as not to distinguish between right and wrong and as not to have some standards in ruling his life) but that in the prophets there is something beyond the ordinary which makes the wisdom of God more wonderful to us. Whence have the prophets the ability to prophesy about hidden things, to penetrate above the heavens, to transcend all bourns? Is this common in men? Since, therefore, he far surpasses the grasp of common men, the prophet there teaches that God's benefit and power together deserve the more praise because *'he reveals hidden and secret things'*.

And in this sense he adds that *'light dwells with God'*. As if he were saying that God is far different from us because we are wrapped in many darknesses or clouds, but for God everything is clear, so that he nowhere hesitates, he does not enquire, he is not impeded by ignorance. So now we grasp the prophet's intention.

But let us learn from this passage to give God the praise which the larger part of the earth arrogate to themselves in sacrilegious audacity but which God shows belongs to himself. Let us remember to give God the credit for all the intelligence and judgment that we have. Even if there exists in us only a drop of common-sense we are to that degree indebted to God; for we should be like stocks or stones unless by his secret instinct he had given us intelligence. But even if anyone excels and is the wonder of almost the whole world, let him also humbly subject himself to God and acknowledge that he is the more indebted to him because he has received more than others. For who singled him out but God? The higher the intelligence with which any is honoured, the more he should magnify God's blessing, taking everything away from himself.

In the third place we learn that the understanding of spiritual things is a rare and singular gift of the Holy Spirit, and that it is especially in this that God's power is conspicuous. So let us beware of that devilish pride with which we see nearly the whole world is unwarrantably drunken and puffed up. Let us in this respect especially glorify God that he not only adorned us with common prudence so that the distinction between good and evil might exist among us, but also raised us above common nature and so enlightened us that we may grasp what would otherwise far exceed our apprehension.

Now when Daniel declares that *'light is with God'*, we should supply a tacit antithesis; for he hints, as I have already mentioned, that men are encompassed by many darknesses and as it were grope their way in obscurity. Here man's dwelling-place is indirectly compared to the sanctuary of God. It is as if the prophet were saying that nowhere is there pure and genuine light save in God alone. Therefore when we remain at home — that is, in our own state — we must needs wander in darkness or at least be surrounded with thick fog. The point of these words is that we should not be content with our own grasp but should await from God that light in which he dwells alone. Yet let us remember that God 'dwells in light inaccessible'[5] — save in so far as he stretches out his hand to us. Therefore, if we desire to be made partakers of the divine light, let us beware of presumption. Let us be mindful of our ignorance, and ask the Lord to enlighten us. His light will not be inaccessible to us when his Spirit leads us above heaven itself.

Afterwards he adds:

23 *'I confess to you, O God of my fathers, and I praise* ['and also I praise'] *you who have given me wisdom and strength; and now you have made known to me what we asked of you; who have revealed to us the business* [or, "the question"] *of the king.'*

Daniel directs his speech to God. *'You'*, he says, *'I confess, O God of my fathers, and you I praise.'* Here he more openly distinguishes the God of Israel from all the fictions of the nations. For it is no empty epithet that he uses when he praises 'the God of his fathers'. Rather he intended to reduce to nothing the multitude of gods all the other nations had invented. Daniel rejects them as empty and false, and shows that only the God of Israel was worthy of all praise.

But he does not base the glory of God on the authority of his fathers, as the papists do. When they want to add some high power, either to George or to Catharine or to their other rubbish, they enumerate how many centuries their error has persisted. They want what a consensus of men has approved to be received as an oracle. But if religion is based on human consensus, what sort of stability will it have? We know that there is nothing more hollow than human thinking. 'If man', says the prophet, 'is weighed against vanity in the scales, vanity will be the heavier.'[6] Nothing, therefore, is more foolish than that principle — that is, of thinking about religion in terms of the consensus of many ages.

But here Daniel commends the God of his fathers because those fathers were the children of God. The sacred adoption by which God chose Abraham and his whole race was a powerful force among the Jews. Daniel, therefore, is not here extolling the persons of men, as if they could, or ought to, add to God what they liked. When he said that *'the God of Israel was the God of his*

---

5. Mg., 1 Tim. 6, i.e., 6:16.
6. Mg., Ps. 62, i.e., 62:9.

fathers' it was simply because he was of the progeny which God had adopted. In sum, he so opposes the God of Israel to all the idols of the gentiles as to set the mark of distinction in the covenant itself and in the heavenly doctrine by which God revealed himself to the holy fathers. In that the gentiles lacked any oracles and followed their own dreams, Daniel here rightly speaks of *'the God of his fathers'*.

Afterwards he adds, *'because you have given me wisdom and strength'*. As for 'wisdom', it is clear enough why Daniel gave thanks to God. It was because he had received (as he says a little later) the revelation of the dream, and also because he had previously been endued with the prophetic spirit and visions, as he related in chapter 1, verse 17. But here it may be asked what he means by *'strength'*. For he had not enjoyed a high position among men or been a commander in war. In short, he had given no proofs of outstanding power for which he could thank God. But Daniel was looking to the principle on which he took his stand, that the God of Israel was to be known as the true and only God from the fact that whatever power and wisdom there are in the world flow from him, as from a spring. It is according to this principle that he is now speaking of himself and all others. For it is as if he were saying, 'If there is in me any strength or understanding, I ascribe it entirely to you, for it is yours.' And certainly, although Daniel was never king or commander, yet the invincible greatness of mind that we see in him should not be counted as nothing. And so he acknowledges deservedly as divine whatever in this respect was conferred on him. In short, his purpose is to make himself completely empty that he might attribute to God what is his alone. But he puts it briefly, as has been said, because he had comprehended the proof of the divinity already under 'wisdom' and under 'power'.

Afterwards he adds, *'because you have made known to me what we asked of you; you have revealed to us the king's question.'* It seems contradictory that he should praise God that he himself had received the revelation of the dream and then join the others with himself. The revelation was not common to them all; it was his alone. The solution is easy. First he makes it clear that it was given peculiarly to himself to know the king's dream and to grasp its interpretation. This confessed, he extends the blessing to his friends; and deservedly, for, although they did not yet know what God had conferred on Daniel, Daniel had nevertheless received the favour for them all — they had all been rescued from death, and also their prayers had been heard. It strengthened and confirmed their faith when they knew they had not prayed in vain. And we said that there was no ambition in their prayers, with each one praying for something for himself so that he himself could gain honour and esteem before the world. Nothing of that sort. It was enough for them to glorify God's name among the unbelievers. That they were also rescued from death was an added benefit from God. Therefore Daniel deservedly says that the king's dream and its interpretation had been revealed to him, and this he afterwards transfers also to his friends.

Grant, O almighty God —for although so many testimonies of your glory are daily before our eyes, we are blind and bury the light under our ingratitude —grant, I say, that we may now at last learn to open our eyes —no, open them for us by your Spirit — that, reckoning the many and great and remarkable benefits in which you show yourself to us and assert the testimony of your eternal divinity —that, reckoning, I say, all this, we may progress in the school of godliness and so learn to ascribe to you all praise for all our faculties, that no praise may remain for ourselves but that we may exalt you alone. And the more you condescend to declare yourself liberal to us, so much the more may we apply ourselves to worship you fervently and devote ourselves entirely to you, leaving no remnant of praise in ourselves but caring only that all the glory may rest with you alone and that it may shine in all the world, through Christ our Lord. Amen.

Lecture 8

24 *And so Daniel went in to Arioch, whom the king had appointed to destroy* ['to kill'] *the wise men of Babylon. Therefore he came and spoke thus to him, 'Do not destroy the wise men of Babylon. Take me to the king, and I will show the interpretation to the king.'*

Before Daniel brought the message to the king he performed (as was seen yesterday) his proper duty of piety. He declared his gratitude to God for revealing the secret. But now he says that *he came to Arioch, who had been sent by the king to kill the magi, and asked him not to kill them, for he had the revelation* — on which we will speak later. Here it is to be noted that some of the magi had already been killed, as I have said. For Arioch would never have dared defer even for a few days when once he had received the king's command. But after Daniel had asked for time a delay was granted. Arioch, by the king's order, ceased to persecute the magi. Daniel now asks him to spare the rest.

Yet this does not seem very wise, for it was desirable for those magical arts to be completely abolished. We saw earlier that they are tricks of the devil. In reply it can be said that, although Daniel saw many faults and corruptions in the magi and their art or science (or false and deceiving profession of science), yet in that the principles were true, he did not wish without more ado to destroy what had proceeded from God. But to me Daniel seems to have another purpose. For although the magi could have been completely wiped out without great loss, he was looking rather to the case itself; and this is why he wished to spare them. It often happens that the wicked, who deserve a dozen deaths, are brought to trial; but, if there is no just case against them, we ought to spare their persons — not because they deserve it but because we must always keep to equity and right dealing. Therefore it is probable that when

76

Daniel was aware of the king's tyrannical command for the magi to be slaughtered, he saw that there had been no case for it and that they were being killed from savage and cruel violence. I therefore reckon that Daniel did not spare the magi for their own sake. He certainly wanted to save them, but for another reason — it was to be expected that God would inflict punishment on them. Their iniquity had not yet matured enough for them to be dragged off to punishment just on account of the king's anger. It is not surprising, then, that Daniel wanted to block this barbarity so far as he could.

Afterwards he goes on:

25 *Then Arioch with haste took Daniel in to the king, and spoke thus to him, 'I have found a man of the sons of the captivity of Judah, who will make known the interpretation to the king.'*

Here the question could be raised how, when he took Daniel before the king, Arioch could speak as if all this was new. For Daniel had already asked the king (as we have seen) to be given time to pray. Why, then, does Arioch now boast that *'he has found a man of the captives from Judah'*, as if he were talking about someone obscure and unknown? But it may be that Daniel had asked for time from Arioch. For we know from histories how difficult it was to gain access to kings. They thought it a profanation of their majesty if they behaved amiably and kindly. So the conjecture is probable that Arioch was an intermediary when the king granted Daniel time. Or we could say that the words should not be referred simply to Arioch, but that Daniel wanted to show what boasting there is among courtiers who always commend their own office grandiloquently. Then Arioch would be refreshing the king's memory; he had come upon Daniel and had at last obtained what the king fervently desired. But I do not labour the point much, for either Arioch was explaining more clearly to the king that Daniel was the one who could interpret the dream or he was connecting it with what had already happened — either Daniel had made his request directly, or Arioch had himself sought from the king that Daniel should be given time. He says *'sons of the transmigration'* or *'captivity'*, in the customary manner of Scripture, for 'captives', although the term is collective.

Now he goes on:

26 *The king replied and said to Daniel, whose name [was] Belteshazzar, 'Have you the faculty to make known ["to declare"] to me the dream that I saw and its interpretation?'*

The king uses these words because he had already given up hope of an interpretation when he saw the magi all lacked discernment and understanding in the matter. Yet he had believed that there was no wisdom save in the magi. So when he asked them in vain, he could hardly hope for anything better from another source, being imbued (as I said) with that error. Here he asks in amazement, as of something impossible, 'Do you really have the faculty?' There is no doubt that God wrung this question out of the proud king, so that his grace might shine the more brightly in Daniel. The less hope the king had, the more worthy of reverence the revelation. As we shall see later, the king was, so to say, thunderstruck, and, quite stunned, lay prostrate on the earth before this prisoner. This is why Daniel relates that the king put the question like this.

Now he goes on:

27 *Daniel answered the king and said, 'The secret that the king demands, the wise men, the magi, the astrologers, the genethliacs* [for we need not take a lot of trouble about these names; even the Jews resorted to guess-work. There are, indeed, some who are bold enough with their definitions (for they make all sorts of rash affirmations) but they cannot distinguish the difference between these species with any certainty. It is, therefore, enough for us to hold that this statement concerns the magi, who were the wise men at that time (that is, they won that reputation then), and it also concerns the genethliacs and astrologers] *could not tell the king.*

28 *But there is a God in heaven who reveals secrets; he has shown King Nebuchadnezzar what will happen in the end* ["in the extremity"] *of the days. Your dream and the vision of your head upon your bed is this.'*

Here Daniel replies that it not surprising that the king had not found among his magi what he was looking for — because God had inspired him with this dream, above the grasp of the human mind. Some interpreters think this is simply a condemnation of the magical arts. But I do not know if this fits. I think it is rather a comparison between the king's dream and the limits of the science of the magi. (I always exclude superstitions, which vitiate true and genuine science. But so far as the principles were concerned, we have already said that astronomy and the study of the natural order cannot be condemned absolutely.)

The substance of it seems to me that the king's dream was not within the scope of human science and that mortals do not possess such perception as to be able to apprehend what the dream meant. God had revealed hidden things; such things need a special revelation of the Spirit. Therefore the presupposition of Daniel's statement — that the magi and astrologers and the like were not able to explain the king's dream and were not fitted to be its interpreters — was that the dream was not natural and had no affinity with human reasoning, but was a special revelation of the Spirit. Similarly Paul,[1] when

1. Mg., 1 Cor. 2:14.

considering the gospel, puts all human understanding in its proper place; for those who are very clever or who are learned think themselves able to understand anything. But the heavenly doctrine of the gospel is a mystery, which cannot be grasped by even the most learned and clever men. This means the same as Daniel's words, that the magi and astrologers and genethliacs were not up to explaining the king's dream because it was neither natural nor human.

And this appears more clearly from the context when he adds, *'there is a God in heaven who reveals secrets'*. For I take בְּרַם, *beram,* here as an adversative particle. He sets the revelation of God against the divinings and interpretations of the magi, for all human sciences are imprisoned, so to say, within their boundaries and limits. Daniel is therefore saying here that a singular gift of the Holy Spirit is needed. The God who revealed the king's dream with certainty to Daniel distributes understanding and insight to anyone, according to his good pleasure. How is it that some are very intelligent but others dull or slow? How is it that some make good advance in human learning and arts whereas others are at a standstill and nearly useless? How is this, except because God shows by these differences that it is in his hand and will either to enlighten men's minds or to leave them dull and stupid?

Since, therefore, God gives all the understanding there is in the world, what Daniel says here is not consistent with the general sense. Unless this antithesis referred to the species it would be either superfluous or tame. Therefore, let us keep to what will be said in the next verse, that the magi and astrologers could not explain the king's dream because God had raised King Nebuchadnezzar above the common grasp in order to show him by his dream what was to come. Therefore, *'there is a God in heaven who reveals secrets; he',* he says, *'is showing King Nebuchadnezzar what is to be'.* He confirms what I have already said, that the king could not infer what God showed him by the dream. For it often happens that when men's minds run on with a subject they collect some certain deductions. But Daniel excludes human means and says that this dream proceeded from the Spirit of God.

He adds, *'what will happen in the last',* or, in the extremity, *'of days'.* It is asked what he means by 'extremity'. Interpreters agree that this should be referred to the advent of Christ; but they do not explain why the advent of Christ is designated by this word. Yet it is not at all obscure that the advent of Christ is called the extremity of days, for it was a sort of renovation of the world. Yet today the world is in upheaval, as it was long ago even before Christ was manifested. But, as we shall see later, Christ came for this end, that he might renew the world. And because the gospel is, as it were, the perfection of all things, we are said to be in the last, or extreme, days. Therefore Daniel compares all the ages preceding Christ's advent with this 'extremity of days'. And so God wished to show the King of Babylon what would come to pass at last after monarchy had wiped out monarchy. He wished to show that there would at length be an end to these changes, because the kingdom of Christ would come. I touch on this head only briefly, for there are many things still to be said.

'The dream', he says, *'and the vision of your head upon your bed is this.'* It might seem absurd that Daniel here claims that he will explain to the king what his dream was and what its interpretation and yet talks about other things. But he adds nothing irrelevant and it should not be made a question why he says that 'this was the vision of the king and this his dream'. For he had to arouse the king more and more, to make him more attentive to the dream and its interpretation. And it is also to be noted that the prophet was insisting on this so that the king might be convinced that God was the author of the dream he was asking Daniel about. For words are poured out in vain unless men are quite convinced that what is being expounded to them proceeds from God. Today many gladly hear anything that can be said about the gospel, but it does not touch them inwardly. What they conceive is evanescent and at once slips away from them. Hence reverence is the foundation of true and solid understanding. Daniel is therefore not digressing from giving the exposition of the dream and relating the dream itself; but he is preparing the proud king to hear him by showing that he did not dream for nothing and that it was not simply the product of his thoughts, but he had been divinely taught and warned about things hidden.

Now he goes on:

29 *'Upon your bed, O King, your thoughts mounted up to what shall be for you hereafter; and he that reveals secrets told you what shall be.'*

He again confirms what I have just mentioned (for he wants to impress this on the king's mind) — God was the author of his dream — so that the king may prepare himself with due soberness and modesty and even docility to hear the interpretation. For unless he had been seriously touched he might have despised Daniel's interpretation. For we see men profiting nothing, either out of pride or carelessness, even if God speaks familiarly with them. We must keep to this ordering, so that we may be prepared to listen to God and learn to put, as it were, the curb on ourselves whenever we hear the sacred name of God, lest we either reject or at least shrink from considering what he sets before us. This, then, is why Daniel again repeats that King Nebuchadnezzar had been divinely taught about things to come.

In the first clause he says that *'the thoughts of the king mounted up'*. It is a Hebrew and Chaldaean expression. They say that thoughts mount up when they turn things over in their brains or heads — as we saw before, 'This vision was in your head'; because the seat of reasoning is in the head. Hence Daniel says that the king was anxious about the future. Great monarchs think about what will happen after their death (and some-one may dream for himself the empire of the whole world!); and it is likely that King Nebuchadnezzar was turning over these ideas. But at once it follows that he was unable to get any further in his cogitations without God revealing the future; for it is his proper office (he says) *'to reveal things secret'*. And certainly we shall see that men torture themselves in vain when they turn over and over inside themselves things which transcend their minds. King Nebuchadnezzar would go on exhausting himself for nothing unless he were taught by an oracle. Great importance lies hidden in these words, *'he that reveals secrets told the king what shall be'* — that is, 'it is not for you to claim this dream as your own or as a product of your mind; God has given you this special grace of wishing to acquaint you with mysteries which would otherwise have been always hidden from you. For you would never have penetrated to such heights.'

Afterwards he adds:

30 *'And I* [that is, "to me"] *not in wisdom which may be in me before all the living, this secret* [is] *revealed to me* [it is a superfluous repetition, but it does not obscure the sense], *but that I might explain the interpretation to the king and you may know the thoughts of your heart.'*

Here Daniel forestalls an objection which Nebuchadnezzar might make: 'If it is for God alone to reveal secrets, where, may I ask, do you come in, a mere mortal?' Daniel therefore forestalls him and transfers all the glory to God and frankly confesses that there is nothing of his own in the interpretation that he brings, but that he is, so to say, led forward by the hand of God and is its interpreter, not from his natural intelligence, but because it pleased God to make him his minister in this matter and to use his work. *'To me'*, therefore, he says, *'was revealed this secret.'* By these words he declares plainly enough that he undertook the interpretation of the dream by a special gift of God.

And he expresses more clearly that the gift was supernatural, as they say, when he said, *'not in the wisdom which may be in me'*. For had Daniel surpassed the whole world in understanding he would still not have been able to divine what the Babylonian king had dreamed. Certainly, he was eminent in intelligence and learning; he was endowed with the highest gifts, as has already been said; but he could not have arrived at what he now begged from God in his prayer — he could not, I say, arrive at it either by his zeal or by his study or by any human means. So we see that Daniel here expressly excludes not only what men falsely claim for themselves but also everything that God confers 'naturally'. For we are aware that irreligious men are also given outstanding intelligence and remarkable gifts; but these are called 'natural', because in giving such examples God wishes his gifts to shine in the human race. But Daniel also acknowledges that he was endowed with an uncommon mind (because so it had pleased God) and that he was also learned (because God had blessed his studies). Although he confesses this, yet he puts the revelation on a higher level. Thus we see that the gifts of the Spirit vary among themselves, for Daniel was almost a dual man, so to say, in the gifts with which God had willed to adorn him. That he advanced so well in all the sciences, that he had such a lively quick wit, we have already shown to have been entirely from the mere liberality of God. But these things also he puts in their proper place and proclaims God's singular gift in the exposition of the dream.

'This secret', therefore, *'was not revealed to me on account of a wisdom which may be in me above all mortals'.* Daniel is not asserting that he surpasses all mortals in wisdom, as some falsely twist these words. He is leaving it undecided; as if to say, 'This should not be ascribed to wisdom. Were I the cleverest of all mortal men, all my cleverness would be of no use. Even were I a complete idiot, God would have willed to appoint me his minister to interpret your dream for you. So do not look to me for a human solution, but accept what I am going to say as if I were fallen straight out of heaven, for I am the instrument of God's Spirit.' This is the simple meaning of the words. But from this we learn also to give God the praise due to him alone — that it is his office to enlighten our minds to understand heavenly mysteries. For although we may be endowed with the highest intelligence by nature and although this is God's gift, yet it is a limited gift, so to say, one which does not mount up to heaven. So we must learn to leave to God what belongs to him, as Daniel admonishes us to do in this verse.

Afterwards he adds, *'but that I might reveal the interpretation to the king and make known the cogitations of your heart'.* Daniel uses the plural,[a] but indefinitely; as if he were saying, 'God has so far kept you in suspense, but it was not for nothing that he put this dream in your head. The two things are joined — that God revealed this secret, and that now he has brought me in as its interpreter.' We see what Daniel intended. For Nebuchadnezzar might here complain, 'Why does God torment me so? What is the point of this perplexity, that I should dream and yet the dream go from me and its interpretation be unknown to me?' Because Nebuchadnezzar could have quarrelled with God, Daniel forestalls him and shows that his dream or vision was not given him in vain but that God would now show what was lacking — that is, that Nebuchadnezzar might remember his dream and at the same time know what its purpose was and what its meaning.

Grant, almighty God (since you will that we should differ from the
brute beasts and therefore engrave the light of understanding on

a. Calvin confuses the meaning of the verb ('I might reveal') with its indefinite plural form in Hebrew.

our minds) grant that we may learn to acknowledge and magnify this singular gift, and that we may employ ourselves in the knowledge of those things that will lead us to reverence your rule; and that we may also distinguish the ordinary sense which you have given us from the illumination of your Spirit and the gift of grace, so that you alone may be glorified, that we may be implanted by faith in the body of your only-begotten Son; and we ask from you also the increase and augmentation of the same faith until at last you bring us to the full manifestation of light, when, made like to you, we see and enjoy your glory face-to-face, in the same Christ our Lord. Amen.

Lecture 9

31 *'You looked, O King, and behold, a lofty image, a large image, and its brightness* [or, "appearance", as it is commonly called. So, its brightness] *was precious* [or, "excellent"]; *it stood before you and its appearance was terrible.*
32 *The head of this image was of good gold* [good gold],[1] *its chest and its arms of silver, its belly and its thighs of bronze* [bronze].[1]
33 *Its legs of iron* [iron],[1] *its feet partly of iron and partly of baked clay.*
34 *You were watching until a stone was cut out, which was not from hands* ["which was not cut out by the hands of men"], *and it struck the image on its feet, which* [were] *of iron and clay, and broke them.*
35 *Then the iron, the clay, the bronze, the silver, and the gold were broken at the same time, and were like sweepings* [or, "chaff"] *from a threshing floor in summer; and the wind carried them away and their place was not found; and the stone that struck the image became a great mountain and filled the whole earth.'*

Although Daniel relates the dream here, he does not come to the interpretation yet. But we cannot go further without discussing that. When we reach the interpretation we shall confirm what was said before and elaborate it as the context demands.

Here Daniel tells of the image which King Nebuchadnezzar saw. It consisted of gold, silver, bronze, and iron; but its feet were a mixture, partly

---

1. In these three cases Calvin gives the nominative after the ablative (governed by the preposition). Why? Was it merely to replace a close translation with a more correct one, as at 5:2ff.? In the second case the reason might have been to remove the ambiguity in *aere*, which is the ablative of both *aer* ('air') and *aes* ('bronze'), but this can scarcely apply in the other two.

of iron, partly of baked clay. Of the nature of the vision we have already spoken, but I will repeat it briefly. King Nebuchadnezzar did not see the image in question with his eyes but it was a kind of revelation which he knew for certain had been set before him by a god. He could have shaken off his anxiety and been free, but God held him as it were tightly bound in torments until Daniel should come as its interpreter.

So '*Nebuchadnezzar saw an image.*' Anyone of sound judgment and wanting to expound the mind of the prophet honestly will indisputably understand this of the four monarchies following one after another. The Jews,[2] when taxed with this oracle, confuse the Turkish and Roman empires. But their ignorance and dishonesty are easily refuted. For when they want to get out of being forced to confess that the Christ has been manifested to the world, they ferret out disgusting calumnies which need no refutation. But yet something shall be said about them in the proper place. Meanwhile, what I said is true, that interpreters who possess even a moderate judgment and honesty explain one and all this passage of the Babylonian, Persian, Macedonian, and Roman monarchies. And Daniel himself shows this clearly enough by what he says afterwards. Yet it is asked why God figured these four monarchies by the image. For it seems incongruous; the Romans had nothing in common with the Assyrians. Again, it is well known how it happened that the Medes and Persians succeeded the Chaldaeans — that Babylon was stormed and Cyrus, as victor, transferred the empire to the Persians and Medes. So it could seem absurd that he sets forward just the one image. But it is probable — in fact, it can be known easily enough — that God was not here thinking of a consensus (of which there was none among the four monarchies), but of the state of the whole earth. Therefore, under this figure God intended to depict the future state of the world up to the advent of Christ. This is why God connects these four empires, which yet were so diverse that the second was born from the destruction of the first, the third from the destruction of the second. That is one point.

Now, it can also be asked secondly why Daniel gives the Babylonian kingdom the honourable title of '*gold*'; for we know that it was just one huge tyranny; and we know the Assyrians were the same. But now they were linked with the Chaldaeans. For we know that after Nineveh was destroyed the Chaldaeans made Babylon the capital of the kingdom, so that they might be assured of the seat of empire. If we consider the foundations of the monarchy, although we certainly find that the Assyrians were monstrous beasts, full of avarice, cruelty, and theft, yet the Chaldaeans surpassed them in all these vices.

---

2. By 'the Jews' Calvin intends rabbinic commentators in particular. The intemperate language he commonly uses against them (see also p. 95, etc.) was extreme even for his outspokenly polemical age.

Why, then, call that empire *'the head?'* Why call it *'the golden head'?* As for the name of 'head', it is not surprising that Daniel gave it the supreme position as being superior to contemporary monarchies. That here it is also superior to Nineveh is not surprising, for that city had already been destroyed and here we are dealing with the future.

So the Chaldaean empire was first in the order of time and was called 'gold' in a relative sense. As the world went on growing worse and worse, so the Persians and Medes, who held the whole East under Cyrus, were worse than the Assyrians and Chaldaeans. Even the heathen poets speak of four ages: gold, silver, bronze, and iron. They do not mention clay, but there is no doubt that they borrowed their ideas from Daniel. If anyone objects that Cyrus excelled in the highest virtues and was of an almost heroic spirit, so that the histories celebrate his prudence and activity and other gifts, I reply that here we are not concerned with the person of a single man but with the continuing condition of the Persian Empire. It is therefore probable enough that, comparing the empire of the Medes and Persians with the Babylonian Empire, and calling it 'silver', it is because morals had grown worse, as has been said. Experience also shows that the world always grows worse and little by little deteriorates into vices and corruptions.

As for the Macedonian Empire, it should not seem strange that it is compared to bronze; for we know what a savage spirit Alexander had. That his affability won him favour with the historians is neither here nor there. If we reckon what his nature was, he certainly breathed out cruelty from his childhood. What a thing it was, to see in a boy envy or jealousy! When he used to see his father subdue the cities of Greece by war or persistence or other perverse tricks, he wept for envy because he thought his father had left him nothing to do.[3] When a boy could be so puffed up with pride, we infer that there was no humanity in him. And what was his purpose and end in undertaking an expedition to make himself king of kings, except that he could not be content, I do not say with his own riches, but with the whole world? We know that he wept when he heard from the crack-brained philosopher that other worlds existed. 'What! I have not yet possessed one world!'[4] If one world was not enough for a little manikin, how could he fail to discard all humanity, as events showed. He spared no bloodshed; wherever he invaded, he was like a raging tempest, destroying everything.

Again, we should not restrict to the person of Alexander what is said of the monarchy of which he was prince and founder. It should be extended to all his successors. And we know the horrible savagery there was among them. For before his empire was divided up into four parts (that is, into the kingdoms

3. Plutarch, *Lives: Alexander 5*.
4. Valerius Maximus, *Memorable Words and Deeds* 8:14 ext. 2.

of Asia and Syria and Egypt and Macedonia) we see how much blood was shed. God took away all Alexander's progeny. He might have lived at home and begotten children and so have left a noble and celebrated memory to posterity. But God exterminated all that line from the earth. Even his eighty-year-old mother died by the sword — his wife and sons and brother (who was of unsound mind); in short, it was a horrifying example of God's wrath on the offspring of Alexander, to show all ages how much his cruelty had displeased him. But if we follow through the Macedonian Empire to its final end when Perseus was overcome and then when Cleopatra was killed in Egypt and Ptolemy, too, was killed, Egypt was brought under the power of the Roman Empire and so were Syria and Asia — if we comprehend all that time we shall not be surprised at the prophet Daniel calling that monarchy 'bronze'.

That he calls the Roman Empire 'iron' is for the reason I have already noted, which refers to the whole world in general. Men were so vicious in nature that vices and perverted morals went on increasing until they reached the highest pitch. And if we consider how the Romans behaved and how cruelly they ruled, we have the reason why their dominion is here called 'iron' by Daniel. For although a certain political economy flourished among them in appearance, yet we know how ambitious they were, how avaricious, how cruel. Scarcely will there be found a nation which was so loaded with these three diseases as the Romans. Since they were so given up to these and other diseases it is not surprising that the prophet defamed them by preferring the Macedonians and the Persians and Medes and even the Assyrians and Chaldaeans.

Now, that he says *the feet of the image were partly of iron, partly of baked clay* should be referred to the downfall which took place when God overthrew that monarchy and tore it into little bits, so to say. The Chaldaean Empire fell. Afterwards, when the Macedonians had subdued the East, they attached that monarchy to themselves, so that the Medes and Persians served them. The same thing happened to the Macedonians. They were in the end subdued by the Romans and all the kings who succeeded Alexander were overcome. But when it was God's will to overthrow the Roman monarchy, it was in a different manner. It fell in such a way as easily agrees with this prophecy; without an external enemy it collapsed of itself. So that it is quite clear that it was broken down by Christ, as the dream of King Nebuchadnezzar sets out. It is, of course, quite certain that there has been nothing stable in the world from the beginning, and the saying of Paul was true that the figure of this world is passing away.[5] By the word 'figure' he means that whatever is illustrious in the world is nevertheless a fleeting shadow. Therefore he adds that all that dazzles our eyes is passing away. But yet, as I said, it was by a different method that God had willed to destroy the Chaldaean Empire and

5. Mg., 1 Cor. 7:31.

87

then the Persian and at last the Macedonian; for in the case of the Romans it was more clearly shown that by his advent Christ had taken away whatever was splendid and magnificent and wonderful in the world. This, then, is why God expressly ascribes feet of clay to the Romans. So much for the four empires.

Now, in the third place it might be doubted why Christ is said *'to have broken the image from the mountain'*. For if Christ is the eternal wisdom of God, by whom kings reign,[6] it does not seem at all congruous that by his advent he destroyed a political order, which we know God approved and indeed appointed and established by his power. I reply, that earthly empires are upheld and destroyed by Christ 'accidentally', as they call it. For if kings perform their office well, it is certain that Christ's kingdom is not against their rule. How, then, does it come about that Christ strikes kings with an iron rod and breaks and crushes them, and reduces them to nothing?[7] Because their pride is untameable and they lift up their heads above the heavens and would like, if they could, to drag God down from off his throne. This is why they feel the hand of Christ against them, because they cannot subject themselves to God — that is, they will not.

But yet another question may be raised: when Christ was revealed, those monarchies, the Chaldaean and Persian, had long since fallen; and the successors of Alexander had also been destroyed. The solution is straightforward if we hold what I said at first — that here under a single image is depicted the condition of the whole earth. Although this did not happen in a moment, we shall find it true and that the prophet's words were not empty, that Christ would destroy all the monarchies. That the seat of the oriental empire was changed and Nineveh demolished, that the Chaldaeans gained supremacy, all this was done by the just judgment of God. Christ was even then King of the world. That monarchy was broken by his power. The same must be said of the Persians. For when they had fallen from a strict and sober life into a foul and infamous licentiousness; when they savagely ravaged other nations; when they were insatiable for plunder; then at last the rule had to pass from them and Alexander executed the judgment of God. The same happened to Alexander and his successors. The prophet therefore means that before he was revealed to the world Christ already held supreme power in heaven and on earth, that he might break all the pride of violence and bring it to nothing.

'But Daniel says that the image perished when the Roman Empire was broken down. And yet we still see that both in the East and in other regions supreme monarchs are reigning with fearful power.' I reply that we must remember what I said yesterday, that the dream was given to King Nebuchad-

6. Mg., Pr. 8:15.
7. Mg., Ps. 2:9.

nezzar so that he might understand what was going to happen up to the renewing of the world. God did not intend to teach the King of Babylon more than the knowledge that there would be four monarchies, which would terrorize the whole world and by their splendour put all the other worldly powers in the shade and attract all eyes and minds to themselves; and that afterwards the Christ who overturns those monarchies would come. God intended therefore to inform King Nebuchadnezzar of these facts only.

And we must note the purpose of the Holy Spirit. There is no mention here of any other kingdoms, because they had not yet grown to sufficient height to be fit to be compared with the four monarchies. As long as the Assyrians and Chaldaeans ruled, they had no rivals among their neighbours. The whole East obeyed them. It was incredible that Cyrus, coming from a backward region, could so easily gain such wealth and occupy so many provinces in almost a moment. He was like a whirlwind, destroying the whole East. The same must be said of the third monarchy. If Alexander and his successors are taken as a whole, there was no kingdom in the world to match its power. The Romans had for some time to negotiate and struggle with their neighbours and did not have peace within their own territories. Then, when Italy and Greece and Asia and Egypt became subject to the Romans, they became the most famous empire of all. For then the whole power and glory of the world were swallowed up by their arms.

Now we can see why Daniel mentioned these four kingdoms and why the advent of Christ constituted the *terminus ad quem*. (When I say 'Daniel', it should be understood of the dream.) Without doubt God wished to comfort[a] for the Jews, lest their spirits should fail when the lightning, first of the Chaldaean monarchy, then of the Persian, then of the Macedonian, and finally of the Roman, struck and destroyed the whole earth. For what must have been their thoughts at the time that King Nebuchadnezzar dreamed about four empires? The kingdom of Israel was already completely destroyed; ten tribes led away into exile; the kingdom of Judah also reduced almost to a wasteland. The city of Jerusalem still stood, certainly; but where was the kingdom? In complete ignominy and disgrace; the seed of David reigned in the tribe of Judah only on sufferance — and only partly reigned, at that. Later, although they were given liberty to return, we know how wretched and afflicted they were. And when Alexander, that tempest, swept through all the East, we know that they lived in extreme peril. Later they were often pillaged by his successors. The very city was reduced almost to a wilderness, its temple profaned. And when their condition was at its best they were still tributaries, as we shall see later. It certainly was necessary for their minds to be upheld in such great and confused disorder.

a. Reading *consolare* for *consulere* ('care for, have regard to').

This, then, is why God gave the King of Babylon the dream about the monarchies. If Daniel himself had dreamed it, the believers would not have had such strong ground to confirm their faith. But the king's dream was gossiped about over almost all the East, and when its interpretation became well known, the Jews could take heart for their own time and also conceive a good hope from the advance warning that the four monarchies would not change by chance. For God, who foretold King Nebuchadnezzar the future, also determined what should occur and what he willed to take place. Since the Jews knew that the Chaldaeans were reigning by the decree of heaven, and that a worse empire would come, and thirdly that they would have to be in servitude to the Macedonians, and finally that the Romans would be conquerors and lords over the whole earth (always, as I said, by heavenly decree) — when, then, they considered all this and heard also that the Redeemer promised to them would be King for ever and that all the monarchies, however brightly they might shine for a while, would have no stability, it was no ordinary encouragement to them. So now we grasp God's purpose in wishing what was still hidden to be proclaimed everywhere — that the Jews might hand on to their sons and grandsons what they had heard from the mouth of Daniel, and also that this prophecy might last and be a monument of remembrance to them in every age.

Now, as for the words themselves, he says *'there was an image lofty and large; its brightness was precious and its form terrible'*. By these statements God wished to forestall any doubt the Jews might have when they saw the empires, each so resplendent in its own age. When the Jews, who were then captives, saw the Chaldaeans so formidable to the whole world and regarded so highly, almost worshipped, by the other nations, what were they to think? That there was no hope left; God had raised their enemies to such power that their greed and cruelty were like a bottomless whirlpool. They could make up their minds that they were sunk in a deep abyss without hope of release.

And even when the empire was transferred to the Medes and Persians and they were given leave to return home, we know how few made use of this bounty, and the rest were ungrateful. However that may be, when the few Jews were returned to their own land, they had daily to fight against their neighbours; troubles thronged upon them; and if they had followed their common-sense they would not have stirred a foot out of Chaldaea and Assyria and the other eastern countries; better there than in their own country with all their neighbours hostile to them. And at that time, since they were tributary and regarded almost as slaves and offscourings and with their condition so despicable, the temptation still remained. For if they were the people of God, why did he not at least have enough regard for them as to save them from such savage tyranny? Why did he not give them rest and freedom from so many troubles and injuries? But when the Macedonian kingdom came to power, they were wretched indeed.

For they were exposed almost daily to pillage and every sort of cruelty was used against them. As for the Romans, we know how insolently they ruled. For although Pompey in the first invasion did not despoil the temple, yet later they became bolder, and Crassus a little later left absolutely nothing. At last came the horrible, hardly natural, massacres. When, therefore, the Jews considered these things, it was necessary for them to be given the consolation that at last the Redeemer would come, who would destroy all these empires.

That Christ is called *'a stone cut without men's hands'*, and then that he is marked out by other titles, I am not able to explain now.

Grant, almighty God, since we are strangers in this world, and our minds could easily be obsessed and our judgment darkened when we see the glaring power of the ungodly and how terrible they are to us and to all others; grant (I say) that we may lift our eyes on high and consider the great power you place in your only-begotten Son — that is, that he may reign over us and govern us by the power of his Spirit, and that he may keep us in his faith and protection, and that he may overthrow the whole earth for our salvation; so that we may quietly rest under his rule and bravely fight, with the patience which he commands us and commends to us, until at last we enjoy the fruit of victory promised to us and which will be shown to us in your heavenly kingdom. Amen.

Lecture 10

We have explained God's purpose in giving King Nebuchadnezzar the dream about the four monarchies and the reign of Christ which would bring them to an end — that it was done not so much for the king's sake as that the remnant of the faithful might have some comfort and support in the great upheavals which still remained for them, and indeed were imminent. For they had been promised redemption and the prophets had extolled in magnificent terms that singular benefit of God. So their spirits might well have failed amidst those great changes which afterwards took place. Therefore the Lord wished to support their minds, so that among all the upheavals and agitations they might still remain firm and wait patiently and quietly for their promised Redeemer. But God also wanted to make all the Chaldaeans inexcusable; for the king's dream was well known everywhere and yet practically no-one profited from it, so far as the eternal kingdom of Christ was concerned. And this was the chief point of the dream, as we shall see later. God's intention above all was to have a care for his elect, lest they should despair in the face of those 'revolutions' (as they call them) which could seem to contradict so many prophecies promising them, not just simple liberty, but steady and perpetual and continuous happiness under God's hand. Let us therefore bear in mind God's purpose in this dream.

Now the explanation must be treated. We have mentioned some of its parts; but Daniel himself shall open the way for us to progress further. First he says:

36 *'This is the dream; and we will tell its interpretation before the king.*
37 *You, O King, are the King of kings, to whom the God of heaven has given a kingdom, power, and might* [others translate it with the nouns as adjectives,

92

or epithets: "he has given a strong and mighty kingdom"] *and glory* [לך, *lach,* is superfluous].

38 *And wherever the sons of men live and the beasts of the field and the birds of the heavens* [that is, "birds"; it is a numerical enallage[1]] *he has given into your hand and made you ruler over all* [literally, "made you the lord in them all"]. *You are that golden head.'*

Daniel here declares that the golden head of the statue was the kingdom of Babylon. We know that the Assyrians held dominion before the monarchy was transferred to Babylon. But because they were not sufficiently powerful to be regarded as sole rulers in that part of the East, the Babylonian Empire is put first. Next it should be carefully noted that God did not wish something that had already happened to be related here. His intention was that the people should in the future depend on this prophecy and rest upon it. It would therefore be superfluous to narrate anything about the Assyrians, an empire which had already fallen. But the Chaldaeans were to have dominion for a certain time yet, that is, about seventy years, or sixty at least. So God wished to hold the minds of his servants in suspense until the end of this monarchy; afterwards to stir up a fresh hope until the second monarchy should pass away: so that later on they would still rest patiently under the third and fourth monarchies; and in the end they would know that the time was ripe for the advent of Christ. This is why Daniel here puts the Chaldaean monarchy first in order and rank.

There is no difficulty in this, for he says that King Nebuchadnezzar was the golden head of the statue. But why he calls him *'the golden head'* we can gather from the next context — that the soundness was then greater than under the empire of the Persians and Medes. It is, of course, true that the Chaldaeans were savage robbers, and we know how detestable Babylon was to all the pious and sincere worshippers of God. But, since things always deteriorate, there was still a tolerable condition in the world under that monarchy. This is why Nebuchadnezzar is called 'the golden head'. But it should not be referred to him personally. It extends rather to his whole kingdom and to all his successors, among whom was Belshazzar, that worst of despisers of God. It is by comparison that he is here said to be a part of the golden head. But to show that he was not flattering the king, Daniel at once ascribes the reason why Nebuchadnezzar was the golden head — because God had put him in command of all his lands. But this seems to be common to all kings whatsoever. For none rules but by the will of God. This is partly true; but the prophet means that Nebuchadnezzar was raised up in a special way to be far above all other monarchs.

Now he goes on:

1. enallage: substitution of one grammatical form for another.

39 *'And after you another kingdom will rise, inferior to you* [that is, "to yours"], *and another, a third kingdom, which will be bronze; and it will rule in the whole earth.'*

In this verse Daniel includes a second and a third monarchy. The second, he says, would not be inferior to the Chaldaean kingdom in power and wealth. For although the Chaldaean Empire stretched far and wide, it was an annex of the monarchy of the Persians and Medes. Cyrus first subdued the Medes, and, although he made his father-in-law Cyaxares his associate on the throne, he expelled his maternal grandfather and took possession of the whole Medean kingdom without a struggle. Afterwards he conquered the Chaldaeans and Assyrians as well, not to mention the Lydians and other nations of Asia Minor. And so we see that his kingdom is called inferior, not because it had less splendour or wealth to human eyes, but because the future state of the world under that second monarchy would be inferior; just as corruptions and vices grow worse and worse. It is true that Cyrus was a wise ruler; but all the same, he was bloodthirsty and very covetous, a man so carried away by ambition and avarice that he forgot all humanity and attacked indiscriminately, like wild beasts do. And if we judge his character aright, we shall find it was as Isaiah said,[2] that he had an insatiable appetite for human blood. At the same time, we must note that the passage is not talking only of kings personally but of their advisors and also of the whole people. And so Daniel justly declares that the second kingdom will be inferior to the first, not as surpassing Nebuchadnezzar in dignity or wealth, but because the world had not degenerated to the state it afterwards reached. For the further these monarchies spread, the more did licence abound in the world — we learn this easily enough in practice.

From this it is clear how foolish, almost mad, are all who want to have very powerful kings. It is like someone desiring a most turbulent river, as Isaiah said when he was rebuking this foolishness.[3] The swifter a river runs and the deeper and fuller it is, so much the more will it flood and damage the whole countryside. Therefore they are quite insane who desire supreme monarchs, for it is inevitable that the wider the dominion of any one man, the more he will fall away from lawful order. And this happened under the monarchy of the Persians and Medes.

Now follows the description of the third monarchy. It is called *'bronze'*, not so much from its hardness as because it is inferior to the second. To the extent that silver differs from bronze, the prophet teaches the second differs from the third. The rabbis confuse the two monarchies,

2. Mg., Is. 13:18, i.e., 13:15-18.
3. Mg., Is. 8:7, i.e., 8:7-8.

wishing under the second to comprehend the Grecian kingdom, as they call it. But they show crass ignorance and also dishonesty; for they are not deceived by mere ignorance, but deliberately want to overthrow what Scripture clearly teaches here about the advent of Christ. They are ashamed of nothing. So they mix up history confusedly and make dogmatic pronouncements about things unknown — unknown, I say, not that they can deceive those of even mediocre attainment in history, but they are so brutish that they see absolutely nothing. And among other things, I will briefly mention this. Instead of Alexander the son of Philip they put Alexander the son of Mammea who took possession of the Roman Empire when it had already lost half its provinces. He was an ignoble youth, and was killed in his tent very ignominiously by his own troops. Nor did he ever rule, but lived like a pupil under his mother's thumb. And yet the Jews are not ashamed to distort and apply to Alexander the son of Mammea what belongs to the Macedonian king. But both the malice and the ignorance are easily refuted from the context, as we shall see later.

Daniel here briefly relates that there would be a third monarchy. He does not describe what it would be like; he does not explain it overtly; but in another place we shall see what he is foretelling. He now interprets the king of Babylon's dream according to the vision that had been presented to him about the four monarchies. But afterwards an angel confirmed it to him in a vision, and more clearly at that, as we shall see in its place. There is therefore no doubt that what is said about the bronze empire belongs to the Macedonian kingdom. But how can we say that so surely? Just from the description of the fourth empire, which is more complete and, as it were, indicates specifically what we shall see again elsewhere, that the Roman Empire was like feet partly of clay, partly of iron.

Therefore he says:

40 *'And the fourth kingdom will be strong as iron; for, even as iron breaks and smashes everything, and even as iron breaks everything to pieces, it will crush and break.*
41 *And that you saw the feet and toes partly of earthen clay* [or, "of brick"] *and partly of iron, the kingdom will be divided and the strength of iron will be in it, as you saw iron mixed with clay brick* [or, "with clay"].
42 *And the toes of the feet* [or, if it is permissible to repeat the word, "the toes of the feet"][a] *were partly of iron and partly of earth* [or, "of clay", of the baked clay of which he had spoken]; *so part of* [that] *kingdom will be strong and part will be weak.*

a. The repetition (of 'toes') is in the accusative, presumably to correspond with its form in v. 41. Its first occurrence in v. 42 is in the nominative.

43 *That you saw iron mixed with clay* ["earthen"] *brick, they will mix themselves among themselves in the seed of man and the one will not cohere with the other, just as iron does not mix with brick.'*

Here the fourth empire is described. This can refer only to the Romans. For we know that the four successors of Alexander were at last conquered. First was Philip, King of Macedonia; next Antiochus. But Philip lost nothing of his own kingdom; he only relinquished it to the free cities of Greece. It was therefore still entire, apart from paying tribute to Rome for some years for the expense of the war. Antiochus was also forced to accept conditions from his conqueror and was driven beyond Mount Taurus. But Macedonia was reduced to a province when Perseus was defeated and captured. The same thing happened later to the kings of Syria and Asia. The last to suffer was Egypt, occupied by Augustus. For their line had reigned up to this point and Cleopatra was the last of them, as is known well enough. So, in that these three monarchies had been swallowed up by the Romans, what the prophet says here fits very well — as iron smashes and breaks and destroys everything, so these three monarchies would be smashed and crushed by the Roman Empire. It is not out of the way that among the monarchies he mentions the government of the republic; for we know that only a few actually held power among the people. It was usual to call any sort of government an empire, and also to call that people the lord of the whole earth.

The prophet compares them to 'iron', not on account of their hardness (although he expressly puts this as a reason); but there is also another reason for the similitude, in that they were worse than all others, and surpassed both the Macedonians and the Persians and Medes in cruelty and ferocity. For although they celebrated their own virtues in magnificent terms, yet if anyone of sound judgment considers how they behaved, he will find that theirs was a more savage tyranny than any of the others. They boasted that they had as many kings as there were senators; but we should do better to describe them as a bunch of robbers and tyrants. Hardly one in a hundred showed the slightest sign of uprightness either when he was sent into some province or when he became a magistrate. So far as the body of that empire was concerned it was a filthy sink. And this is why the prophet will say that that monarchy was composed partly of iron and partly of earthen clay. We know under what intestine quarrels they laboured. And in this respect the prophet needs no further interpretation, for he says that this mixture of iron and clay, which cohere badly, was a sign of dissidence; there would never be agreement. Therefore, *'the kingdom will be divided'.*

Yet he adds that there would be some mixing, because *'they will mix themselves in human seed';* that is, there will be interrelationships and the mutual union which ought to promote friendship, but it will all come to nothing.

Some here point to the alliance between Pompey and Caesar; but this is weak. The prophet is speaking of continuous government. If we look for stability in any empire, it ought certainly rather to flourish in a 'democratic' state, or at least an 'aristocratic', than in a dictatorship. When all are subservient, the king cannot safely trust his subjects and be without continual apprehension. But when all are associates in an empire and even the lowest look for some good from the common rule, there, as I said, a greater stability should flourish. But Daniel declares, even if there were a common government by senate and people (for, 'as the dignity in the senate, so the majesty in the people'[4]), that empire would be transient. Next, even though some were relatives or associates, it would not prevent them from fighting bitterly among themselves, to the extent of destroying their own empire. So a living picture of the Roman Empire is here painted for us by the prophet when he says that *'it was like iron'*, and yet that *'it was mixed with brick'*, or clay. For by their civil wars they destroyed themselves after they had reached the peak of fortune. So much for the four monarchies.

Now, when it is asked why Daniel said that *'the stone which was cut out of the mountain would destroy all these empires'* — for it does not seem at first sight to fit the kingdom of Christ, in that it came long after the monarchy of Babylon had been destroyed, and the Persians and Medes shamefully overthrown by Alexander, and finally, when all Alexander's conquests were split up into four kingdoms, the Romans had subdued all those lands. So it seems absurd when he says 'a stone will come from the mountain which will break up all the empires'. But the solution is straightforward, as I said above. Daniel is not relating what was going to be completed in one moment; he just wants to teach that the kingdoms of the world are transient and that there is only one eternal kingdom. He is not concerned with the time or the method of the fall of the Chaldaean and Persian empires; he is comparing Christ's kingdom with all those monarchies he had mentioned. And we must always bear in mind what I have touched on — the prophet spoke according to the grasp of common people and accommodated his style to believers, to whom he wished to give a helping hand, so that they might stand fast under the severe shocks that were imminent.

And so, when he speaks of all lands and all nations, if any one objects that there were other empires in the world at that time, the reply is easy — the prophet was not here describing what was going to happen in future ages to the whole world but only what the Jews would see. For the Romans ruled in many places before they went over to Greece. We know of two provinces in Spain; we know that after the end of the Second Punic War they dominated

4. Probably an echo of one or more of Cicero's dicta linking *dignitas* and *maiestas*, e.g., *Part. Orat.* 105 (cited by Quintilian, *Institutio* 7:3:35).

the Adriatic Sea and without doubt, therefore, all the islands in it; besides this they possessed Cisalpine Gaul and other regions. But no account is taken of this empire until it became known to the Jews. For they might have fallen into utter despair at seeing no end imposed on so many storms which almost overwhelmed the world; they were of all men most miserable, and the various and constant calamities did not cease in all the world. We must therefore remember this, for otherwise this whole prophecy would be weak, and it would be fruitless also for us.

I return now to the kingdom of Christ. It is said that the kingdom of Christ would crush all earthly empires — not absolutely, but by 'accident', as they say. For here Daniel takes up a principle that was well known to the Jews — that those monarchies are opposed to the kingdom of God. For the Chaldaeans destroyed the temple of God and tried their utmost to exterminate godliness from the world. As for the Persians and Medes, although they allowed the people freedom to return, yet we know that a little later the kings of the Persians and Medes raged against that unhappy people, so that the larger part chose to live in captivity rather than in their homeland. At last came the Macedonian fury. Although they spared the Jews for a little, we know how violent and frequent were the invasions into Judaea of the kings of Syria and the kings of Egypt, and how cruelly they treated those poor wretches; how they plundered and despoiled them of all their possessions. How much innocent blood was shed! We know that at last the cruelty of Antiochus reached the extent of ordering all the prophetic books to be burned, as if the whole of religion were to be destroyed.[5] So it is not surprising that Daniel here opposes the kingdom of Christ to such monarchies. As for the Romans, we know in what way and how arrogantly they despised the name of Christian; they tried by every means to eradicate the gospel and the teaching of salvation out of the world, because it was an abomination to them. We know all this. Therefore, to warn the faithful what would be their future condition until the advent of Christ, Daniel says that all the empires in the world would be against God, and that all the supreme kings and monarchs would be so many wicked and cruel enemies set on extinguishing all godliness — if, indeed, that were in their power. And so he exhorts them to bear the cross, lest they should at last give way when confronted by such miseries and unhappinesses; to continue in spite of it all on the course of their calling until the promised Redeemer should appear. We have said that this was 'accidental', because certainly all the kingdoms of this world are founded on the power and beneficence of Christ; but there had to be set up a memorable proof of God's wrath against all who so furiously and inimically raise themselves against the Son of God, the supreme King.

5. Mg., 1 Macc. 1:59, i.e., 1:56.

Now Christ is compared to *'a stone cut out of the mountain'*. Some, rather inappropriately, restrict this to the generation of Christ, in that he was born from his Virgin Mother without sexual intercourse with a man. And so he says, *'cut from the mountain without the hand of man'* (as we saw) because he would be sent by God, so that his is to be distinguished from all earthly empires in that it is divine and heavenly. Now therefore we can grasp the point of the metaphor.

As for the word *'stone'*, Christ is not called 'a stone' in the same sense as in Psalm 118:22 and Isaiah 8:14 and Zechariah 3:9 and elsewhere. For there the name 'stone' is ascribed to Christ because the Church is founded on him. In those places also the perpetuity of his kingdom is indicated just as here, but, as I have said, the terms should be distinguished. For it is added that Christ was 'a stone cut without the hand of man', because at the outset he almost lacked beauty and form as far as human perception is concerned.

And there is also a tacit antithesis between the greatness which the prophet will soon mention, and his beginning. *'There shall descend'*, he says, *'a stone cut from the mountain, and that stone became a great mountain and filled the whole earth.'* We see that the prophet warns them that the beginnings of Christ's kingdom would be contemptible and mean in the eyes of the world. There was nothing excellent to be seen. For, as it is said in Isaiah, 'There is born a shoot from the stock of Jesse';[6] the line of David lacked all dignity, the royal name completely buried, the crown trodden under foot, as it is said in Ezekiel.[7] So Christ first appeared abject and lowly. But wonderfully and beyond all expectation and thought he grew to an immense magnitude, so as to fill the whole earth. So now we see how appositely Daniel speaks of the kingdom of Christ.

But we must speak of the rest tomorrow.

> *Grant, almighty God, that we may so remember that we sojourn in this world, that no splendour of worldly wealth and power and wisdom may dazzle our eyes; but let us always direct our gaze and all our senses to the kingdom of your Son and utterly cleave to it. Then nothing will hinder us from hastening on the course of our vocation until at last we pass through immeasurable space and arrive at the goal which you have set before us and to which today the proclamation of your gospel invites us. And at last you will gather us into that blessed eternity which has been won for us by the blood of the same your Son, nor shall we ever be eroded away from him but, upheld by his power, we shall at last be raised above all the heavens by him. Amen.*

6. Mg., Is. 11:1.
7. Mg., Ezk. 21:17, i.e., 21:25-27.

Lecture 11

We must now explain more clearly from the words of the prophet himself what' we said yesterday about the eternal kingdom of Christ. When he relates the dream, he says a stone cut from the mountain without hand was the fifth kingdom, by which the four kingdoms in the vision shown to King Nebuchadnezzar would be broken and destroyed. Now we must see whether this is the kingdom of Christ or not. The words of the prophet run thus:

44 *'And in the days of those kings the God of heaven will raise up a kingdom which will never be dispersed* [or, "be destroyed"], *and this kingdom will not be left to a foreign people. It will crush and wear away all those kingdoms, but it will itself stand for ever.*
45 *Moreover, you have indeed seen the stone cut out of the mountain and not by hand, which broke* ["and broke", literally; but the copula should be resolved into a relative pronoun] *the iron, the bronze, the clay, the silver, and the gold to pieces. The great God has shown the king what will take place in the future. And the dream is true and the interpretation is faithful.'*

The Jews agree with us that this passage can only be understood of the eternal kingdom of Christ, and they gladly, nay greedily, appropriate to the glory of their race everything they read in the Scriptures. They often distort many of the testimonies so as to be able to boast foolishly of their privileges. They therefore do not deny that the dream given to the Babylonian king related to the kingdom of Christ. Where they differ from us is in still waiting for their Christ. This compels them to corrupt the prophecy in several respects; for, if they allow that the fourth empire, or fourth monarchy, should be referred to the Romans, they will be forced to assent to the gospel, which testifies that the Christ has been

100

revealed who was promised in the Law. For Daniel here plainly asserts that the Christ would come after the end of the fourth monarchy. So they fly to the wretched refuge that the fourth monarchy should be understood of the Turkish kingdom which they call 'the kingdom of the Ishmaelites'. And to do this they muddle together the Roman and the Macedonian empires. But what authority is there for constructing one out of two such different empires? They say the Romans sprang from the Greeks. If we grant that, then what was the origin of the Turks? Did they not come from the Caspian mountains and greater Asia? The Romans look to Ilium for their origins. But Troy had vanished when this prophecy came to be fulfilled. And what is the point of this, when they had no identity after a thousand years? And the Turks after an even longer period, in fact six hundred years later, suddenly broke forth like a flood. How could they make one kingdom out of such a variety of events and distances of time? Then again, they bring forward no characteristic that is not common to all nations. They recall us to the very beginnings of the world to make their conflation of one nation out of two. This mixture, therefore, completely lacks both reason and authority. There is no doubt that by the fourth kingdom Daniel intended the Romans. For we saw yesterday how that empire at last perished from internal discord rather than from natural decay. It was not a single monarchy, but a democracy, and all thought themselves kings; and they were interrelated. Such a connection ought to have been a very firm bond of perpetuity. But Daniel had before declared that, even if they were interrelated and had mutual alliances, yet the kingdom would not be a community but would perish through its own quarrels. In short, it is clear enough that the prophet's words can be interpreted only of the Roman Empire, and cannot be forced to mean the Turkish Empire.

I will now also refer briefly to what our brother Dominus Antony[1] suggested to me from a rabbi, one Barbinel,[2] who seems to have been smarter than others. He tries to show, by six main arguments, that this fifth kingdom cannot refer to our Christ — that is, to Jesus, the son of Mary. First, he takes the ground that since the four kingdoms were earthly, you cannot compare the fifth kingdom with them unless it is in the same category. Otherwise, he says, it would be an improper and absurd comparison. As if Scripture does not everywhere compare God's heavenly rule with earthly kingdoms! For it is not necessary and not even proper for a comparison to match in every detail. Although God showed the Babylonian king the four earthly monarchies under a figure, it does not follow that the nature of the fifth kingdom had to be exactly the same; it could be completely different. Indeed, if we consider it all carefully,

1. That is, Chevalier — see p. 46, n. 3.
2. Isaac ben Judah Abarbanel (or Abrabanel or Abravanel), Spanish Jewish commentator on the Pentateuch and the Prophets (1437–1509), who in 1497 produced a commentary on Daniel, *Maʿyene ha-Yeshuʿah* (Wells of Salvation) (Ferrara, 1551); see B. Netanyahu, *Don Isaac Abravanel* (Philadelphia, 1972), pp. 209–16.

we shall necessarily observe some difference between those four and the last. So it is a frivolous argument by the rabbi to infer that Christ's kingdom had to be visible because otherwise it would not correspond to those kingdoms.

His second line of attack against us is this: 'If religion was the difference between the kingdoms, it follows that the Babylonian, the Persian, and the Macedonian all had the same. For we know that all those nations worshipped idols and were addicted to superstitions.' The answer to such a weak quibble is easy: The four kingdoms did not differ simply on account of different religions but in that God despoiled the Babylonians by his power and transferred the monarchy to the Medes and Persians. Later, the Macedonians came into power by the same providence of God. And finally the Romans, all those kingdoms having been wiped out, obtained the kingdom in the whole of the East. And we have already shown what was the prophet's purpose. He wanted simply to teach the Jews not to despair when they saw all sorts of agitations in the world — more, a wonderful and fearful confusion, for those ages would be subject to many changes. But at last the king would come who had been promised. So the prophet wanted to exhort the Jews to patience and to keep them, so to say, in suspense, waiting for Christ. So he did not distinguish the four monarchies in terms of religion, but in that God, as it were, rolled the world round in a wheel when the one lot expelled the other, so that the Jews might apply their minds and all their senses to the hope of their redemption promised to them in the advent of Christ.

The third argument on which this rabbi rests can be refuted without any ado. He infers from the words of the prophet that the kingdom of our Christ, the son of Mary, was not the kingdom spoken of by Daniel, who expressly states that this kingdom would neither pass away nor change: *'it shall not be left to another* [or, "foreign"] *people'*. But the Turks, he says, occupy a good part of the globe; also, religion itself is divided among the Christians, and many abhor the teaching of the gospel. It follows, therefore, that Jesus the son of Mary was not the king spoken of by Daniel — that is, in the dream given to the Babylonian king, which Daniel explained. But he is too foolishly imagining and taking for granted what we will also deny to him, that the kingdom of Christ is visible. For although the children of God are dispersed, and cannot boast a great reputation, yet it is certain that Christ's kingdom stands fast and unharmed, that is, in its nature, because it is an invisible and not an external kingdom. It was not for nothing that Christ declared, 'My kingdom is not of this world.'[3] In saying this he meant to exclude his kingdom from the common rank and number. Therefore, although the Turks have spread far and wide; although, too, the world is full of despisers of God; and the Jews also occupy a part; yet the kingdom of Christ does not cease to be, is not 'transferred to foreigners'. So the reasoning is not only weak but even puerile.

3. Mg., Jn. 18:36.

There follows the fourth argument. He regards it as quite absurd that Christ, who was born under Octavian, or Augustus, Caesar, should be the king prophesied by Daniel. 'For', he says, 'the beginning of the fifth and fourth monarchies would be identical; which is absurd. The fourth monarchy had to last a certain length of time and then to be succeeded by the fifth.' Here he betrays not only his ignorance but his brutish dullness; as God blinded all that people that they might be mere impudent dogs. (I have often spoken with many Jews. I never saw the least speck of godliness, never a crumb of truth or honesty, not even discerned any common sense in any Jew whatsoever.) But he, who thinks himself so clever and ingenious, betrays his shameful ignorance. He thought the beginning of the Roman monarchy lay in the person of Julius Caesar. As if the Macedonian kingdom was not abolished when the Romans possessed Macedonia and turned it into a province! — when they brought Antiochus to heel! When the third monarchy, that is, the Macedonian, began to decline, the fourth, the Roman, succeeded. We must grasp this firmly — and reason dictates it — for unless we accept that the fourth monarchy began when the third gave up its place and rank, how will the other things agree with one another? We must therefore observe that the prophet was not thinking of the Caesars when he spoke of the monarchies. Indeed, what we saw about the ties of blood cannot in any way be applied to the Caesars — as I said yesterday, those who restrict it to Pompey and Julius Caesar are inept and lack good judgment in this matter. For the prophet is speaking generally of the state and continuation of the whole people. Although all were related among themselves, the empire was not stable; they were inwardly destroying themselves when they fought against their own flesh and blood. This being so, we gather that that rabbi was foolish when he added the absurdity that the Christ was not the son of Mary who was born under Augustus. I pass over in silence the feeble idea that Christ's kingdom began at his birth.

He puts forward a fifth argument: Constantine and other emperors professed the faith of Christ. 'If', he says, 'we accept that Jesus the son of Mary was the fifth king, how comes it that the Roman Empire still continued while he was king? For when the religion of Christ flourishes, when he is worshipped and acknowledged as the sole King, that kingdom ought not to be separated from his kingdom. When therefore under Constantine and his successors Christ obtained glory and power among the Romans, his monarchy could not be separated from the Romans.' But the solution is easy. The prophet here measures the end of the Roman Empire from the time when it began to be torn apart. So far as relates to the beginning of Christ's kingdom, I have already said that it should not be referred to the time of his birth but to the preaching of the gospel. And from the time the gospel began to be proclaimed, as we know, the Roman monarchy was dispersed and at last vanished away. Hence, the empire did not last up to Constantine or the others, for its condition was different. We know, too, that neither Constantine nor the other emperors were Romans. As early as Trajan the empire began to be transferred to an alien. Rome was ruled by foreigners. We know with what monsters God afterwards burdened the Roman people. None more infamous, more shameful, than many of the emperors. If anyone scans all the history books he will scarcely find elsewhere such monstrous rulers as Heliogabalus, or others like him at Rome. I am silent now on Nero and Caligula; I am speaking only of the foreigners. So the Roman Empire was abolished after the gospel began to be preached and Christ was made known everywhere in the world. So we see the same ignorance here that that rabbi showed in his other arguments.

The last is this: because the Roman Empire still in some measure exists, what is here said about the fifth monarchy cannot refer to the son of Mary. For it is necessary that the fourth empire should come to an end if the fifth king is to begin his reign from the time Christ rose from the dead and was preached to the world. I reply, as I have already said, that the Roman Empire ceased and was abolished from the time when God transferred all the power with great shame and disgrace to foreigners — not only to swineherds but to horrifying monsters; so that it would have been better for the title of 'Roman' to have been completely wiped out than for it to continue in such disgrace. So we see that the sixth and last argument vanishes away.

I wanted to bring together these things by the way, so that you may know what inept reasoners the Jews are when they fight against God like this and furiously rush forward to attack the clear light of the gospel.

Now I return to Daniel's words. He says that 'a kingdom would come which would destroy all other kingdoms'. Yesterday we explained how Christ destroyed those old monarchies which came to an end long before his advent. For Daniel does not want to teach what Christ was going to do at any one moment but what would happen from the time of the exile until the revelation of Christ. If we keep that purpose firmly in mind, the context will present no difficulties. The sum of it is: although the Jews would witness many very powerful empires which would fill them with fear and terror, in fact almost stupefy them, yet these would have no stability or firmness in them because they were opposed to the kingdom of God's Son. Isaiah pronounces a curse on all kingdoms which do not serve the Church of God.[4] When, therefore, all these monarchies with devilish boldness raise their crests against the Son of God and true piety, they have to be destroyed and God's curse through the prophet realized and made public in them. Thus Christ destroyed all the empires of the world. Today the Turkish Empire is prominent in wealth and population and power. But it was not God's purpose to show what would happen after the revealing of Christ. He only wanted the Jews to be admonished not to give

4. Mg., Is. 60:12.

way under such a heavy burden when new tyrants arose in the world and they found themselves in constant and unremitting danger. God wished to arm their minds with courage. And the only way they were to do this was to look for the promised redemption and know that all the empires of the world, not founded on God or joined to the kingdom of Christ, are passing and transient.

'The God of heaven', he says, 'will raise up a kingdom which will never be dispersed.' Here it is important to notice the character of perpetuity in the kingdom of which Daniel speaks. It should not be restricted to the person of Christ but relates to all the godly and the whole body of the Church. Christ is certainly eternal in himself, but he communicates his eternity to us, because he upholds the Church in the world and also invites us to the hope of a better life and begets us again by his Spirit to an incorruptible life. Therefore the kingdom of Christ has a twofold perpetuity apart from his person; that is, in the whole body. For although the Church is often dispersed, so that nothing appears to men's eyes, yet it is never completely destroyed, but God preserves it by his hidden and incomprehensible power so that it will always remain until the end of the world. Secondly, there is another perpetuity in individual believers in that they are born again of incorruptible seed, begotten again by the Spirit of God, and they are now not mortal sons of Adam only but bear a heavenly life within themselves, because the Spirit who is in them is life, as Paul says in Romans 8.[5] Therefore we must hold that whenever Scripture asserts that the kingdom of Christ is eternal, it should be extended to the whole body of the Church and does not belong to his person alone. And we see that this kingdom will be eternal from the time when the teaching of the gospel began to be proclaimed. For although the Church would be in a sense buried, yet God gave life to his elect even in the sepulchre. Now, how did it happen that the children of the Church arose, who are as it were a new people, just created, as Psalm 102 puts it?[6] Here it clearly appears how wonderfully the remnant were saved by God even when there were none left in the sight of men.

He adds, 'this kingdom will not be left to a foreign people'. By these words the prophet signifies that this kingdom cannot be transferred to another, as happened in other cases. Darius was overcome by Alexander, and his line was in a sense exterminated. At length God destroyed the accursed Macedonian nation so that none remained to claim descent from that family. As for the Romans, although there was always something of a nation there, they were shamefully ruled by foreigners and barbarians and men replete with disgrace and numberless villainies. But so far as the kingdom of Christ is concerned, neither can he be despoiled of the empire given to him nor can we who are

5. Mg., Rom. 8:10.
6. Mg., Ps. 102:19, i.e., 102:18.

105

his members lose that kingdom of which he makes us consorts. Christ, therefore, both in himself and in his members, rules above any danger of change because in his person he remains always safe and sound. As for ourselves, because we are saved by his grace and he takes us into his faith and care, we are not at risk, as I said, and our salvation is sure. For the inheritance which remains for us in heaven cannot be snatched away from us. We also who are 'kept by his power through faith' (as Peter says)[7] can also through faith be safe and at rest; because whatever Satan devises, although the world might bring up all its heavy weapons to destroy us, we shall remain safe in Christ. We see how the prophet's words should be understood when he says that this fifth empire would not be transferred to another and left to another people.

As for the last clause, when he says, *'it shall destroy and break all those kingdoms and itself shall stand for ever'*, no long explanation is needed. We said in what way Christ's kingdom would destroy all the earthly empires that Daniel had spoken of before — that whatever was against the only-begotten Son of God must of necessity vanish and perish miserably. The prophet exhorts all the kings of the earth to 'kiss the Son'.[8] Since neither the Babylonians nor the Persians nor the Macedonians nor the Romans subjected themselves to Christ (rather they employed all their might in fighting against him and were enemies of godliness), they had to be effaced by the kingdom of Christ. For although the Persian kingdom no longer existed when Christ was revealed to the world, yet its memory was accursed before God. For Daniel is not dealing here only with things that are plain to human eyes but raises our minds higher — that is, that we may know that nowhere but in Christ alone can be found a true support on which we may rest. Therefore he declares that outside Christ whatever is splendid and powerful in the world, and wealthy and strong, is fleeting and passing and of little worth.

In the following verse he confirms that statement — *'God would show the Babylonian king what should be in the last times'*, when he shows him *'the stone cut out from the mountain and that not by hand'*. We have said that Christ was cut from the mountain and not by hand in that he was sent by God, so that men can claim nothing in this respect for themselves — as also, in treating of the redemption of his people, God says in Isaiah, 'Because the Lord did not see a helper in the world, he armed himself with his own arm and with his own power.'[9] Because, therefore, Christ was sent from none other than from the heavenly Father, he is said to be *'cut out and not by hand'*. And we must also hold what I added in the second place — that the lowly and abject beginning of Christ is to be noted, in that he would be like a rough and undressed stone. As for the

7. Mg., 1 Pet. 1:5.
8. Mg., Ps. 2:12.
9. Mg., Is. 63:5.

mountain, I have no doubt that Daniel here wanted to teach that Christ's origin would be sublime and above the whole world. Therefore, to my mind, he meant by the metaphor of a mountain that Christ would not arise out of the earth but would come from the glory of the heavenly Father — as also it is said in a prophet, 'And you, Bethlehem Ephrathah, you are the least among the princes of Judah; yet out of you shall arise for me a Ruler in Israel and his origin from the days of eternity.'[10] Daniel here forestalls the wild imaginings which we all indulge in. For because no such dignity appeared in Christ at the beginning as is seen in the kings of the earth (and even today he rules under, so to say, the ignominy of the cross), many despise him and acknowledge no worthiness in him. Daniel therefore now raises our eyes and minds on high when he says *this stone was cut out from the mountain'*. Nevertheless, if anyone prefers to take *'mountain'* as the chosen people, I will not argue about it; but it seems to me remote from the prophet's genuine sense.

Finally he adds, *'And the dream is true and the interpretation faithful.'* Here Daniel firmly and boldly asserts that he was not offering dubious guesses, but that he was explaining to King Nebuchadnezzar what he had received from God. Therefore he is here claiming prophetic authority, that the Babylonian king might know he was God's faithful and reliable interpreter. And we see that the prophets always spoke with this confidence; otherwise all their teaching would be weak. If our faith is stayed either on the wisdom of men or on other things, it will continually vacillate. Therefore we must take our stand on the foundation that what they set before us proceeds from God. This is why the prophets so earnestly insist on this point, lest their teaching should be thought a human fabrication. Thus also in this place Daniel first says *'the dream is true';* as if he were saying that this was no ordinary dream (from the horn gate, to use the poetic fable);[11] nor was it a violent dream, of the sort that mentally disturbed people have, or those too full of food or drink, or even from some physical condition, like melancholy, and choler, and so forth. He says therefore that the dream of the King of Babylon was a true oracle. Then he adds, *'the interpretation is sure',* where, just as in the next clause, he again claims the authority of a prophet lest Nebuchadnezzar should doubt whether he was being taught divinely to understand the truth of the dream.

Now he goes on:

46 *Then King Nebuchadnezzar fell on his face and worshipped Daniel; and he ordered that there be sacrificed to him an oblation and a sweet odour* [that is, 'a very fragrant odour'].

---

10. Mg., Mi. 5:2.

11. Homer, *Odyssey* 19:562: 'Two are the gates of shadowy dreams; one is fashioned of horn and one of ivory' — the 'ivory' are deceptive, the 'horn' true; Virgil, *Aeneid* 6:893-94.

When it is said that the King of Babylon *fell on his face,* it can be taken partly as praise and partly also as blame. It was a sign of piety and modesty to prostrate himself before God and his prophet. We know how untameable is the pride of kings; we see that they are like madmen, that they do not think they are numbered among mere mortals, so blinded are they by the splendour of their greatness. Nebuchadnezzar was the paramount monarch of the day. It was hard for him to bring his mind to give glory to God. Moreover, the dream which Daniel had explained could not have been pleasant to him. He began to see that his monarchy was both accursed before God and would perish in ignominy; other monarchies, still in the future, had been ordained in heaven; and although he could get some comfort from the destruction of the other kingdoms, yet it was very harsh for sensitive ears to hear that the very flourishing kingdom, which all thought would be perpetual, was of no long duration, even quite transitory. So, that he prostrated himself before Daniel was, as I have said, both a sign of piety that he revered God and embraced the prophecy which could otherwise have been vexatious and bitter to him, and also a sign of modesty in that he humbled himself before God's prophet. For these things, therefore, the Babylonian king can rightly be praised.

But the nature of the blame in this reverence we shall tell tomorrow.

Grant, almighty God (since you have revealed to us by so many and so clear and substantial testimonies that we are to hope for no other Redeemer than him who was revealed by you once and whose divine and eternal power you sealed with so many miracles and pledged, both with the preaching of the gospel and with the seal of your Spirit in our hearts, and daily you confirm the same by experience), grant that we may remain firm and steadfast in him, never swerving from him, and our faith never overthrown, whatever Satan may attempt against us. But let us so persevere in the course of your holy calling that at last we may be gathered into that eternal blessedness and perpetual rest which has been gained for us by the blood of your Son. Amen.

Lecture 12

Yesterday we said it could certainly be thought praiseworthy that King Nebuchadnezzar bowed down before Daniel when he had heard the dream and the interpretation given to it. For he gave some proof of piety in that in the person of Daniel he adored the true God, as will be said later. He also showed he was teachable, even when the prophecy could have exasperated him — for tyrants will suffer scarcely any detraction from their authority. But he cannot be completely excused in all respects. Although he confesses that the God of Israel was the only God, he transfers part of his worship to a mortal man. Those who excuse this do not sufficiently consider that the heathen mix up heaven and earth; although their original impetus may be right, they slip back at once into their superstitions.

There is no doubt that the confession which we shall see at once was partial. For Nebuchadnezzar was not truly and substantially converted to true piety so as to bid farewell to his errors. But he partially acknowledged that supreme power was in the possession of the God of Israel. This reverence did not correct all his idolatries, but by a sudden impulse, as I said, he confessed that Daniel was the servant of the true God. Yet he did not leave his accustomed errors, and a little later returned to even greater madness, as we shall see in the next chapter. In the same way we see that Pharaoh gave glory to God, but only momentarily;[1] he was still stubbornly proud and cruel, and never changed his character. We should judge the King of Babylon in the same light, although on a different level, for King Nebuchadnezzar was not so obstinately proud as Pharaoh. Both showed some sign of reverence in such a way that neither subjected himself truly and heartily to the God of Israel. He worshipped Daniel,

1. Mg., Ex. 9:27; 10:16.

not because he thought he was God, but because heathens confuse white with black — we know, moreover, that even the dullest have had from the beginning some inkling of a unique God. For no-one ever denied there was a supreme deity; but they went on to fabricate a multitude of gods; they even transfer part of the worship of divinity to mortals. King Nebuchadnezzar was entangled in these errors, and it is no wonder that he worshipped Daniel and at the same time confessed that there was only one God.

Today also we see in the papacy that everybody confesses this truth and yet the name of God is torn asunder — not in title, but in fact; for they divide the worship of God, so that each may have a part of the spoil or prey. What experience teaches now is what Daniel relates.

It is, of course, true that such adoration was then common among the Chaldaeans, Easterners always being immoderate in their ceremonies; and we know that kings were worshipped there as gods. But because he uses the word 'sacrifice' and then 'offering', מנחה, *minha,* it is certain that he worshipped Daniel thoughtlessly as if he were some demigod fallen out of the sky. So we must conclude that King Nebuchadnezzar acted wrongly when he ascribed such honour to Daniel. For there is a certain moderation in revering God's prophets; they are not to be exalted above their state. And we know on what condition the Lord raises them up — that he may have sole pre-eminence and that all his doctors and prophets and servants should keep within their own order.

The question is raised about the prophet allowing himself to be worshipped. For if, as we have already said, Nebuchadnezzar sinned, the prophet's tolerance has no excuse. There are some who are uneasy and strive to excuse him. It is true that, if he passed this over in silence, we should have to confess that he had contracted some fault from the corruptions of the court. It is hard to live there without being quickly infected with something. The defence of a man, even the most perfect, ought not to count so much with us as to prevent our holding fast the principle that nothing is to detract from God's honour, and that we act perversely when and so often as the worship which belongs to God is transferred to creatures. It may well be that Daniel rejected and so restrained the foolishness of the King of Babylon; but I leave this undecided, for it is not said; although it seems to me hardly likely that he would be silent when he saw God's honour being partly transferred to himself — for he would then have been an accomplice in the sacrilege and impiety. And this could hardly happen with such a holy prophet of God. But we know that many things were omitted in their narratives; and Daniel was not relating what was done but what the king commanded to be done. He prostrated himself on his face — but what if Daniel showed him this was not lawful? And when he ordered that sacrifices should be made, Daniel could also reject such wickedness. For if Peter rightly corrected the error of

Cornelius,[2] which was more tolerable because Cornelius only wanted to show honour to Peter in the common manner — if the apostle would not tolerate this act but sharply rebuked it, what should be said of the prophet? But, as I said, I dare not decide on either side — except that the conjecture is probable that the servant of God refused this misplaced honour. Certainly, if he allowed it, he had nothing to say for himself but that he had sinned. As we have said already, it is difficult to live amid courtly corruptions without contracting some blemishes, however pure one strives to be — as we see also in the person of Joseph. He, although he had given himself entirely to God, yet smacked somewhat of the Egyptian in his speech, as in the form of oaths.[3] And as this was a fault in him, the same can also be said of Daniel.

Let us go on:

47 *The king replied to Daniel, and said, 'Surely your God* [is] *the God of gods and the Lord of kings and a revealer of secrets; for you were able to reveal this secret.'*

This confession breathes forth nothing but piety and holiness and uprightness and sincerity. It could therefore be seen as testimony to a true conversion and repentance. But as I have just told you, the heathen are sometimes carried away in admiration of God; and then they will confess abundantly and at great length anything that real worshippers of God could ask. But it is only momentary; they still remain entangled in their superstitions. God is extorting words from them when they speak so piously; but inwardly they hold on to their faults and afterwards slip easily back into their former ways — and a memorable example of this will follow later. However that may be, God's will was that his glory should be proclaimed by the mouth of this heathen king, that he should be a herald of his power and divinity. For this was especially of benefit to the Jews; that is, to the remnant that was still sound. For the larger part had fallen away, as is well known. For it was easy for them to degenerate from the true worship of God; and when they were carried away into exile they were already idolaters and apostates, they had already denied the living God. So only a small number of the godly remained, and it was of them and of strengthening their minds that God was thinking when he extracted this confession from the King of Babylon.

But it had also another use, in that both the king and all the Chaldaeans and Assyrians were made the more inexcusable. For if the God of Israel was truly God, why did Bel keep his position? *'God is the God of gods'* — but he is the enemy of false gods, we must at once add. Therefore we see that

2. Mg., Acts 10:26, i.e., 10:25-26.
3. Mg., Gn. 42:15.

111

Nebuchadnezzar here mixed light with darkness and white with black, when he confessed that the God of Israel was supreme among the gods and yet went on worshipping the other gods. For if the God of Israel is given his right, all idols vanish away. Therefore Nebuchadnezzar is self-contradictory when he speaks like this. But, as I said, he is completely carried away and is not in command of himself when he so liberally declares the power of the one God.

Now, as for the words which he uses: *'Surely your God is the God of gods'*, he says. The particle is not at all superfluous, when he says, 'Surely'. In saying this, he affirms it. For if anyone were to ask him if Bel and the other idols were truly to be worshipped as gods, he could reply out of a preconceived idea that it was so, but he would be doubtful. (All the superstitious continue to be puzzled, and if they should defend their superstitions more stubbornly, it comes from the temerity that the devil suggests to them and not from their own judgment. In a word, they are not masters of their minds when they dare to assert that their superstitions are godly and holy.) But here it would appear as if Nebuchadnezzar were renouncing his errors — as if he were saying, 'Hitherto I have thought there were other gods; but now I change my mind. For I am convinced that your God is the chief of all gods.' And certainly, had he sincerely spoken like this, he could have realized that he was doing a serious injury to his idols, if there were any divinity in them. For we know that the God of Israel was bitterly hated and even abominated by heathen nations. When he extols him above all the gods he puts in their places both Bel and the whole rabble of false gods that the Babylonians worshipped. But, as we have said, he was quite carried away and spoke without thinking. It was a sort of 'enthusiasm'; the Lord stupefied him and then transported him into wonderment and at once into the proclaiming of his power.

He calls him also *'the Lord of kings'*, thus claiming for him supreme rule on earth. Therefore he means that the God of Israel not only excels all gods but also that he is at the helm of his world. For if he is 'the Lord of kings', all peoples are under his hand and sway. For the common people as a whole cannot be exempted from God's power if he holds kings themselves under him. Therefore let us hold on to what these words mean — that whatever gods are worshipped are subordinate to the God of Israel because he is above all gods; moreover, that his providence rules the world, so that peoples and kings are under his sway and all things are governed by his will.

He adds that he is *'a revealer of secrets'*. This is one of the evidences of deity, as was said elsewhere. For when Isaiah wanted to prove that there was only one God, he took these two principles; that nothing happens but by the rule of God, and to this he adds the foreknowledge of all things.[4] These two things are joined as by an inseparable chain. Although Nebuchadnezzar did not grasp what the property of divinity really was, yet, because he was impelled by a secret

4. Mg., Is. 48:3, 4, 5, etc.

instinct of God's Spirit, he proclaimed so strongly God's power and wisdom. Therefore he confessed that the God of Israel excels all the gods — because he holds sway in the whole world and because nothing is unknown to him.

And he adds the reason, *'because Daniel could reveal the secret'*. Yet this seems an insecure reason. For he gathers that the world is governed by the rule of God alone because Daniel revealed the secret; but this has nothing to do with power. But the reply is easy. For we said elsewhere that we must not imagine God is like Apollo, who only foretells the future. And certainly it is too weak to ascribe bare foreknowledge to God, as if the outcome of things should depend on something other than his will. But God is said to foreknow the future rather because he will already have determined what he wills to happen. Nebuchadnezzar therefore justly infers that the dominion of the whole world is in God's hand because he pronounces like this on things future. For unless the future lies in his will, he cannot with certainty predict this or that. When therefore he predicts the future, we may conclude with certainty that all things are ordained by him, so that nothing happens fortuitously but that he fulfils all that he has decreed. We must learn from this place that it is not sufficient for anyone to celebrate God's wisdom and power at the top of his voice, as they say, unless at the same time he casts all superstitions out of his mind and holds that there is only one God and tells all others to get packing and depart. For no fuller confession could be demanded than what is made here. And yet we see that Nebuchadnezzar was always entangled in the impostures of Satan, because he wanted to keep his false gods and thought it was enough to give the primacy to the God of Israel.

Let us learn to take care to purge our minds of all superstition, so that the one and only God may occupy all our thoughts. Meanwhile we must note what a serious and dreadful judgment awaits the papists and their like, who ought at the least to be imbued with the rudiments of piety. They confess that there is one supreme God, and yet mix in a huge crowd and so to say cut up his power and wisdom and obscure what is here spoken by a heathen king. For the papists not only divide up the power of God, so that each one of their saintlings can claim some part for himself, but also, when they speak of God himself, they imagine that he foreknows all things yet all things happen contingently because God created man with a free will and then left all events in suspense; so that heaven and earth, congruously with men's merits or sins, now perform their office, now are against men. It is, of course, true that neither rain nor heat nor clouds nor fine weather nor anything else happens except from the judgment of God, and whatever is adverse is a sign of his curse and whatever is prosperous and desirable is a sign of his favour; this is very true. But when the papists lay down the principle of man's will we see that God is despoiled of his right. Therefore, let us learn from this place to allow God no less than is ascribed to him by the heathen king.

He goes on:

113

48 *Then the king magnified Daniel and gave him splendid and great rewards* [or, 'gave him many rewards', as others render it] *and set him over all the province of Babylon, and as chief master over all the wise men of Babylon.*

Here he adds something else — that King Nebuchadnezzar exalted God's prophet and adorned him with the highest honours. The ill-addressed worship which he himself showed and which he ordered others to perform has been mentioned. So far as the rewards and the governorship are concerned, we can condemn neither Nebuchadnezzar's honouring God's servant so highly nor Daniel's allowing himself to be so decorated. All God's servants must, of course, beware of seeking gain from their office. In particular we know that it is a most pestilent disease when prophets and teachers love money or are ready to receive gifts. For where money is not despised, many vices will necessarily flourish; all avaricious and greedy men adulterate the Word of God like merchants.[5] Therefore all prophets and ministers of God should take special care not to devote their thoughts to rewards. But so far as Daniel is concerned, he was able to receive what the king offered, just as it was also lawful for Joseph to accept the prefecture of all Egypt.[6] There is no doubt that Daniel had something other than his own personal advantage in view. For it is not credible that he should be mercenary who bore exile so patiently, who, moreover, preferred at the peril of his life to abstain from the royal food rather than to alienate himself from the people of God. He preferred the ignominy of the cross (for then God's people were oppressed) to wealth and pleasures and honours; so who could think he was blinded by avarice to receive rewards? But because he saw the children of God wretchedly and cruelly downtrodden by the Chaldaeans he wanted to help their miseries, so far as he could. Therefore, because he knew this would be for the relief and comfort of his nation, he allowed himself to be made governor of a province. And the same reason moved him to seek high positions for his friends, as it goes on:

49 *And Daniel asked the king and he set Shadrach, Meshach, and Abednego over the work* [or, 'administration'] *of the province of Babylon. Daniel, however,* [was] *in the king's gate.*

Here could be noted some ambition in the prophet, that he chased after honours for his friends. When the king spontaneously offered him a governorship, he could accept it from fear of offending the proud monarch. There was a certain necessity in it. But what shall we say was the source of his asking the king to give governorships to the others? As I have already intimated, Daniel could

5. Mg., 2 Cor. 2:17.
6. Mg., Gn. 41:40.

here be suspected of ambition. He could also be charged with making gain out of the teaching divinely revealed to him. But he was thinking rather of his own people; he wanted to bring some comfort to the oppressed. For the Chaldaeans then ruled over their slaves tyrannously and we know that the Jews were as good as hated by the whole world. So when Daniel was moved to pity and sought some relief for God's people, there is no reason for us to accuse him of any fault. He was not attached to any private gain; he was not greedy for honours for himself or his friends; but he was intent on his friends' ability to bring help to the Jews in their troubles. Hence, the authority he procures for them had as its sole intention that the Jews should be treated a little better, so that their condition would not be so hard and harsh when they had governors from their own fellow-countrymen, who would study their welfare in a brotherly way. Now we see that in this respect Daniel can be excused rightly and without any dissimulation or sophistry. For the affair is clear enough in itself, and it is easy to infer from it that Daniel was godly and humane, and was not sinning in what he did.

When it is said that *he was in the king's gate,* we should not understand that he was the gate-keeper. Some take it that he was 'in the gate' because it was there that they were accustomed to dispense justice. But they are transferring to the Chaldaeans what Scripture teaches about the Jews. I take it more simply, that Daniel was the governor in the king's residence, so that he held supreme rule there; and that sense is the more genuine. We know also that it was customary among the Chaldaeans and Assyrians for access to the king to be difficult. Hence it is said that 'Daniel was in the gate', in the sense that none could enter the king's palace save by his permission.

Now he goes on:

CHAPTER 3

1 *King Nebuchadnezzar made an image of gold; its height was sixty cubits, its breadth six cubits. He set it up on the plain of Dura* [others make the noun appellative and translate it 'on the habitable field'. But the interpretation is more correct that he placed the image on the plain of Dura] *in the province of Babylon.*

It is probable that King Nebuchadnezzar did not erect this statue quite soon after. The prophet does not say how many years had passed, but it is more probable that when he made the statue no little time had elapsed since he confessed that the God of Israel was the supreme God. Since, however, the prophet is silent, there is no need for us to argue about what is uncertain. Some of the rabbis think that the statue was erected as an expiation, as if Nebuchad-

115

nezzar wanted to drive away his dream — that is, the effect of his dream — by this magic charm, as they call it. But their guess is altogether too silly.

Now it is asked whether Nebuchadnezzar deified himself or erected this statue to Bel, the chief of the gods among the Chaldaeans, or even fashioned some new god. Many incline to the view that he wanted to place himself among the number of the gods. But I do not know how sure this is — to me it certainly is not. It seems rather that Nebuchadnezzar consecrated the statue to one of the gods. Nevertheless, superstition being always joined with ambition and pride, it is likely that Nebuchadnezzar was moved by a lust for glory and by pride to erect this statue. Sometimes superstitious people spend vast sums on building temples and making idols. If anyone should ask what their motive is, their answer will come pat, that they are doing it for the honour of God. Yet there is none that does not put his own fame and reputation first. Therefore the worship of God is treated as almost nothing by the superstitious; they want rather to gain for themselves favour and esteem among men. That such was the purpose of King Nebuchadnezzar I freely admit — indeed, I am almost sure of it. Nevertheless, there was an appearance of piety in it. For he pretended that he wanted to worship God.

From this what I mentioned before becomes clearer — King Nebuchadnezzar had not been truly converted, not in his heart. Rather, he was still stuck fast in his errors, even when he ascribed the glory to the God of Israel. Therefore the confession was isolated and anomalous, as was said; for now what he had nourished in his heart comes out. For he was not reverting to his own nature, as they say, when he set up the statue; rather it was that his impiety was uncovered, which had for a time been hidden. His splendid confession could have been taken as testimony of a change. All would have said that he was a new man, had God not wanted to make it plain that he was still entangled and bound by the chains of Satan — and still addicted to his errors. Therefore God wished to put forward this example that we might know that Nebuchadnezzar was always ungodly, however much he might be compelled to give some glory to the God of Israel.

Grant, almighty God, since our minds have so many hidden corners that nothing is more difficult than thoroughly to cleanse them of all inventions and falsehood, grant, I say, that we may rightly examine ourselves; and shed the light of your Spirit upon us that we may truly recognize our hidden vices and drive them far from us, so that you alone may be our God and true piety may win the victory in us and we may offer you sound and unblemished service; and also that we may live with a sound conscience in the world; each of us so engaged in his own lot as to care for the good of his brethren rather than of himself, so that at the last we may become partakers of the true glory which you have prepared for us in heaven through Christ our Lord. Amen.

Lecture 13

We began in our last lecture to treat of the golden statue that Nebuchadnezzar set up and placed in the field, or the plain, of Dura. We have said that this statue was erected for a religious reason certainly, but the ambition of the king, or tyrant, was the prevailing motive — something we may always remark in the superstitious. Although they always hide behind the name of God and even persuade themselves that they are worshipping God, yet always what drives them on is pride, the wish to be seen in the world. Such was King Nebuchadnezzar's state of mind with this statue. Its very size shows us this. For the prophet says *the height of the statue was sixty cubits and the breadth six cubits.* There must have been a huge outlay for such a massive bulk; for the image was forged of gold. It is, of course, probable that the gold was amassed from his many plunderings and robberies; but however that may be, we may easily perceive what we have already said, that this heathen king offered God worship in such a way that his real wish was that the memory of his own name should be published among the generations to come. And the region in which he put the image suggests the same thing. For without doubt the prophet is indicating a well-known place, much frequented either for its market or for some other purposes.

Now, as for the king's particular aim, we have said that the conjecture of those who think the statue was erected to expiate for the dream is weak. It is more probable, since Jews were living everywhere in Assyria and Chaldaea, that the image was set up lest these foreigners who had been carried into exile from their fatherland should introduce any new ways. This conjecture has at any rate some likelihood. Nebuchadnezzar knew that the Jews were so devoted to the God of their fathers that they were strangers to all the superstitions of the gentiles. So he was afraid that they would seduce many to their opinion.

117

He therefore wanted to thwart them by setting up a new statue and compelling all his subjects to worship it. Meanwhile we see that the knowledge of the God of Israel, whose power and glory he had celebrated only a little before, vanished at once from his mind. For now this victory memorial is erected as an insult to him, as if he had been conquered along with the idols of the other nations. But, as we have said elsewhere, Nebuchadnezzar had never seriously avowed the God of Israel but had been forced to confess by a sudden impulse that he was the supreme and only God, being always sunk the while in his own superstitions. The confession was that of a man thunderstruck; it did not proceed from a true affection of the heart.

Now let us come to the rest:

2 *Then Nebuchadnezzar the king sent to gather together the satraps* [the etymology is unknown to me. But as it is certain that all these are names for civil officers, I will take the liberty of translating freely these words which are not Hebrew and whose origin was hidden from the Hebrews themselves (save that some want to be seen to be very subtle, yet bring forward nothing that is not feeble, even downright silly). So let us be content with this simplicity, that he 'sent to gather together the satraps'], *leaders and quaestors, nobles* [or, 'princes'], *judges, magistrates, peers, and all the governors of the provinces, to come to the dedication of the image which Nebuchadnezzar the king had set up.*

3 *Then the satraps, leaders, princes, quaestors, magistrates, judges, peers, and all the governors of the provinces assembled for the dedication of the image which Nebuchadnezzar the king had set up; and they stood before the image which Nebuchadnezzar had set up.*

Let us proceed with the context, for it is all connected.

4 *And a herald proclaimed loudly* [or, 'in the multitude'; for חיל, *haiil*, can be expounded either way], *'To you it is commanded, O peoples, nations, and languages* [that is, "nations of whatever language you are"],

5 *As soon as you hear the sound of the horn* [or, "trumpet"], *pipe, lute, harp, psaltery, symphonia* [we cannot conjecture with certainty what these were, but they were musical instruments, as it goes on], *and all musical instruments,* [that] *you fall down and worship the golden image which Nebuchadnezzar the king has set up.*

6 *And whoever does not fall down* [that is, "bend his knees"] *and worship, will in the same hour* [that is, "immediately"] *be thrown into the midst of a furnace of burning fire* [or, "fiery"].'

7 *Therefore as soon as* ['in the same hour that'] *all the peoples heard the sound of the horn, pipe, lute, harp, psaltery, and all the musical instruments, all the peoples, nations, and tongues fell down and worshipped the golden image which Nebuchadnezzar the king had set up.*

We see that Nebuchadnezzar wished to stabilize religion among all the nations over which he then ruled, lest disturbances should occur through a pluralist society. And such discord, it was to be feared, might shake the government. And so we may conjecture that the king was thinking especially of his own peace and well-being. Princes are accustomed to look to what suits them rather than to what God demands when they issue edicts on the worship of God. And from the beginning this boldness and rashness has gone on in the world, so that those in authority have always dared to fabricate gods. Then they have gone even further and commanded the worship of the gods they have made.

We should observe the division into three species of gods: the 'philosophic', the 'politic', and the 'poetic'. They call 'philosophic' gods those whom there is some natural reason for worshipping. It is, of course, true that philosophers are completely foolish when they dispute on either the essence or the worship of God. By following their own ideas, they of necessity come to nothing. For God cannot be apprehended by the human mind.[1] It is necessary that he reveal himself to us by his Word; and it is as he descends to us that we on our side rise up to heaven. Nevertheless, the philosophers in their disputations have some show of truth, so that they can seem not to talk irrational nonsense. But the poets have fabled whatever they liked and have filled the world with the silliest, and at the same time the foulest, errors. All the theatres declaimed their empty imaginings, and so the minds of the masses were at once filled with the same crazinesses. We know that the human mind is prone to vanity. But when the devil lights the fire, we see learned and ignorant alike carried away. So it happened that they became convinced that what they used to see represented in the theatre was the truth.

But there was also a stable religion among the gentiles, founded on the authority of past generations. They called these gods which were received by common consent 'politic'. And those who were regarded as sensible said that what the philosophers taught on the nature of the gods was not advantageous, for it uprooted all the public observances and things that had been accepted without question. For both Greeks and Latins, and also some barbarous nations, worshipped certain gods they thought had been born, that is, whom they confessed to have been mortal. But the philosophers at least retained the principle that the gods are eternal. If the philosophers had been listened to, the authority of past generations would have fallen. So even the most sensible of men were not ashamed to say, as I have already related, that philosophy should be kept separate from religion.

In regard to the poets, the philosophers were forced to give in to the whims of the masses; but at the same time they taught that what the poets

1. Mg., 1 Cor. 2:14.

119

feigned and fabled on the nature of the gods was harmful. Therefore, there was in the world an almost common rule for worshipping God; as it were, a basis of piety. It ruled out other gods being worshipped apart from those handed down by past generations. And this is the point of the oracle of Apollo whom Xenophon,[2] in the person of Socrates, especially praises — that in every city their own gods should be worshipped. For when Apollo was consulted as to which religion was best, he commanded (in order that the errors with which all the nations were drunk might be cherished) that there should be no change in the public state, but that the best religion for any peoples and towns was that which had been received from the most ancient antiquity.[3] This was a phenomenal imposture of the devil; he did not want men's minds to be aroused to consider within themselves what was right, but kept them in the lethargy of 'The august authority of the ancients is all you need.' As I have said, the height of sagacity among the heathen was that consensus ruled instead of reason. Yet those who ruled or had power or rank assumed a sort of right to make new gods. So we see many temples dedicated to invented gods, just because they were armed with authority.

So it is not surprising if Nebuchadnezzar took the liberty of setting up a new god. It could be that he dedicated the statue to Bel, who is thought to have been the Jupiter of the Chaldaeans. Nevertheless, he still intended to introduce a new form of religion, under pretext of which his memory would be celebrated in succeeding generations. Virgil obliquely ridicules this fool-ishness when he says, 'And he increases the number of the gods with their altars.'[4] He means that, although men erect many altars in their lands, the number of gods does not increase in heaven. Thus Nebuchadnezzar with his one altar increased the number of the gods; that is, he introduced a new rite, that the statue might be his own monument, so to say, and his name proclaimed so long as that religion should last. Meanwhile we see how unbridled he was in abusing his power. He did not ask his magi what was lawful or even consider in himself whether that religion were legitimate or not. Blinded by pride, he meant to bind a religion on everybody; and what he decreed had to be approved. From this we conclude how false are the heathen when they pretend that their aim is to worship God, for in fact they want to be God's superiors. They allow themselves no lucid, right thinking; they do not apply their minds to the knowledge of God. Whatever pleases them they intend shall be lawful. There-fore they do not worship God himself, but their own production.

Such was the pride of King Nebuchadnezzar, as his edict shows: *King Nebuchadnezzar sent to gather together all the satraps, all the leaders, gover-*

2. Mg., Xenophon, *In Comment.,* i.e., *Memorabilia* 4:3:16.
3. Mg., Cicero, *On Laws* 2, i.e., 2:16:40; cf. 2:11:27.
4. Mg., *Aeneid* 7, i.e., 7:211.

nors, etc., to come to the dedication of the image which King Nebuchadnezzar had set up. The word 'King' is always added, except in one place, as if the regal office raised mortals to such a height that they had the right to fabricate gods. And we see the King of Babylon assuming this right — that the statue which he (not some private person, not a commoner, but the king himself) had set up should be worshipped as God. Because a king enjoys pre-eminence in the world, kings will not acknowledge that they remain in their legitimate rank only if they keep themselves in obedience to God.

And today we see all the earthly kings still swollen with this sort of pride. They do not ask what is consistent with the Word of God and what is genuine piety; but because they consider only the errors handed down by the past, they give them royal approval and think their pre-judgment is final — in case God should be worshipped differently from what seems good to them and their decree.

As for the dedication, we know that it was the custom among the heathen to consecrate their statues and pictures before they worshipped them. Today the same error reigns in the papacy. So long as the images are still with the sculptor or painter, there is no veneration. But as soon as an image is dedicated, whether by private piety (the papists call it 'devotion') or by a public and solemn ceremony, 'God' is made out of a tree-trunk, out of stone, out of pigments. Among their forms of exorcism the papists have definite ceremonies for consecrating statues and pictures.

Nebuchadnezzar, therefore, when he wished this image of his to be considered in the place of God, consecrated it with a solemn ceremony — as was said, this was the custom among heathen races. He is not speaking here of the masses (for not all would be able to assemble); but the governors and nobles are ordered to come, and they bring their many hangers-on. Then they can pass on the king's edict and each one will take care that a monument will be erected in his own territory; so it would appear as if all his subjects were worshipping as God the statue which had been set up by the king.

Now it goes on that *all the satraps, all the governors, leaders, princes, quaestors, magistrates came and stood before the image which King Nebuchadnezzar had set up.* No wonder that the governors fell in with the king's command! They had no other religion save what they had received from their fathers. But many were swayed rather by the obedience they owed to the king than by antiquity. So today, if any king thinks up a new superstition, or if he forsakes the papacy and wants to restore the pure worship of God, immediately you will see a sudden change in all his governors and in all the courtiers and nobles. Why? Because they neither fear God nor reverence him sincerely, but just hang on the king's word and flatter him like slaves. What pleases the king is approved by them all — with loud applause if need be. So it is not surprising if the Chaldaean nobles, who had never had an idea of what the true God is

121

like or had had even a taste of true piety, should be at once quite ready to worship the statue. But from this we gather also that nothing is firm, nothing steady, among heathens, who have not been taught in God's school what true religion is. For they are swayed every moment at the breath of any breeze. As leaves move when the wind blows among the trees, so whoever is not rooted in the truth of God must needs waver and be swayed to and fro when any wind begins to blow. The royal edict is no light breeze but a violent tempest. For none can oppose kings and their edicts with impunity. Hence it happens that those who are not solidly grounded on God's Word and have no grasp of what true piety is are carried away by the onrush of such a blast.

Afterwards he adds that *a herald proclaimed loudly,* or 'in the host'. And this latter rendering fits quite well, for the herald proclaimed in the crowd when there was a great gathering of peoples — the Babylonian kingdom embraced many provinces at that time. *The herald, therefore, proclaimed with a loud voice, 'To you it is commanded, O nations, peoples, and languages'.* This was enough to strike them with terror, when the king commanded that without exception all the provinces should worship his idol. For each watched his neighbour, and any individual who saw such a multitude being obedient would not dare to dissent. Thus fell all liberty.

Now he goes on: *'As soon as you hear the sound of the trumpet* — or, 'the sound of the horn' — *the lute, the pipe, the psaltery, the harp, etc., that you fall down and worship the image. But whoever does not fall down, will in the same hour be thrown into a burning furnace.'* It would make them even more frightened when King Nebuchadnezzar ratified his impious rite with such a savage punishment. Any ordinary death would not suit him; he commanded that whoever did not worship the statue should be thrown into a fire. This threat of punishment shows quite clearly that the king suspected that some were insubordinate. Had the Jews not been intermixed with the Chaldaeans and Assyrians, who had always worshipped the same gods, there would have been no resistance (and also because it was the custom everywhere that the gods approved by the kings were to be worshipped). It therefore looks as if the statue had been set up deliberately for the king to test whether those who had not yet grown used to heathen superstitions would be obedient. He wanted to blot out the memory of sincere godliness from among the children of Abraham and corrupt them once for all, so that they should follow the usual customs and adapt themselves to the king's will and the consensus of the people among whom they lived. But we shall see about this later.

As for the worship itself, it consisted only in a gesture. King Nebuchadnezzar did not demand a verbal profession of belief that it[a] was God — that is, that there was in the statue a divinity to which worship was to be paid. It

---

a. Reading *illam* (= statue or image, both of which are feminine nouns) for *illum* (masculine).

was sufficient to declare this by an outward gesture. We see, then, that all who make a pretence of worshipping idols are rightly condemned of idolatry even if they cover themselves by saying that they do not do it from their heart but only from fear, because they are forced by a king's commands. That excuse is altogether too weak. We see this king, or tyrant, although he had fabricated the image by the cunning of the devil, demands nothing more than that all the people and all the nations should genuflect before the statue. Assuredly in this way he would have alienated the Jews from the worship of the one and true God if he had extorted it from them. For God wills first to be worshipped inwardly by us and then also by outward profession. The chief altar at which God is worshipped ought to be situated within ourselves. For God is worshipped spiritually by faith and by prayers and by other offices of piety.[5] External profession must of necessity be added, not only that we may exercise ourselves in the worship of God but also that we may offer ourselves wholly to him and hold him both in body and mind, as Paul teaches[6] — in short, that he may possess us entirely. This, therefore, on the worship and the punishment.

He goes on again: *As soon as was heard the noise of the trumpets and the sound of the many instruments, all the nations, all the peoples, all the languages, fell down and worshipped the image which King Nebuchadnezzar had set up.* Here we must again remember what I said, that all mortals are ready to yield obedience to their kings. Whatever they are commanded they readily accept, so long as it is not harsh or detrimental; they will often bear the heaviest burdens to please their kings. But it is also to be noted that they are always more inclined to act a vicious part. If King Nebuchadnezzar had commanded that the God of Israel should be worshipped and all temples overthrown along with the altars which had formerly existed under all his jurisdiction, no doubt great tumults would have arisen. For the devil so bewitches men's minds that they stick stubbornly to the errors they have once imbibed. The Chaldaeans and Assyrians and the rest would never have been brought to obedience without the greatest difficulty. But now at the given signal they immediately fall down and worship the golden statue.

Here let us learn to contemplate, as in a mirror, our nature — and to this end, that we may keep ourselves under the Word of God and never be removed from a right faith but stand our ground with invincible constancy, whatever kings may command. Let them threaten us with a hundred deaths; they cannot shake our faith. For unless God holds us back with his bridle, we shall at once slip aside into everything that is worthless. But especially if some king introduces corruptions we are immediately carried away; because, as I said, we are too inclined to faulty and perverted forms of worship.

5. Mg., Jn. 4:24.
6. Mg., 1 Cor. 7:34; 1 Thes. 5:23.

Again the prophet repeats the word 'king', to tell us that all the host did not consider what would be pleasing to God or that worship should be holy and sound but were content with the wish of the king alone. The prophet condemns this over-easiness, and rightly. So we learn from this place not to be moved by men's wills to embrace this or that religion. Our first aim must be to seek diligently what worship is agreeable to God. Hence, we need judgment, so that we do not impetuously throw ourselves into superstitions.

As for the musical instruments, I acknowledge that they were used by the Church of God, and, indeed, by God's command. But the people of God had one way and the Chaldaeans another. For although the Jews used trumpets and lutes and musical instruments in singing the praises of God, yet they were not foisting this on God as an inherently godly rite. There was another purpose in it — God wished to stir them up by every means when they were sluggish (for we know that our interest in godliness is always cool unless we are goaded). God, therefore, used these stimuli to make the Jews worship him with more fervent zeal. But the Chaldaeans thought they had satisfied God if they got together a lot of musical instruments. For, as is usual, they estimated God by their own sense. Whatever pleases us we think will please God too. Hence that immense mass of ceremonies in the papacy. Our eyes are feasted with such splendour and we think we have done our duty to God, as if his delights were the same as ours. This is too gross an error. And so, as far as the lute, trumpet, and the other musical instruments are concerned, with which Nebuchadnezzar adorned the worship of his idol, there is no doubt they were a part of the errors — and we must say the same of the gold. God certainly wanted his sanctuary to be splendid, not because gold or silver or precious stones are pleasing to him in themselves, but he wanted to commend his glory to the people, so that under those figures they might acknowledge that whatever is precious should be offered to God alone, because it is sacred to him. Although, therefore, the Jews had many pomps (so to say), that is, they had magnificent splendour in the outward worship of God, yet the principle remained that God is to be worshipped spiritually. But the heathen, even as they invent stupid gods for themselves out of their own heads, so also they want to worship them according to their own judgment; and they think that the perfection of sanctity is to sing beautifully, to have an abundance of gold and silver, to have a magnificent shape and form in their sacrifices.

The rest we will leave till tomorrow.

Grant, almighty God, because we always wretchedly go astray in our thoughts and, if we try to worship you, do nothing but profane the true and pure worship of your divinity and are so easily drawn away to depraved superstitions, grant, then, that we may remain in the pure obedience of your Word and never turn aside one way or the other; and arm us with the unconquerable power of the Spirit, that we may not yield to any terrors or threats of men, but stand fast in the reverence of your name right to the end; and however much the world may rave after its devilish errors, that we may never turn aside from the right way but stand firm in the right course to which you invite us until the race is run and we come to that blessed rest which is laid up for us in heaven through Christ our Lord. Amen.

Lecture 14

8 *And so immediately* ['in the same hour'] *men, Chaldaeans, came forward and shouted accusation against the Jews* [that is, 'noisily and tumultuously they accused them'. Some translate it 'they accused an accusation'. For אכל, *acal,* since it means 'to eat', they say that when it is joined with this word it can be taken metaphorically for 'to accuse'. But because it also means 'to shout', the sense is applicable here that they were noisy accusers.]
9 *They spoke and said to Nebuchadnezzar the king, 'O King, live for ever.*
10 *You, O King, have placed a decree that every man when he hears the sound of the horn* [or, "trumpet"], *the pipe, the lute, the harp, the psaltery, the symphonia, and music of all instruments, shall fall down and worship the golden image.*
11 *And that whoever does not fall down and worship will be thrown into the midst of* [or, "within"] *a furnace of burning fire.*
12 *There are men, Jews, whom you have set* [that is, "made governors"] *over the administration* [or, "work"] *of the province of Babylon —Shadrach, Meshach, and Abednego. These men have given no thought to you, O King* [others translate it "paid no respect"]. *They do not serve your god* [or, "your gods" — there is little difference] *and they do not worship the golden image which you have set up.'*

   Although he does not here openly state the intention of those who accused Shadrach, Meshach, and Abednego, we can infer by probability from the outcome that it was a concerted plan when the king erected the golden image. For we see that they had been watched; and, as was said yesterday, Nebuchadnezzar seems to have followed the usual aim of kings. Although they proudly despise God, yet they use religion as a weapon to keep their authority strong; and for this end alone they make a pretence of worshipping God to keep the people in their duty. Because there were Jews intermixed with the Chaldaeans and Assyrians, the king wanted to forestall any disaffection. And so he put the statue in a well-frequented place as a trial and test of whether the Jews were willing to attach themselves to Babylonian religious forms.

Meanwhile, this passage teaches us, at least by probable conjecture, that the king had been stirred up by his counsellors, because they thought it shameful that foreign slaves should be governors of the province of Babylon. For they had been taken into exile as lawful spoils of war. Since, then, the Chaldaeans thought this all wrong, they were moved by envy to suggest their advice to the king. For how came it that they detected so suddenly that the Jews had not shown worship and veneration to the statue, especially Shadrach, Meshach, and Abednego? What happened shows plainly that they were, so to say, keeping a watch to see what the Jews would do. So we can easily infer that they had prepared this slander from the start, when they were the originators of the king's scheme to make a statue.

From the turbulent way they accused the Jews we can also see that they were filled with envy and hatred. It might well be said that they were burning with zeal, in the way that the superstitious have of wanting to impose a law on everybody; and cruelty made them even worse. But it is clear that mere jealousy took possession of the Chaldaeans, and made them accuse the Jews so loudly.

But it is uncertain whether they spoke of the whole nation in general, that is, of all the exiles, or only pointed out these three. It is probable that the accusation was restricted to Shadrach, Meshach, and Abednego. For if these three had been broken down, victory over the rest would have been easy. For few so stronghearted could be found in the whole people. Therefore it is likely that those clamourers wanted to attack the men whom they knew to be spirited and steadfast above the others. They also wanted to degrade them from the position of honour in which they were unwilling to see them. But it is asked why they spared Daniel; for it is not consistent that he dissimulated when the king ordered his statue to be worshipped, that is, which he set up. It could be that they let Daniel alone for the time being, knowing that the king had exalted him. And they brought the accusation against these three, because they could be oppressed more easily and with less trouble. I think it was this craftiness that moved them not to name Daniel along with the three, lest favour towards him might soften the king's anger.

Now the form of the accusation is given: *'O King, live for ever.'* This was the common salutation. Afterwards is added, *'You, O King'*. This is emphatic, as if they were saying, 'You have issued a decree under your royal power *that whoever hears the sound of the trumpet* (or, "horn"), *lute, pipe, psaltery, and musical instruments shall fall down before the golden statue. But whoever refuses to do this shall be thrown into a furnace of burning fire. But here are Jewish men whom you have made governors in the administration of the province of Babylon.'* To make them more offensive they add that they charge them with ingratitude, in that, raised to such an honour, they despise the king's command and seduce others by their example to a like disobedience. So we see that this was said to magnify their crime: *'the king had made them governors of the province of Babylon. These men do not worship the golden image and do not serve your gods'* — this is the chief crime. And in all this speech we see that the Chaldaeans' only aim was to condemn Shadrach, Meshach, and Abednego for the one crime of not obeying the king's command. They are not talking about their own religion, for it would not have served their turn if it were called in question whether the gods they worshipped were worthy of such worship. So they omit what will not help them and seize up the weapon that the king had been despised because Shadrach, Meshach, and Abednego did not worship the image when the king had commanded by his edict that this be done.

Here again we see that the superstitious do not apply their mind or diligence to a genuine investigation of how they may worship God properly and with piety. They neglect this and only follow where their own audacity and wishes lead. Since then such rashness is set before us by the Holy Spirit as in a mirror, let us learn that our worship can only be approved by God if it rests upon truth. Hence the authority of men must be regarded as worthless. For unless we are sure that the religion which we follow is pleasing to God, whatever can be contributed by men will be weak. Now when we see those saintly men accused of the crime of ingratitude and also of rebellion, there is no reason for us to take the same thing hard today. Those who slander us accuse us of stubbornness, of despising the commands of kings — who want to involve us in their own errors. But, as we shall see again, we have an easy and ready defence. Meanwhile we have to undergo this infamy before the world as if we were pig-headed and intractable. And as for ingratitude — if they load us with a thousand insults, their calumnies must be borne patiently for the time, until the Lord our champion sheds his light on our innocence.

Now he goes on:

13 *Then Nebuchadnezzar with anger and rage* [some translate it 'fury'] *commanded Shadrach, Meshach, and Abednego to be summoned. And these men brought* ['them' is to be understood] *before the king.*
14 *And Nebuchadnezzar spoke and said to them, 'Is it true, Shadrach, Meshach, and Abednego, that you do not serve my gods* [or rather, "my god"], *and that you do not worship the golden image which I have ordered* [or, "set up"]?
15 *Now, behold, you will be ready* [others read it as a question: "will you be ready?"], *as soon as you hear the sound of the horn* [or, "trumpet"], *pipe,*

lute, harp, psaltery, symphonia, and music of all instruments, [that] *you fall down and worship the image which I made. Because, if you will not worship, in the same hour you will be thrown into the midst of a furnace of burning fire. And who is that god who will rescue you from my hand?'*

This narrative clearly shows us that kings pretend piety only with an eye to their own greatness, putting themselves into the place of their gods. For this is like some abnormality, that King Nebuchadnezzar here insults all the gods, as if there were no power in heaven but what he approves. *'What god'*, says he, *'can rescue you from my hand?'* Why, then, did he serve any god at all? Simply to keep the people under his control and so establish his tyranny; not because any feeling of piety had crept into his mind.

Daniel first relates that the king was furious with anger. For nothing is more irritating to kings than to see their commands rejected. They want everyone to be yielding, even if they command what is very unjust. Yet afterwards the king seems to control himself, when he asks Shadrach, Meshach, and Abednego whether they are not prepared to worship his god and the golden image. When he addresses them in this hesitating sort of way and still offers them a free choice, there is a certain moderation in the words. For he seems to be clearing them from the accusation, on condition they will allow themselves to be persuaded for the future. Nevertheless, his rage was still boiling under the deceptive appearance of moderation. For he at once adds, *'If you will not obey, behold! you will be thrown into a furnace of burning fire.'* Finally he breaks out into that sacrilege and horrible blasphemy, that there was no god who could rescue these saintly men from his hand.

We see in the person of Nebuchadnezzar the sort of pride with which kings are puffed up, even when they pretend some zeal for godliness. For certainly, no reverence for God himself touches them, but they want whatever they order to be accepted by everybody. And so, as I said, they put themselves into the place of God rather than strive to reverence God and assert his glory. This is the point of the words he uses: that *'he set up a statue which he had made'*. It is as if he said, 'It is not for you to decide whether or not you should worship the image. My command is sufficient for you. I have not set up this image without forethought and good cause. Your duty is just simply to obey me.' We see, then, that he arrogates to himself supreme power even in inventing a god. For it is not here a question of politics; Nebuchadnezzar wants the statue to be worshipped as God just because he had decreed so, just because he had published his edict.

But we must always bear in mind what I touched on — that we are given such an example of pride so as to learn that we should not rashly take this or that line in religion; we must listen to God and rest on his authority and will. For if we abandon ourselves to men there will be no end to our errors. Therefore, although kings are so proud and so savage, we must hold fast this rule, that nothing pleases God but what he himself has commanded in his Word; and the principle of true piety is obedience offered to him alone.

As for the blasphemy, it shows more clearly what I said — that, although kings profess some devotion to piety, they despise every divinity and have no other intention than to exalt their own greatness. They make use of a god's name so as to get greater veneration for themselves; and if it advantaged them to change a hundred gods every day, no religious feeling would stop them. For earthly kings, therefore, religion is mostly a pretext; there is no reverence for God in their minds, and no fear, as this heathen king demonstrates. *'Who is that god?'* he says. He makes no exception. If anyone replies that he was speaking comparatively, and defending the glory of his own god whom he worshipped, yet when he utters this blasphemy against all gods, an intolerable arrogance, a devilish rage, is driving him on.

Now let us come to the chief head, where Daniel relates how much constancy Shadrach, Meshach, and Abednego showed:

16 *Shadrach, Meshach, and Abednego replied, and said to the king, 'O Nebuchadnezzar, we are not anxious about this word* [or, "matter"], *what we shall reply to you.* [Others translate it, "It is not necessary for us to reply to you on this matter." And they want the *lamed*, ל, to be superfluous, as it frequently is.]
17 *Behold! our God, whom we serve, is powerful* [that is, "able"] *to free us from the furnace of burning fire, and he will rescue us from your hand, O King.*
18 *And if not, be it known to you, O King, that we do not serve your gods and we will not worship the golden image which you have set up.'*

The chief thing to consider in this story is that these three holy men remained steadfast and courageous in the fear of God even when they knew that they stood in instant peril of death. Death was set before their eyes, yet they did not swerve from the right course, but set the glory of God above their own lives — nay, above a hundred lives, if they had needed to expend so many and it had been granted them. Daniel does not relate all their words but gives only a brief summary. Yet this reflects brightly enough the unconquerable power of the Holy Spirit, with which they were armed. It was indeed a fearful threat when the king said, *'If you are not prepared at the sound of the trumpet to fall down before the statue, it will be your end and you will immediately be thrown into a furnace of fire.'* When the king thundered like that they might, being only human, have lost their nerve. For we know how dear life is to us and what a horror of death will pervade our minds. But Daniel recounts all these details that we may know that when the servants of God are led by the Spirit they have too much fortitude to yield to any threats or give way to any terrors.

They reply to the king, 'There is no need for a long deliberation.' For by saying that they are not anxious, they mean that the matter is settled. As also in that memorable saying of Cyprian related by Augustine,[1] when the courtiers were persuading him to save his life (for the emperor acted reluctantly when he condemned him to death) — so when these flatterers were urging him to save his life by denying godliness, he replied that in so holy a matter there could be no deliberation. And this is how these holy men speak: *'We are not careful'* — that is, 'we will not embark on a consultation as to what is useful, what expedient; nothing of that sort. We have already decided that we will not be drawn away from the sincere worship of God for any reason at all.' If we wish to read, 'It is not necessary for us to reply to you', the meaning will be the same. For they show that the fear of death is set before them in vain; because they have determined, and it is deeply fixed in their hearts, not to move an inch from the true and lawful worship of God. Moreover, they use a twofold reason in rejecting the king's proposal. They say that God has sufficient power and strength to set them free; and second, even if they have to die, yet they do not prize their life so highly as to deny God for the sake of prolonging it. They declare themselves ready for death if the king stubbornly urges them to worship the statue.

This is a most noteworthy passage. For first this reply is to be remarked: when men tempt us to deny God, we must shut our ears and admit no deliberation. For as soon as we even debate whether it is lawful to leave his pure worship we begin to injure God severely, whatever our reason may be. Would that it were well known to all that God's glory is so transcendent, so vital, that everything must be put in its proper place when there is any thought of diminishing or obscuring that glory. But today the fallacy deceives very many into thinking it right to weigh in the scales, so to say, whether it might be best to swerve from the true worship of God for a time when some advantage on the other side suggests itself. As today we see pretenders (of which the world is full) have their excuses to cover their crime when either they worship idols with the ungodly, or deny true piety, now indirectly, now openly and plainly. 'O, what will happen?' he who possesses some rank will say; 'I see how much I can profit if I just pretend a little bit and do not betray what I am. For such openness would not only harm me personally but others as well. If the king has none to try to placate his wrath sometimes, the wicked will be more and more free to drive him on to all barbarity. There must be some middlemen to listen and to watch what the wicked are planning. Then, if not openly, at least covertly they can avert danger from the heads of the godly.' When they make these observations, they think they have satisfied God.

As if Shadrach, Meshach, and Abednego could not have found some

1. Augustine, *Sermon* 309:4:6.

excuse! As if they could not have thought, 'Look! We possess some power to help our brethren. How much barbarity and cruelty there would be if professed enemies of religion succeeded us. They will do all they can to overturn and blot out of the world our nation and the memory of godliness. Would it not be best if we were to yield for a time to the tyrannous and violent edict of the king rather than leave a place open for furious men to occupy who will quite overwhelm our unhappy nation, which is suffering more than enough already?' Shadrach, Meshach, and Abednego could, I say, have assembled all these pretences and dissimulations to excuse their perfidy if, to escape the peril, they had bowed the knee before the golden image. But they did not do so. Therefore, as I have already said, God's right remains sound when his worship is set firm and without any doubtfulness; and once we are convinced of this there is nothing important enough to make it lawful and right for us to swerve in the slightest degree from the profession which he commands us in his Word and which he demands of us. To sum up: the lack of concern which ought to confirm true worshippers of God is here opposed to all cunning and devious plans which they think up who, for the sake of living, lose the cause for living, as the heathen poet said.[2] For what is the point of living except to serve the glory of God? But we lose that cause for living for the sake of life — that is, when we desire overmuch to live in the world and do not look to the purpose of living. And so Daniel sets the simplicity which the children of God must follow against all the reasonings which dissimulators use to cover and cloak their crime.

Therefore, *we are not careful*. Why? because we have already decided that the glory of God is more to us than a thousand lives and whatever our fleshly sense can supply. Therefore when this high-heartedness flourishes, all evasions flee away. Nor will they worry themselves who are called into danger for the testimony of the truth. For, as I have already said, their ears will be closed to all the enticings of Satan.

And when they add that *'God is powerful enough to save them; and if not, yet they have prepared themselves for death',* they show what ought to lift our minds above all temptations — that our life is precious to God. And he will be able to save us if he so wishes. Since, then, we have protection enough in God, let us realize there is no better way to save our lives than by putting ourselves entirely under his protection and casting all our cares upon him.

Then, in the second clause we must notice that, even if the Lord shall wish to irradiate his glory by our death, this is a lawful sacrifice, which is to be offered to him. Sincere piety flourishes in us only if our souls are in his hands, that is, if our life is always ready to be sacrificed.

2. Juvenal, *Satires* 8:84.

This, then, is what I briefly want to note now; I will, the Lord willing, expound it tomorrow.

> *Grant, almighty God, that, when we see the ungodly carried after their impure imaginations with such force and swollen with so much arrogance, we may learn true humility and so subject ourselves to you that we may wait always for you to speak and not undertake anything save by your command; and also that, when we shall have learned what worship pleases you, we may persist in it steadfastly to the end, moved from our place or led astray from our way by no perils, by no threats, by no violence; but persevering in obedience to your Word we may prove our zeal and submission; and then, that you may acknowledge us your children, so that finally we may be gathered into that eternal inheritance which you have prepared for all the members of Christ your Son. Amen.*

Lecture 15

We said yesterday that the constancy of Shadrach, Meshach, and Abednego was grounded on two things: that they were entirely convinced that God was the keeper of their life and that his power would free them from imminent death if that was right; and also that they had boldly and fearlessly determined to die if God wished such a sacrifice to be offered to him. But what Daniel relates of these three is pertinent also to us. It is therefore right to infer this general doctrine when danger threatens us for the testimony of the truth: first, that we learn that our life rests in God's hand; second, that we prepare ourselves boldly and without fear to encounter death. As for the first, experience teaches us that very many defect from God and profession of the faith because they cannot make up their minds that there is strength enough in God to set us free. It is true, of course, that everyone will say, 'God has a care for us and our life is placed in his hand and will.' But hardly one in a hundred will have this fixed deep and sure in his heart. For each one seeks out some way to preserve his life, as if God had no power. Hence only he really profits in the Word of God who learns that his life is in God's care and that his guardianship suffices. Whoever has got to this stage will be able to face a hundred risks, for he will not hesitate to follow whither he has been called. The one thing that will free us from all fear and apprehension is that God can rescue his servants from a thousand deaths, as it says in the Psalm: 'To him belong the issues from death.'[1] Death seems to consume everything; but from that gulf God rescues whom he will. This conviction should be enough to give us a firm and unassailable constancy.

But it is necessary for those who cast the care of their life and safety on

1. Mg., Ps. 68:21, i.e., 68:20.

God to be sure of their ground, so that they do not doubt they are defending a good cause. And this also is expressed in the words that Shadrach, Meshach, and Abednego speak: *'Behold, our God, whom we serve'*. By mentioning the service of God they declare that they have a sure support; because they are not acting rashly but are servants of the true God and are oppressed for the sake of defending godliness. This is the difference between martyrs and the madmen who are often steadfast when they pay the just penalty for their mad attempts to turn everything upside down.[2] (For we see many disturbed by their excesses.) If they should happen to pay the penalty, they are not to be numbered among the martyrs of God. For, as Augustine says, the cause makes the martyr, not the punishment.[3] There is therefore an implied weight in these words, when the three assert that they serve God; for in this way they glory that they are undergoing the peril which they see before them not rashly but on behalf of the true worship of God.

Now I come to the second: *'If it is not God's will to rescue us from death, be it known to you, O King, that we do not serve your gods.'* I said at first that, if we are to be ready and constant to undergo any contest, our life must be committed to God, as it is right to submit to his will and hand and to be protected by his guardianship. Moreover, a desire for this earthly and fleeting life ought not to hold us back and hinder us from a free and frank profession of the truth. The glory of God should be more precious to us than a hundred lives. We cannot be witnesses of God unless we lay aside the desire for life, at least so as to put God's glory first. Meanwhile, we must note that this cannot be done unless we are overcome by the hope of the better life. For when the promise of the eternal inheritance does not take possession of our hearts we can never be torn from the world. For we desire to exist, and that affection cannot be taken from us unless faith overcome it. As also Paul says: 'Not that we desire to be unclothed, but clothed upon.'[4] Paul accepts that men cannot naturally be brought to wish to leave the world gladly unless, as was said, faith is victorious. But when we understand that our heritage is in heaven and that we are pilgrims on the earth, then we put off that affection for the earthly life to which we are too much addicted. There are, therefore, two things which prepare the children of God for martyrdom so that they do not hesitate to offer themselves and their lives to God in sacrifice: if they are convinced that their lives are guarded by God and that he will be their sure deliverer, if it is expedient; and second, when they rise above the world and aspire to the hope of eternal and heavenly life so that they are prepared to renounce the world.

And a high-heartedness is to be observed in the words, when they say,

2. The reference is to Anabaptists.
3. Augustine, *Against Cresconius* 3:47:51, and often.
4. Mg., 2 Cor. 5:4.

135

'*Be it known to you, O King, that we do not serve your gods nor will we worship the statue which you have set up.*' For here they indirectly accuse the king of taking too much to himself when he wishes religion to stand or fall by his will. 'You have set up a statue — but your authority is unimportant, for we know that the god whom you wish to be worshipped under the statue is a fiction. The God whom we serve has revealed himself to us. Hence we know that he is the maker of heaven and earth; he redeemed our fathers from Egypt; it was also his will to chastise us when he cast us into exile. Therefore, because we have a strong assurance of faith, we care nothing for either your gods or your power.'

He goes on:

19 *Then Nebuchadnezzar was filled with wrath and the form of his face was changed* [צלם, *zelem*, is here taken differently from what it was before. For Daniel had several times used this word for 'image'. But here it means the face or figure of the king. Therefore 'the figure of his face was changed'] *towards Shadrach, Meshach, and Abednego, and he ordered* [or, 'decreed'] *the furnace to be heated seven times* [that is, 'sevenfold'] *more than it was accustomed to be heated.*

20 *And he commanded men outstanding in strength* [or, 'strong in power'], *who* [were] *in his guards* [חיל, *haiil*, is here taken for 'retinue' or 'guards'. Properly it means 'an army'; but, because the king was not then fighting, there is no doubt that Daniel meant the retinue of the king. Therefore, 'he chose the strongest of his guards and'] *commanded* [them] *to bind Shadrach, Meshach, and Abednego and throw* [them] *into the furnace of burning fire.*

At first sight it looks here as if God were deserting his servants, because he does not openly succour them. The king orders them to be thrown into the furnace of fire. No help appears from heaven. So this was a lively and extremely effectual trial of their faith. But they had already been trained, as we saw, to endure anything. For they responded so bravely, not simply because they trusted that God would help them here and now, but because they had made up their minds to die. For a better life so possessed their minds that they willingly cast away the present. Hence it was that they were not terrified by the king's fearful command but kept on their course — that is, of undergoing death fearlessly for the service of God. There was no third way open to them when they were given the choice of either casting themselves into death or renouncing the service of the true God.

By this example we are taught to meditate on and practise the life immortal while we have time, so that, if it seems good to the Lord, we shall not hesitate to lay down our lives for the confession of the truth. For we are so timid. Then when it becomes a reality we are seized by fear and shock —

just because, when no danger presses, we invent an empty security for ourselves. Therefore as long as we are given time we must apply our minds to the meditation of the future life, so that we count the world as nothing and, as often as there is need, are prepared to shed our blood for the testimony of the truth. For this story is told to us not only that we should proudly make known and esteem and admire the virtue of the three saints, but their constancy is set before us as an example to imitate.

As for King Nebuchadnezzar, here again Daniel shows, as in a mirror, how great is the pride of kings and how arrogant they are when they see a custom not being practised according to their good pleasure. Surely a mind of iron should have melted at the reply, when he heard what we have already seen, that Shadrach, Meshach, and Abednego surrendered their lives to God, and when he heard that they could not be torn away from their faith by fear of death. But he is merely filled with wrath. As for his fury, we ought to consider how effective Satan is when he possesses and occupies men. There is no moderation in them, even if otherwise they show great and outstanding hope of virtue. Nebuchadnezzar had been endowed with many virtues, as we have seen. But when the devil was disturbing him, nothing could be seen in him but wildness and barbarity.

Meanwhile let us also remember that our constancy is pleasing to God even if it is not immediately fruitful before the world. Many indulge themselves and their pleasures because they think they would be rash to give themselves to death uselessly. And many excuse themselves for not fighting more bravely for God's glory with the pretext that it would be a mockery of service and their death would be unfruitful. But we hear what Christ declares,[5] that it is a sacrifice pleasing to God when we die for the testimony of the heavenly doctrine, even if the generation before whom we bear witness to the name of God be adulterous and perverse, even hardened against our constancy.

Such an example is set before us in these three holy men. Although Nebuchadnezzar is the more furious at their open confession, yet that frankness was pleasing to God. Nor had they any cause to be sorry, even if they should not see the fruit of their constancy as they wished.

The prophet also brings out a circumstance that demonstrates the king's fury — *he ordered the furnace to be heated sevenfold more than usual;* also, *he delegated from his guards six of the strongest to bind the holy men and throw them into the furnace of fire.* But from the outcome it at once becomes clear that all this was not done without the secret moving of God. The devil could otherwise obscure the miracle unless all doubtfulness were removed. But by the king ordering the furnace to be heated sevenfold more than usual and choosing the strongest guards and putting them in charge of the execution,

5. Mg., Mt. 5:11; 10:32; Mk. 8:38.

God, when he freed his servants, had already removed all doubtfulness beforehand; so that from the darkness an even clearer light emerges from Satan's trying to obscure it. Thus God is wont to frustrate the ungodly; and the more cunningly his glory is attacked so much the more he irradiates his glory and his doctrine. Just so here, as in an image, Daniel describes King Nebuchadnezzar omitting nothing when he wanted to strike terror into all the Jews by this most cruel punishment. And yet his plans were good for nothing but to reveal more clearly God's power and grace towards his servants.

Now he goes on:

21 *Then those men were fettered* [or, 'bound'] *in their cloaks* [some translate it, 'sandals' or 'shoes'; others 'breeches'. But from the word itself the larger part take it for 'breeches'. But we should not worry overmuch about the words but only the substance. Afterwards, and with] *their turbans* [for we know that Easterners wore turbans, a custom they still practise. They wind bandages round their heads. Although not many appear among us, yet we know well enough what the Turks wear. Finally he adds the general name], *in their robes; and were thrown into the furnace of burning fire.*
22 *Because the king's command was urgent* [or, literally, 'hastened'] *and he had ordered the furnace to be excessively heated, the men who were lifting up Shadrach, Meshach, and Abednego were killed by the hot ashes* [some translate it, 'flames'] *of the fire.*
23 *And these three men, Shadrach, Meshach, and Abednego, fell down bound into the midst of the fire of the furnace* [that is, 'within the furnace of fire'].

Here Daniel relates the miracle by which God rescued his servants. But there are two parts to the miracle: these three holy men walked safely in the midst of the fire; but the flame or the hot ashes consumed the guards who had thrown them into the furnace. The prophet carefully records the things which demonstrated the power of God. He says, *since the king's command was urgent* (that is, since the king so wrathfully commanded the furnace to be heated) those men carrying out the execution were engulfed in the hot ashes of the fire. For in the eighteenth chapter of the book of Job שביבא, *sebiba*, is taken for 'hot ashes', or 'sparks', or 'extreme heat'. The prophet's meaning is not at all obscure; the extreme heat licked up and consumed the strong guards; but Shadrach, Meshach, and Abednego walked within the actual burning coals, in the fire and flame. They were not just at the edge of the fire. It is as if the prophet were saying that the king's guards were killed merely by the fumes, but the fire had no effect on those saintly servants of God.

He says, then, that *these three fell down into the furnace of fire.* When he says *fell down,* it is certain that they could not help themselves or seek any way to escape. Then he adds, *fell down bound.* So they would naturally have been suffocated as they met the fire and quickly burnt up. But they remain sound and, when they are free, they walk in the furnace. Therefore we see such a manifest power of God that the devil could never obscure it with his lies. By the fact that the extreme heat, or the ashes of the fire, or the sparks, devour the guards, God also confirms that the whole was his doing. Meanwhile the purpose of the story is that the three holy men were saved miraculously and unexpectedly.

This example is set before us that we may learn that nothing is safer for us than to make God the guardian and defender of our life. Yet we must not positively hope that we shall be preserved from danger, for we see that these holy men determined both things — they hoped for liberation from God if this were useful, but also they did not hesitate to meet death without any fear if so it pleased God. But still, we must deduce from this story that God is protector enough if he wishes to prolong our life. And we know that our life is precious to him. Therefore it is in his choice either to rescue us from danger or to take us to a better life if he thinks good. In Peter we have an example of both things.[6] Peter was once taken out of prison when he was to be executed the next day. God at that time showed that he had a care for the life of his servant. At last Peter suffered death; there was no miracle then. Why? Because he had finished the course of his vocation. So often as is expedient, God will use his power and save us; but if he leads us to death, let us make up our minds that there is nothing better for us than to die, and that it is harmful to prolong our lives. This, then, is the sum of the teaching that we infer from this story.

Afterwards he goes on:

24 *Then Nebuchadnezzar the king trembled greatly* [or, 'was terrified'] *and rose in haste* ['quickly']; *he spoke and said to his counsellors* [some translate it 'friends', and indeed, because the word can be derived both from 'counsel' and from 'custom', we can take it for the companions who were near the king. But because a little later he indicates counsellors by the same word, let us follow this to avoid variety], *'Did we not throw three men into the furnace bound* ["fettered"]?' *They replied and said to the king, 'True, O King.'*
25 *He replied and said, 'But I see four men unbound, walking in the fire, and they are unharmed; and the face of the fourth is like a son of God.'*

Here Daniel relates that God's power was manifested to the heathen men, both to the king and his courtiers, who had plotted the death of the holy men. Therefore he says that *the king trembled greatly* at the miracle. God often forces the ungodly to acknowledge his power. Although they stupefy themselves and harden all their senses, yet whether they want to or not, they are forced to feel God's power. Daniel shows that this happened to King Nebuchadnezzar.

6. Acts 12:3-19.

He trembled greatly and arose, he says, *quickly, and spoke with his companions, 'Did we not throw into the furnace three men bound?'* When they replied, 'It is so', there is no doubt that Nebuchadnezzar was led by a divine prompting (that is, by a secret instinct) to question his companions, no doubt either that the confession was forced from them. For Nebuchadnezzar could immediately have gone to the furnace; but God wanted to force this confession from his enemies so that they, along with the king, should confess that Shadrach, Meshach, and Abednego were rescued, not by any earthly means, but by a wonderful and most unusual power of God. Let us therefore note that these ungodly men were witnesses to the power of God, not spontaneously, but because God put this question into the king's mouth, and also that he did not allow them to escape or to hedge; they had to confess that it was true.

And Nebuchadnezzar says that *'four men walked in the fire, and the face of the fourth was like a son of God'.* Here there is no doubt that God sent one of his angels to encourage the holy men by his presence lest they should give way. For it was a fearful sight, to see the furnace burning like that and themselves to be thrown into it. God, therefore, wished to relieve their anguish with this comfort and to soothe their distress by giving the angel to be their comrade. We know that sometimes many angels are sent for the sake of one man, as we read of Elisha.[7] And it is a general rule, 'He has given his angels charge for you, to keep you in all your ways.'[8] Again, 'The angels camp around those that fear God.'[9] This was especially true of Christ, but it is extended to the whole body of the Church and to each individual member. God therefore has his armies ready to keep his people safe. But we read again that often one angel was sent to a whole nation. God does not need angels when he uses their activity; but this is how he helps our infirmity. Sometimes we do not ascribe to his power as much as we should, and so he sends his angels, who correct our doubts, as we said.

One angel was given to these three men. When Nebuchadnezzar calls him 'a son of God', he was not thinking that he was Christ. But we know that it was a common view among all nations that angels were sons of God, because a certain divinity shone in them. Therefore they indiscriminately call any angels 'sons of God'. It is according to this common custom that Nebuchadnezzar says that *'the fourth man is like a son of God'.* For he who was blinded by so many depraved errors (as we saw earlier) could not recognize the only-begotten Son of God. If anyone should say that this was a case of divine inspiration, it would be weak and forced. Let the simplicity suffice us that King Nebuchadnezzar was speaking in the usual way, and saying that one of the angels had

7. Mg., 2 Ki. 6:15.
8. Mg., Ps. 91:11.
9. Mg., Ps. 34:8, i.e., 34:7.

been sent to these three men, because angels used then to be called 'sons of God', as I said. Scripture speaks like this,[10] but God never allowed the world to become so overwhelmed that no seed of sound teaching was left, at least as a testimony to the heathen — that is, that it might make them more inexcusable, as we shall treat more fully in the next lecture.

> *Grant, almighty God, since our life is but a moment, a mere nothing and a vapour, that we may learn to cast all our cares on you and so depend on you that we may not doubt that when it shall be good for us, you will be our Saviour from all the dangers that threaten us. Then, that we may also learn to despise and be indifferent to our life, especially for the sake of witnessing to your glory, so that we may be ready to go as soon as you call us from this world. And may the hope of the heavenly life be so fixed in our hearts that we may willingly leave the world and aspire with all our mind to the blessed eternity which you testify by the gospel is laid up for us in heaven and which your only-begotten Son has gained for us by his own blood. Amen.*

10. Mg., Ps. 89:7, etc.

Lecture 16

26 *Then Nebuchadnezzar approached the entrance to the furnace of burning fire. He spoke and said, 'Shadrach, Meshach, and Abednego, servants of the Most High God, come out and come here.' Then Shadrach, Meshach, and Abednego came out of the midst of the fire.*

Here is described the sudden change in a king no less proud than cruel. We saw earlier how audaciously he demanded impious worship from God's servants, and, when he saw they did not obey his command, how he raged against them. Now Daniel shows that within a short while his pride was controlled and his cruelty calmed. But we must note that the king was not so changed that he straightway put off his character and ways. Affected by the present miracle, he certainly gave God the glory; but it was only momentary; he did not come to his senses. Examples of this sort should be carefully noticed, for many measure a person's character from one action. But the worst despisers of God can subject themselves to them temporarily, and that not dissimulating, to be seen by men, but with an earnest disposition. For God compels them by his power; yet they still keep their inward pride and unruliness. Such was the conversion of King Nebuchadnezzar. Astounded by the miracle, he could no longer resist God. But it did not last, as we shall see a little later.

And so we can see that the ungodly, who are not regenerated by the Spirit of God, are often compelled to worship God, but with only part of themselves; it does not remain the uniform tenor of the whole course of their lives. But when God reforms his own he assumes at the same time the government of them until the end and animates them to perseverance and strengthens them by his Spirit. Yet we must notice that God is glorified by this temporary

142

and evanescent conversion of the reprobate because, whether they will or no, they do yield to God for a time. And from this is known how great his power is. God therefore adapts to his glory what does not profit the reprobate but rather brings them into more serious judgment. Nebuchadnezzar was less excusable when once he had acknowledged the God of Israel to be the supreme and only God. Then he at once relapsed into his superstitions.

It says therefore that *he approached the entrance of the furnace and thus spoke: 'Shadrach, Meshach, and Abednego, servants of the Most High God, come out and come here.'* A little before, he had wanted his statue to be worshipped and to be regarded as the supreme deity in heaven and on earth — just because it was his will. For we saw him arrogate to himself so much that he subjected religion and the worship of God to his choice, or rather licence. But now, as if he were a new man, he calls Shadrach, Meshach, and Abednego 'servants of the Most High God'. What position did that put him in and all the Chaldaeans? Simply that they were worshipping fictitious gods and idols, which they had invented for themselves. But God wrung this saying out of the cruel and proud king, just as criminals are forced by torture to say what they do not want to say. So Nebuchadnezzar confessed that *'the God of Israel is the Most High God'*, as if he had been on the rack, and not spontaneously, not from a settled state of mind. He was not dissimulating before men, as we said; but his mind was neither pure nor whole; he was only speaking effusively from this partial impulse. It also must be added, that this was an impetuous rather than a voluntary impulse.

Afterwards, Daniel relates that his friends *came out of the midst of the fire.* With these words he again strengthens the miracle. For God could have extinguished the fire of the furnace. But he wanted it to burn in the sight of everyone so that the power of the liberation should be the more plain.

And we must note that *the three men walked in the furnace* until the king ordered them to come out, because God had given them no command. They saw that they stayed safe and sound in the midst of the furnace; they were satisfied with God's present blessing; and they were not free to leave until they were summoned by the king's voice. Just as when Noah was in the ark he saw that his safety lay in a grave and undertook nothing until he was commanded to leave.[1] Similarly Daniel makes it clear that his friends did not leave the furnace until the king told them to. Then at last they understood that what they heard from the mouth of the king was pleasing to God — not that he was a prophet or a teacher but because they had been thrown into the furnace by his command. So when he now calls them out, they know that their cross has been ended and so they pass, as it were, from death to life.

He goes on:

1. Mg., Gn. 8:16, i.e., 8:13-18.

27 *And the satraps, princes, governors, and counsellors of the king* [others translate the last 'governors', but wrongly. Properly it means either counsellors or familiars among the courtiers, as appears from many places. Therefore, 'counsellors of the king'] *gathered together to look at those men, that the fire had not had power over their bodies, and the hair of their head was not scorched, and their clothing was not changed, and the smell of fire had not reached* [or, 'had not penetrated'] *to them* [or, 'to their things'; for this relative can be expounded either of the persons or of their bodies and clothes. But there is little difference in the substance.]

Daniel relates that the satraps and princes, and governors, and counsellors of the king had assembled. The word 'assemble' is equivalent to 'confer'. So, with such an important matter to deliberate, they meet together. And this detail also strengthens the miracle. For if they had been stunned by it, what would have been the good of this power, this great power of God being set before the eyes of the blind? God strikes them with wonder, yet not so that they are completely stunned. This is what Daniel means when he says that *they were assembled.* After they had discussed it among themselves, he says that they came to look into this instance of the incredible power of God.

He enumerates many details which show more clearly that those three men were saved in no other way than by a singular blessing of God. For he says that *the fire had not had power over their bodies;* then, that *the hair of their head was not scorched;* third, that *their clothing was not altered;* and finally, *the smell of the fire had not penetrated to them,* or, 'to their clothes'. For he expresses more by this word *'smell'* than if he had simply said 'the fire had not penetrated'. For it could happen that fire might not consume a body which yet it might scorch or singe. But when not even the smell of the fire reaches the body the miracle becomes even more plain. So now we grasp the prophet's intention. In sum, he relates that the reason why this blessing of liberation was crystal clear was not because Shadrach, Meshach, and Abednego came safe out of the furnace, but because the satraps, governors, and princes were witnesses of the power of God. And its testimony could be worth more than if all the Jews had been spectators of this grace of God. For it would not have been accredited[a] by the Jews. But since it was certain that these were professed enemies of true godliness, they would surely have hidden the miracle had it been in their power. But God drags them unwillingly, forcing them to be eyewitnesses, forcing them to confess what could not admit of any doubt.

He goes on:

a. Or, 'believed' *(neque enim creditum fuisset Iudaeis).*

28 *Nebuchadnezzar spoke, and said, 'Blessed be the God of these men, namely, of Shadrach, Meshach, and Abednego, who has sent his angel and rescued* ["saved"] *his servants, who trusted in him, and changed the king's word* ["they transgressed", that is, "they withdrew faith and authority from the king's edict"] *and delivered their bodies rather than serve or worship every god* [that is, "worship any god whatsoever"] *except their own God.'*

This was no common confession. From the outcome it is plain that King Nebuchadnezzar had been carried away by a sudden impulse and there was no living root of the fear of God in his heart. I repeat this, that we may know that repentance is not placed in one or another act but in perseverance; as Paul says, 'If you live by the Spirit, also walk in the Spirit.'[2] There he demands from believers the constancy of showing that they are truly regenerate by God's Spirit. Nebuchadnezzar, therefore, as if carried away by enthusiasm, celebrated the God of Israel; but he still mixed up his idols with the true God. Thus there was nothing sincere in him. The ungodly do not dare to go on more stubbornly against God when they have felt his power, but they want to placate him by a fictitious penitence and without putting off their own character.

It is quite clear that Nebuchadnezzar was always like himself, save that God extorted this confession from him: *'Blessed'*, he said, *'be the God of Shadrach, Meshach, and Abednego.'* Why not rather call him his own God? This could be excused if he had truly given himself to the God of Israel and abjured his former superstitions. But this he did not do. Therefore, his confession was fictitious. Not that he wanted to gain grace or favour with men, as I said, but he deceived himself, as hypocrites are wont to do. He declares the God of Shadrach, Meshach, and Abednego to be blessed. Had this been done sincerely, he would have at the same time cursed his idols; for the glory of the true and only God cannot be extolled without all idols being reduced to nothing. For in what does the praise of God lie, except that he may be exalted above all others? If any other is opposed to him as God, his majesty is already buried as if in thick darkness. Hence we may infer that Nebuchadnezzar was not touched with a true repentance when he blessed the God of Israel.

He adds *'who sent his angel and rescued his servants'*. Here Daniel shows more clearly that Nebuchadnezzar had not been converted in such a way that he embraced the God of Israel and really worshipped him with all his heart. Why? Because piety is always founded on the knowledge of the true God; and this demands teaching. Nebuchadnezzar knew that the God of Israel was the Most High God. How? Simply from his power. For he had the sight of it set before his eyes; he could not make light of it if he wanted. And so he confesses that the God of Israel is the Most High God just because a miracle

2. Mg., Gal. 5:25.

145

tells him so. But, as I have told you, this is not sufficient for genuine piety unless teaching is added to it — no, is put first. I confess, of course, that men are prepared for believing by miracles. But if bare miracles are seen apart from knowledge out of the Word of God itself, faith will be transitory. And this is illustrated clearly enough from the example before us. We can see that it was only partial faith in King Nebuchadnezzar, because he focussed all his attention on the miracle and was content with the mere spectacle without asking who the God of Israel was and what his Law comprehended. Nor was he interested in a mediator. In short, he neglected the whole substance of piety and seized rashly on only one part.

This we also daily see in many irreligious men. God often humbles them so that they may flee to him for help. But yet their minds remain entangled and they do not give up their superstitions or care what the true service of God is. For our obedience to be approved by God, the principle must be held that nothing pleases him which is not of faith.[3] But faith cannot be conceived from any miracle, from any sense of the divine power. It needs teaching as well. Miracles avail only as preparation or as confirmation of godliness; they cannot of themselves bring men to the true service of God.

It is surprising that the heathen king says that *an angel had been sent by God*. But it is clear enough from the writings of profane authors that something about angels had always been known. This was, so to say, a prolepsis, a certain anticipated conviction. Just as all nations were convinced of the existence of a deity, so also there was some trace, even though obscure, of belief in angels. And when, a little before, Daniel had said that the fourth within the furnace was called 'a son of God' by the Babylonian king, then, as I explained, Nebuchadnezzar already professed that he held some idea about angels. Now he says more expressly that 'God sent his angel'. How angels bring help to the elect and believers was then briefly said — and it is not my custom to dwell at length on points of doctrine. It is enough, so far as the present passage goes, that even the ungodly, who had learned nothing either of God himself or of godliness, had been imbued with the principles that God was wont to use the activities of angels to help his servants. For this reason Nebuchadnezzar now says that *an angel was sent by God, to rescue his servants*.

Now he adds, *who trusted in him*, which is also noteworthy, because it repeats the reason why these three men were so wonderfully saved — because they put their hope in God. Although Nebuchadnezzar was almost like wood or stone so far as the teaching of faith is concerned, yet God wished by this stone, by this log, to teach us and to strike shame into us and accuse us of the sin of unbelief because we cannot surrender our life to his will and boldly meet dangers, whenever there is need. For if we were convinced that

3. Mg., Rom. 14:23.

God is the guardian of our life, assuredly no threats, no terrors, no deaths would prevent us from going on in our duty. But distrust is the cause of cowardice; and so often as we swerve from the right way, so often as we defraud God of his honour, so often as we treacherously default, our unbelief betrays itself and is almost tangible.

Therefore, if we want our lives to be protected by the hand of God, let us learn to surrender ourselves entirely to him. He will not deceive our hope, so long as we rest in him. We see certainly that the outcome for Shadrach, Meshach, and Abednego was uncertain. Yet this did not diminish their hope and trust. They used this either/or: *either* God will rescue us from the furnace of fire; *or,* if we must die, he will save us in a more wonderful way by taking us into his kingdom. Although they did not dare to promise themselves what was hidden from them, yet they placed their souls in the hand and guardianship of God. They deserved the compliment Nebuchadnezzar paid them that *'they trusted in their God'.*

Afterwards he adds that *'they changed the king's edict'* — that is, held it as nothing but rather rejected it because they possessed a superior authority. For whoever looks to God will easily disregard all mortals and whatever is splendid and lofty in the whole earth. And this sequence is noteworthy, where trust is made the foundation, and the greatheartedness and constancy in which Shadrach, Meshach, and Abednego had been trained are added to it. For whoever rests in God can never be moved from carrying out his duty. And although he meets with many hindrances, yet he is, as it were, borne on high by the wings of trust. Now he who knows that God stands on his side will be superior to the whole world so that the sceptres or diadems of kings will be no threat, no power a fear. Rather he will rise above whatever earthly loftiness he encounters and never swerve from his course.

Afterwards he adds, *'they offered their bodies not to serve or worship any god but their own God'.* What the heathen king was forced to praise in these three men many professing Christians today want to weaken. For they imagine a faith buried in the heart, bearing no fruit of confession. Some people want to defraud God of his lawful honour; but at the same time they try to blindfold him, so to say, in case he should espy the injury they are doing him. There is no doubt that God intended these details to be related by his prophet so as to make their trickery more detestable to us. They are convicted by God's Word; they are unworthy. Here Nebuchadnezzar is appointed their master, and censor, and judge.

And this also is to be carefully noticed. Nebuchadnezzar praises these three men for refusing to worship any other god than their own. Why, then, did he intermingle their God with a whole host of gods? For he did not depart from his errors and give himself completely to the God of Israel and embrace his pure worship. Why praise in others what he did not practise himself? But this is all too common. For we see virtue praised and yet left out in the cold, as someone says.[4] For many want to do their duty with their tongues alone. And although Nebuchadnezzar seemed to himself to be speaking in earnest, he had not examined himself. Nevertheless, this removed any pretext for excuse, for afterwards he could not plead ignorance and error when he had asserted with his own mouth that no other god was to be worshipped. Therefore, nowadays it shames those who want to be thought Christians if they do not distance themselves from all ungodly superstitions and consecrate themselves entirely to God and retain his true worship. It should also be recalled that King Nebuchadnezzar did not simply praise the constancy of these three men for not worshipping that god, but at the same time he acknowledged that the God of Israel was the true God. From this it follows that all others are fictitious and mere nothings. But this was spoken to no effect, for God had not deeply touched his heart in the way that he works in his elect when he regenerates them.

He goes on:

29 *'And by me was placed* [that is, "is placed"] *the edict* [or "decree"; we have spoken about this word] *that every people, nation* [others translate it "family"), *and language, which brings* [anything] *against* [שלה, *salah*, signifies "to err". From this is derived the present word, which many translate "error", others "rashness". But it means "perverse speech". 'Whoever, therefore, brings a perverse speech] *against the God of these men, that is, Shadrach, Meshach, and Abednego, shall be cut to pieces and his house reduced* [into] *a latrine* [or, "into a dunghill"]. *For there is no other god who can save in this way.'*

Here Nebuchadnezzar is pushed on (we have to use this word) even further. He does not sincerely adopt the service of the one God and forsake his errors, as was said. It is just as if God were violently pushing him on when he published this edict. In itself the edict is pious and laudable. But we have already said that Nebuchadnezzar was carried away by a blind and wild impulse, because piety had struck no root in his heart. He was always obsessed by the miracle and so had only a partial faith and with it a truncated fear of God. Why, then, did Nebuchadnezzar now seem a defender of God's glory? Because he was terrified by the miracle. Therefore, with no other impulsion, he could not be firmly kept in the fear of the one God. In short, the zeal he shows is nothing but a transient mood.

And it is useful to know this. For we see many carried away by an impetuous enthusiasm in wanting to assert the glory of God. But because they

4. Mg., Juvenal, *Satire* 1, i.e., 1:74 *(probitas laudatur et alget).*

lack discrimination and judgment, this cannot be set to their credit. Many go much further astray, as we see happening in the papacy. There a lot of edicts of kings and princes go flying around; but if any one asks why they are so ardent that they do not even spare human blood, they plead their zeal for God. But that, without the light of true knowledge, is mere madness. We must therefore hold that no law can be passed nor any edict promulgated on religion and the service of God in which a right knowledge of God does not shine. In this edict Nebuchadnezzar was entirely reasonable; but, as I have already said, it was just a partial mood in him. Those who now wish to be regarded as Christian princes run riot under pretext of zeal, shedding innocent blood like cruel wild beasts. Why? Because they do not distinguish between the true God and idols. But tomorrow many more things will be said on this, and therefore I will now pass over lightly what will be treated more fully. For then it will have its opportune place.

Therefore, *'every people, and nation, and language, which brings a perverse speech against their God'*. Nebuchadnezzar again extols the God of Israel. But where had he learned that God is the Most High? Just from one instance only of his power. And he neglected the main thing, to understand from the Law and the prophets who that God is and what is his will. Thus we see that he asserts God's glory in one respect only. The principal thing in his service and true piety he neglects and omits.

He adds no light penalty: that *'he shall be reduced to pieces and that his house shall be turned into a dunghill who speaks insultingly of the God of Israel'*. Whence we gather that his severity is not to be completely condemned when he asserts the worship of God with savage penalties. But there ought to have been a fair judgment of the case. But this also I will put off until tomorrow.

Now what is added, *'because there is no other god who can save in this way'*, the more confirms what I have already touched on, that King Nebuchadnezzar in his edict was not thinking of the Law, not regarding the other parts of piety, but was just so much moved and impelled by the miracle that he could not bear, let alone wish, anything disrespectful to be said against the God of Israel. Therefore, this only was blameworthy in the edict, that he did not ask who that God was, so that he might have a reason for publishing the edict.

Finally he adds:

30 *Then the king made to prosper* [*zalah*, צלח, literally signifies 'to act prosperously'. From this is derived this word, which means to replace in a prosperous state. Therefore 'he gave to fare prosperously these three men'] *Shadrach, Meshach, and Abednego in the province of Babylon.*

This seems unimportant, but it was not added for nothing; it teaches us that the miracle was confirmed throughout the whole province and region. All

149

the Chaldaeans knew that these three men who had been thrown into the furnace of fire were then possessed of regal authority and were restored to their honourable position. Since this had actually happened, the power of God could not be hidden. It was just as if God had sent out three heralds through the whole region who proclaimed everywhere how wonderfully they had been rescued from death, and that by a remarkable blessing of God. From this it could also be understood that all the gods that were then worshipped in Chaldaea were nothing, that is, since that 'supreme god' whose statue Nebuchadnezzar had set up was despised, whereas this constancy to the true God, who had saved his servants from death, had been approved.

> *Grant, almighty God, since you have become known to us in the teaching of your Law and gospel and also daily condescend to reveal your will familiarly to us, that we may remain fixed in true obedience to that teaching in which perfect righteousness is manifested to us, and that we may never be moved from your service; and whatever shall happen, that we may be prepared rather to undergo a hundred deaths than to swerve from the true profession of piety in which we know our salvation rests; and that we may so glorify your name that we may be partakers of that glory which is won for us by the blood of your only-begotten Son. Amen.*

Lecture 17

CHAPTER 4

1 *Nebuchadnezzar the king, 'To all the peoples, nations, and languages, who live in all the world; peace be multiplied to you.*
2 *The signs and wonders which the Most High God has done with me it is beautiful to relate before me.*
3 *How great* [are] *his signs! And his wonders how mighty! His kingdom an age-long kingdom* [that is, "permanent"], *and his dominion with age and age.'*

Some attach these verses to the end of chapter 3; but there seems no reason for it. From the context it is quite clear that here an edict under the name of the king is related, with at the same time a statement of what happened. Daniel therefore here represents the king speaking. Afterwards, he relates what happened to the king, and finally he reverts to the first person. So those who separate these three verses from the context of chapter 4 seem not to have sufficiently considered the prophet's purpose and language. It could seem forced and harsh when he now represents the Babylonian king speaking, then speaks in his name, and afterwards again brings in the king. But this alternation gives a meaning that is neither ambiguous nor obscure, and there is no reason why it should worry us. We now see how all these statements cohere, and we will expound them in their right places.

The substance of the chapter is that although Nebuchadnezzar had been taught clearly enough that the God of Israel was alone to be worshipped, and although he had been forced at the time to confess this, yet, because he did not leave his superstitions and because his conception of the true God was only momentary, he was given the just penalty for such ingratitude. But God

151

willed to blind him more and more, as he is wont to do with the reprobate and even sometimes with the elect. For when they add sins to sins, God slackens the reins and gives them their head. Afterwards he either stretches out his hand, or draws them back by his hidden power, or even by his rods forces them to order and humbles them. This is how he acted with the King of Babylon. We shall see his dream afterwards.

Here we must briefly note that the king was warned so that he might feel at last that he had no excuse for having been so obdurate. God could indeed justly have taken him in hand as soon as he saw that he was not truly turned to him. But before he executed the final punishment on him (which we shall see in its place), he wished to warn him, in case there might be any hope of repentance. And although he seemed to accept with the profoundest meekness what God had revealed through the dream, which Daniel himself interpreted, yet what he professed by mouth was not what he had in his mind. And he shows this clearly enough, because when he should have been fearful and vigilant, he still did not stop being proud but boasted that he was the king of kings and Babylon the queen of the whole world. Therefore, because he spoke so daringly, something he had been warned about by the prophet, we see that the dream had done him no good at all. But this is how God wished to make him more inexcusable. Although no fruit appeared at once, yet after a long, long time, when God touched his mind, he could better acknowledge that his punishment had been inflicted by God. Therefore this dream was an entrance and, so to say, preparation into repentance. As the seed seems to putrefy in the earth before it bears fruit, so also God sometimes works by lingering processes and causes that teaching, which for a long time seemed useless, to be at last fruitful and efficacious.

Now I come to the words. The preface to the edict runs: *Nebuchadnezzar the king, 'To all peoples, nations, and languages, who live in all the world'* — that is, under his sway; he did not mean this to be understood of Scythia or France or other distant countries; but he spoke proudly, because his empire spread far and wide. Similarly we see that the Romans, who did not rule so extensively, called Rome the seat of the empire of the whole earth. Hence, Nebuchadnezzar is here grandiloquently proclaiming the size of his monarchy, for he sends his edict *'to all peoples, and nations, and languages, who live in the world'*.

Afterwards he adds, *'the signs and wonders which the Most High God has done with me it is beautiful to relate before me'*. There is no doubt that in the end he knew that the punishment had been exacted for his ingratitude in only carelessly giving glory to the one and true God, after he had slipped back into his superstitions — or rather, when he had never given them up. So we see that King Nebuchadnezzar was chastised quite often before he profited from God's beatings. We must not be surprised if God often strikes us with his hand, for the actual outcome and our experience show that we are slothful, or, to speak more truly, completely doltish. When God intends to lead us to repentance, it is necessary for him often to repeat the strokes; for either we are unmoved even when chastised by his hand or, if we seem to be awakened for a time, we quickly sink back into our former torpor. It is therefore necessary for the scourge to be repeated and repeated.

And this we see in the present story as in a mirror. But it was a singular blessing of God that Nebuchadnezzar at last yielded after God had often chastised him. It is not known, however, whether this confession came from a true and genuine penitence. I leave it undecided. Yet there is no doubt that Daniel quoted this edict to show that the king was at last compelled to confess that the God of Israel was the only God. And this he declared to all the peoples and nations under his sway. Meanwhile it is also to be observed that the edict of the king of Babylon was praised and commended by the Spirit. For Daniel had no other purpose here, and quotes the edict for no other end, than to show the fruit of conversion in King Nebuchadnezzar. Therefore it is beyond controversy that King Nebuchadnezzar was testifying to his repentance when he celebrated the God of Israel among all his peoples, and threatened punishment to all who should speak insultingly against God.

This passage was often cited by Augustine against the Donatists.[1] They wanted to go unpunished when they wantonly disturbed the Church, when they corrupted pure doctrine, even when they took licence to act like bandits. For it was known at the time that some had been murdered by them and others castrated. So they gave themselves licence to do anything, but wanted their crimes to go unpunished. In particular they held this principle, 'No punishment is to be inflicted on those who differ from others on religious doctrine.'

We see some nowadays contending for this all too greedily. It is quite clear what they really want. For if anyone examines them closely, they are ungodly despisers of God. At the least, they want nothing to be assured in religion; therefore they strive to weaken and, so far as is in them lies, to pluck up all principles of godliness. They earnestly contend for impunity and deny that heretics and blasphemers should be punished, so that it may be lawful for them to spew out their venom. Such is that dog Castellio[2] — and his mates and the rest of that ilk. The Donatists were just the same in their own day. And so, as I have already mentioned, Augustine in many places cites this testimony and shows that the slackness of Christian princes is shameful when they tolerate

1. Mg., *Epistle* 166 *(To the Donatists) et al.,* i.e., *Epistle* 105:2:7. Cf. *Epistles* 93:3:9; 185:2:8.
2. Castellio: former school-master in Geneva, who led a group protesting against the execution of Servetus. Their book, *Whether Heretics Should Be Persecuted,* was published in 1554.

heretics and blasphemers and do not, with King Nebuchadnezzar, assert the glory of God with lawful punishments. Although he was never even truly converted; he promulgated this edict by a certain secret impulse. However that may be, all modest and peaceable men should know well enough that Nebuchadnezzar's edict was praised by this commendation of the Holy Spirit. If this is so, it follows that it is the duty of kings to defend the worship of God and to take vengeance on irreligious despisers who either try to annihilate his worship or adulerate true religion with their errors, and so break the unity of the faith and disturb the peace of the Church. This appears clearly enough from the prophet's context.

But first Nebuchadnezzar says, *'The signs and wonders which God has done with me it is beautiful to relate.'* In the beginning he had partly declared what things God had wonderfully wrought with him. But that was transient. Now, therefore, after being reproved by God a second and a third time, he at last confesses that it is glorious to declare the wonders and signs of God. Afterwards he breaks out into an exclamation: *'How great are his signs! How mighty are his wonders! His kingdom is a kingdom of an age, and his dominion with age and age.'* There is no doubt that Nebuchadnezzar wished to rouse his subjects to read the edict very carefully and to realize how important it was that they should devote themselves to the true and only God.

It is without any doubt the God of Israel whom he calls *'God Most High'*. Yet it is not known whether he renounced his superstitions. I rather incline to the opposite conjecture, that he had not put off his errors but had been compelled to give glory to the supreme God. Hence he acknowledged the God of Israel in such a way as yet to conjoin with him lesser gods as allies or comrades — just as all unbelievers think there is some supreme deity but imagine a host of gods. Thus Nebuchadnezzar confessed that the God of Israel was the Most High God; yet he did not correct the idolatry which then flourished under his rule; in fact, he made a confused mixture of the false gods with the God of Israel. So he did not leave his corruptions. Of course, he celebrated the glory of the Most High God magnificently. But this was not enough without abolishing all the superstitions, so that only the religion appointed by the Word of God should have a place and his worship flourish pure and sound. In sum, this preface could be an indication of a great conversion; but we shall see at once that Nebuchadnezzar was not inwardly purged from his errors. So much the more ought we to be affected when we see the king still entangled in many errors, yet so carried away by wonder at the divine power that, when he cannot express his thoughts, he cries out, 'How great are his signs and how mighty are his wonders!'

He adds, *'his kingdom is a permanent kingdom and his dominion is of age and age'*. Here it is already confessed that God's power does not depend on man's choice; only a little before he had said that the statue he had set up was to be worshipped because he had so decreed for the sake of his power. Now he lays aside much of this pride by confessing that God's kingdom is perpetual.

Now the narrative continues (for hitherto it has been a preface, that the edict might be more useful among his subjects and they should pay attention to this great matter):

4 *'I, Nebuchadnezzar, was at home quiet* [or, "happy"] *and prosperous* [or, "fresh"] *in my palace.*
5 *I saw a dream, and it terrified me* ["I was frightened." The copula can be resolved into a relative pronoun: "I saw a dream which terrified, or frightened, me"], *and upon my bed the thoughts and visions of my head disturbed me.*
6 *And a decree was put out by me that there should be led* [that is, "brought"] *to me all the wise men of Babylon who might reveal the interpretation of the dream to me.'*

Here Nebuchadnezzar explains how he at last came to know the Most High God. He is not referring to previous evidences he had had; but, because his pride was at last tamed by this final dream, this is his only subject now. Yet there is no doubt that he will have recalled the earlier dreams and condemned his own ingratitude that he had buried such powerful acts of God and consigned to perverse forgetfulness the great blessings that God had given him. So here he is speaking only of the last dream, which we shall see in its own place.

But before he gets to the dream, he says that *'he was quiet'*; שלה, *seleh,* means 'quiet' and also it means 'happy'. And because prosperity makes men over-confident, it refers metaphorically to over-confidence. David, when he pronounces the same verdict on himself, uses the same word — that is, one derived from this: 'I said in my unhappiness',[3] or 'in my quiet'. שלוה, *saluah,* some translate 'abundance'; but rather it signifies either 'quiet' or 'prosperity'. Here, then, Nebuchadnezzar indicates a detail of time to tell us that he was seized by God when prosperity had made him drunk and almost stupefied. And it is no wonder that this happened. For it is a common and old proverb 'Satiety begets wildness'[4]; we see that replete horses are recalcitrant and try to throw their rider. Men are just the same. For if God treats them more kindly or liberally, they run wild; they are contemptuous of all mortals and shake off the yoke of God himself. In short, they forget they are men.

And if this happened to David, what will it be like for the irreligious or those who are still too much devoted to the world? For David confessed that he had been so deceived in his peace and prosperity that he told himself he

---

3. Mg., Ps. 30:7, i.e., 30:6.
4. Erasmus, *Adages* III.vii.53.

had nothing to fear: 'I said in my prosperity [or, "in my quiet"] I shall not be moved.' And then he adds, 'You, O Lord, chastised me and I was troubled.'[5] If, then, David promised himself continual peace in the world because God spared him for a time, how suspicious we should be of our tranquillity, lest we lie becalmed in our filthiness! It was not for nothing that Nebuchadnezzar declared that *'he was quiet at home, prosperous in his palace',* for this was the cause of his security and pride and despising God so self-confidently.

Afterwards he adds that *'he saw a dream and was troubled'.* Here without doubt he meant to distinguish his own from ordinary dreams, which often come either from an over-active brain or from what we were thinking about the day before or from other causes, as we saw elsewhere. (For we need not repeat here what we have already treated quite fully.) Enough to grasp this briefly, that the dream by which God forewarned him of the future punishment which threatened was distinguished from other dreams, which are either violent, or fleeting and irrational. Therefore he says that *'he saw a dream',* yet in such a way that he was awake. For he adds, *'he had thoughts upon his bed and he was troubled by the visions of his head'.* This accumulation of words comes simply to this, that the vision or dream was a heavenly oracle; and on this we must speak more fully later.

He goes on that *'a decree was put out by him that all the wise men of Babylon should be called who would explain',* or, 'reveal', *'the interpretation of the dream'.* Doubtless the king often dreamed; but he did not every day assemble the magi, arioles, and astrologers, and the rest who possessed the art of divination — or at least claimed they did. He did not consult them about every one of his dreams. But God had engraven on his heart a distinctive mark by which he had sealed this dream; and this was why the king could not rest until he had heard its interpretation. Thus earlier we saw how the authority of the first dream (that on the four monarchies and Christ's eternal kingdom) was confirmed, so that the king felt it had come from heaven. But there is a certain difference between this dream and that which we explained earlier. For God wiped the dream of the four monarchies out of King Nebuchadnezzar's memory, and it became necessary for Daniel both to bring the dream before the king and at the same time to supply its interpretation. At that time Daniel was less well known. For although he had made such progress that he stood out among all the Chaldaeans, yet King Nebuchadnezzar would have admired him less if he had been only the interpreter of the dream. God therefore wished to gain greater respect for his prophet and the prophetic message by enjoining two duties on him — to divine what the dream was and to explain its meaning and purpose. In this other dream Daniel is the interpreter only. For God had already sufficiently proved him to be endued with a heavenly spirit, so that

5. Mg., Ps. 30:7.

156

Nebuchadnezzar would no longer summon him as just one of the magi, but would distinguish him from all the rest.

After this he says:

7 *'Then came the magi, astrologers, Chaldaeans* [that is, "the wise men"], *and philosophers* [or, "mathematicians". So far as the words are concerned there is, as we said earlier, no need to expend much energy, since we cannot tell for certain what each of these professions might have been. Assuredly, although what they taught was sheer imposture, yet they covered their shame with these honourable titles. They called themselves "mathematicians" as a common name, yet strictly speaking they had neither art nor science, but only cheated wretched men with their tricks. By these terms Daniel embraced all the magi and arioles and astrologers and augurs, who professed the art of divining], *and I* [he says] *have declared the dream before them, and they have not revealed its interpretation to me.'*

Here Nebuchadnezzar acknowledges that he had summoned all the magi and arioles in vain. It follows that all their science was a deceit; or at least, the fact that Daniel could explain the dream came not from some human activity but from a heavenly revelation. And I accept this conclusion because Nebuchadnezzar expressly intended to declare that Daniel had not been taught by man to interpret dreams but that it was a unique gift of the Spirit. For he took it for granted that if there were any science or method of divining, it would lie with the magi and arioles and augurs and the other Chaldaeans, who boasted they possessed perfect wisdom. It was almost beyond controversy that the astrologers and the rest enjoyed such art in divination that nothing within the grasp of men escaped them. Hence the opposite also follows, that Daniel was divinely taught, because if he had been only a magus or astrologer, would he not also have devoted prolonged study to the art? Hence Nebuchadnezzar meant to exalt Daniel above all the magi, as if he were saying that he was a heavenly prophet.

And this also appears better from what follows, when he adds:

8 *'Until at last Daniel was brought before me, whose name is Belteshazzar after the name of my god, and in whom is the spirit of the holy gods. And I related the dream before him.*
9 *"Belteshazzar, chief* [or, 'master'] *of the magi, because I know that the spirit of the holy gods* [is] *in you, and no secret causes you distress* [some translate it 'is a trouble to you'. I will speak of the word later], *explain the visions of the dream which I saw and its interpretation."'*

Here the king of Babylon addresses Daniel very pleasantly, because he sees he has been let down by his own doctors. From this we infer that he would never have come to the true God unless compelled by necessity. For Daniel was neither unknown nor absent far. We saw, in fact, that he was in the palace. So why, when the king could have had Daniel at the very outset, did he pass him over? Why did he summon the other magi from all sorts of places, and that by an edict? From this it clearly appears (as I said) that he never gave glory to God save when constrained by deepest necessity. Therefore, he never freely subjected himself to the God of Israel, and it is quite clear that the tokens of godliness he sometimes showed were momentary impulses. His asking Daniel so humbly shows us he had a servile character. When the proud do not need outside help, they are puffed up and no-one can bear their insolence. But when they are brought to extremes they would rather lick the dust than not get the favour they need. Such, then, was the character of this king. He despised Daniel in his heart and deliberately neglected him in favour of the magi. But afterwards he saw he was still in difficulties and could get remedy from nowhere but Daniel, his last resort. So now he forgets his loftiness and speaks pleasantly to the holy prophet of God.

But I will go on with the rest tomorrow.

Grant, almighty God, since here you place before our eyes a remarkable example, from which we may learn that the greatness of your power cannot be sufficiently celebrated by human words, and since we hear that the heathen and cruel and proud king was its herald; grant that, after you have condescended to reveal yourself to us familiarly in Christ, we may apply ourselves in a true spirit of humility to giving you the glory, and devote ourselves completely to you, so that not only with lips and tongue but also in our actions we may declare that for us you are not only the true and only God but also our Father, after you have adopted us in your only-begotten Son, until at last we enjoy that eternal heritage which is laid up for us in heaven, through the same Christ our Lord. Amen.

Lecture 18

9 ' *"Belteshazzar, master of the magi, because I knew that the spirit of the holy gods is in you and no secret escapes you* [or, 'defeats you'. I will speak of this word soon], *relate to me the visions of my dream which I saw and its interpretation."* '

Yesterday we said that King Nebuchadnezzar was a suppliant to Daniel because he had been brought to extremities. He did not enquire of him first, but consulted his own magi. Therefore, the one he had despised he is now compelled to respect.

He calls him *"Belteshazzar"*. Without doubt this name deeply wounded the prophet. As a little child he had been given another name by his parents; by it he knew he was a Jew and drew his origin from the holy and elect nation. That his name was now changed was (as I said elsewhere) without doubt done by the cunning of the tyrant, so that little by little he might forget his race. By changing his name, King Nebuchadnezzar intended to make this holy servant of God fall away from his nation. Whenever he was called by this name it was certainly no small stumbling-block. But he had no remedy for the ill; he was a prisoner and knew that he had to deal with a victorious people, proud and cruel. Moreover, in the former verse he had said that Nebuchadnezzar named him after his own god. Because Daniel had a real name which his parents had given him by God's determination, Nebuchadnezzar wanted to blot out that holy name and so called him, as an honorific, 'Belteshazzar' — a word likely to have been derived from the name of his idol. It doubled the holy prophet's sorrow, that he was stained with such a foul blot as to include a notorious idol in his name. But he had to bear this evil along with the other scourges of God. Thus God exercised his servant in many ways in bearing the cross.

159

Now, that he calls him *"the chief of the magi"* also without doubt pierced the mind of the holy prophet. He wanted nothing more than to be distinguished from the magi, who deceived the whole world by their impostures and tricks. For although the astrologers possessed learning and had some praiseworthy principles, yet we know that they corrupted all their learning. Therefore Daniel did not like to hear himself reckoned as one of them; but he could not free himself from the slander. So we see that his patience was divinely tested in various ways.

Now Nebuchadnezzar adds: *"Because I knew that the spirit of the holy gods is in you"*. Many translate it 'angels', and this interpretation does not displease me, as I have mentioned elsewhere. For it was known among all the nations that there was some supreme God; but they supposed angels were lesser gods. However that may be, Nebuchadnezzar here betrays his ignorance in not arriving at the knowledge of the true God but being still entangled in his former errors and keeping many gods, as from the beginning he had been imbued with that superstition. This place might be translated in the singular, as some in fact do; but it would be too forced and the reason why they do it is too weak. For they think that Nebuchadnezzar was truly converted. Yet that there is nothing in this is demonstrated by the whole context. Obsessed with this opinion, they want to clear him of all blame. But since it is certain that Nebuchadnezzar included in this edict many proofs of his old ignorance, there is no reason for us to change anything from the straightforward meaning of the words. So he ascribes a divine spirit to Daniel but still imagines a plurality of gods.

"The spirit of the holy gods is in you", he says, *"and no secret defeats you."* אנס, *anas,* some translate as 'to be troublesome'. But properly it means 'to force' or 'to compel'. Therefore those who render it, 'There is no secret that is beyond you' depart from the genuine sense. Those who translate it 'to be troublesome' might have a tolerable translation; but they would do better to render it as, 'No secret makes you anxious or perplexed.' If the grammarians are right that א is a servile letter, that meaning would fit well. For נסה, *nasa,* means 'to test' or 'to prove'; it also means 'to elevate'. We could translate it, 'No secret is too high for you', or, 'for your mind', or 'No secret is a test for you', as if he were saying that Daniel was endued with a divine spirit so that whatever he put forward was not tested; that is, there was no thought of examining his learning, because an answer was easy and ready for him. But yet it is necessary to keep to what I said, 'no secret makes you anxious or constrained'.

Nebuchadnezzar knew this. Why then did he not call him as soon as he began to be worried? Daniel can free him from all worry; so his ingratitude is betrayed by his summoning his magi for advice and neglecting Daniel. We see, then, that he was always trying to escape from God until he was dragged to him by violence. Hence it is plain that he was not truly converted. For penitence is voluntary; they are said to repent who with a changed mind return freely to the God they had deserted. This cannot happen without faith and without the love of God.

Lastly he asks that *"he will relate the dream and its interpretation"*. But the dream was not unknown and he himself tells it to Daniel. There is, therefore, something unnecessary in the words; but the meaning is not ambiguous — Nebuchadnezzar just asks that his dream shall be explained.

He goes on:

10 *'"And the visions of my head upon my bed; I saw, and behold a tree in the middle of the earth, and its height was great.*
11 *The tree grew* ['was multiplied'] *and became strong and its height reached* [that is, 'so that its height reached'] *to heaven, and the sight of it to the extreme of all* [or, 'the whole of'] *the earth.*
12 *Its branch was beautiful and its fruit abundant* [שׂגיא, *saggui*, means 'great' or 'much'], *and on it was food for all; beneath it shaded* [literally; that is, 'took shade'] *the beasts of the field; and in its branches lived* [or, 'nested'] *the birds of heaven, and from it all flesh was nourished."'*
The following verses should be joined on:
13 *'"I saw* [also] *in the visions of my head upon my bed, and behold, a watcher and a holy one came down from heaven.*
14 *He cried in strength* [that is, 'strongly'], *and spoke thus: 'Cut down the tree, and strip off its leaves* [for I do not like to repeat 'branches', as some do. I admit that the word עֲנַף, *anaph*, which occurs here is taken both for foliage and for branches. But עֲפָא, *apha*, means 'a branch'. Hence the repetition will not be unnecessary, 'strip off', or 'tear away, its leaves'], *break off its branches, and scatter its fruit; let the beast flee from its shade* ['from under it', literally], *and the birds from its leaves* [or 'from its branches'].
15 *Yet leave the bottom of its roots in the earth, and in a band of iron* [that is, 'an iron band'] *and bronze, in the grass of the field, and let it be washed with the rain of heaven, and let its portion be with the beast in the grass of the earth.*
16 *Its heart from human* [simply, 'from man'] *let them change* [that is, 'shall be changed', as we saw elsewhere] *and a heart of a beast be given to it. And let seven times pass over it.'"'*

Here Nebuchadnezzar tells his dream, the interpretation of which will follow in its place. But since the narration would be weak, even useless, unless we had already said something about the substance, we must just touch on that. The rest may be deferred.

First of all, under the figure of a tree Nebuchadnezzar himself is indi-

161

ᴄᴀⅼᴇd. Not that it corresponds in all respects to the king, but because God established empires in the world to the end that they should be like trees of whose fruit all mortals may eat and under whose shade they may rest. But this appointment of God flourishes in order that tyrants, however far they may be from a right and moderate rule, are forced, whether they will or not, to be 'trees'; because it is better to live under the most savage tyrant than without any government at all. We may all imagine we are equal; but what is the result of such anarchy in the end? None will give place to another; each will attempt whatever he can. The sum of it will be a licence to pillage and plunder and defraud and murder. In short, the reins will be loosed to all men's desires. That is why I said a tyranny is better and can be borne more easily than anarchy, where there is no government, none to rule and keep the rest in their obligations. And so those who think that the king is here described as endowed with outstanding virtues are arguing too subtly. King Nebuchadnezzar was not exceptionally righteous and just. But under this figure God intended to show for what purpose he would have the world ruled by a political order; and this is why he appoints kings and monarchs and other officials.

Second, he wished to show that, although tyrants and other rulers who forget their duty do not exhibit what God has laid on them, yet God's grace always shines through in all empires. Tyrants strive to blot out all the light of fairness and justice and to confuse everything. But the Lord holds them in a secret and incomprehensible way, so that they are forced to do something useful to mankind, whether they will or not. This is what we should hold from the figure or image of the tree.

What he adds, *"the birds of heaven dwelt in its branches"* and *"the beasts lived from its food"*, should be referred to men. For although the beasts of the field feel some advantage from the political order, yet we know that political constitution was ordained by God for the sake of men. There is therefore no doubt that this whole passage is metaphorical. In fact, strictly speaking, it is an allegory; for allegory is nothing but a continued metaphor. If Daniel had only depicted the king under the figure of a tree, it would have been a metaphor. By continuing his parallels in the same vein, the story becomes allegorical.

He says, then, *"the beasts of the field live under the tree"*, because we are protected by the shelter of government. Otherwise no heat of the sun would burn and scorch unhappy men worse than if they were denuded of this shelter, under which God wishes them to be at peace. Also *"the birds of heaven nest in the branches and foliage"*. Some too subtly make a distinction between birds and beasts. For me it is enough that what the prophet denotes is that men of whatever rank feel no little advantage from the safeguard of princes. If they were without this support, it would be better for them to live among wild beasts than to destroy themselves mutually. But that would necessarily happen, if we reckon how much pride is innate in all, and how blind is our self-love, and how turbulent are desires. Since this is so, God shows in this dream that, whatever our rank may be, we need the shelter of government.

By *"fodder"* and *"food"* and by *"shelter"* he is signifying the various advantages which fall to us from the political order. Someone might object that he did not need rulers in some area of life or other. But if we consider all the circumstances of life, we shall see that this benefit from God is necessary for us in every respect.

What he adds, that *"its height was great"*, and that *"it increased so that it reached even to heaven, and its aspect extended to the furthest ends of the earth"*, is restricted to the Babylonian monarchy. There were other empires in the world at that time, but they were weak or at least only second-rate. The Chaldaeans were so dominant that no other rulers came anywhere near their greatness and power. Since, then, Nebuchadnezzar was so outstanding, it is not surprising that here he specifies the height of the tree, 'which reached even to heaven'. And again that the height was visible to the end of the earth.

But that some rabbis have wanted Babylon to be set down in the middle of the earth, situated on the same line or parallel as Jerusalem, is altogether silly. And those who say that Jerusalem was the centre point of the earth are as unbalanced as babies. Yet men like Jerome[1] and Origen[2] and other old writers hold it as a certain principle that Jerusalem was the centre of the earth. For they think it was situated at the middle point of the world. But they deserve the mockery of the Cynic who, when he was asked to indicate the centre of the earth, touched the earth beneath his feet with his stick. And when it was objected that this was not the umbilicus of the earth, said: 'Then measure the earth yourself!'[3] But as for Jerusalem, it is certain that nothing like they imagine can be found out. That arrogant Barbinel[4] wanted also to seem a philosopher. But there is nothing weaker than the Jews, when they step outside grammatical explanations. The Lord has so blinded them and delivered them to a reprobate mind that he intended them to be mirrors of terrible blindness and monstrous stupor. And that worthless fellow shows his absurdity in the least detail.

Now, that he said that *"its branches were beautiful and its fruit abundant"* can be referred to the common opinion of the masses. For we know how their eyes are dazzled by the splendour of princes. Anyone who excels the rest by his great power is worshipped by everybody; they are carried away by their

1. Jerome: *Commentary on Ezekiel* 5:5: 'The prophet here declares that Jerusalem is situated in the middle of the earth, showing that it is the umbilicus of the earth.'

2. Origen, *Fragm. ex Catenis* on Ps. 74:12, ed. J. B. Pitra, *Analecta Sacra*, vol. III (Venice, 1883), p. 99.

3. Source not found.

4. Barbinel: see p. 101, n. 2.

admiration so as to have no judgment left. When his Imperial Majesty or his Royal Majesty comes forth, everyone is at once struck dumb and senseless. For they do not think it right for them to look at what may lie within those princes. Since there was so much wealth and power in King Nebuchadnezzar, no wonder that the prophet says *"his branches were beautiful and his fruit abundant"*. But all the same we must remember what I said formerly, that the blessing of God is conspicuous in princes, even if they are far from carrying out their obligations; for God does not allow his grace to be completely extinguished in them. Therefore, they are forced to bear some fruit. Any sort of firm rule is a much more beautiful sight than where there is a common equality, every man watching his neighbour suspiciously. And to this also is relevant what he says, that *"it was food and drink for all"*, as I explained earlier.

The second point of the dream follows. Hitherto he had described the beauty and excellence of Nebuchadnezzar's state under the figure of the lofty tree which provided shade for the beasts and fed them with its fruit, besides giving safe nests to the birds of heaven in its branches. Now follows the felling of the tree: *"I saw"*, he says, *"in the visions of my head upon my bed, and behold, a watcher and a holy one came down from heaven."* There is no doubt that by 'watcher' he means an angel. He is also called 'a holy one'; but this is a periphrasis for 'angel'. They are deservedly called by this name, because they are continually on the watch to execute God's commands. They do not have to sleep; they neither eat nor drink, but live a spiritual life. The reason why they do not need sleep is that we contract sleep from drink and food. In short, because angels have no bodies they are, on account of their spiritual nature, always awake.

This statement is not only spoken about their nature; it also expresses their office. Because God always has them on hand at his beck and call, and because he appoints them to fulfil his commands, they are called 'watchers'. In the Psalm we have, 'Angels who perform his will'[5] — because they run hither and thither with a speed incomprehensible to us, and fly from heaven to earth, from one extreme to the other, from east to west. So, because angels are so willing and ready to execute God's commands, they are deservedly called 'watchers'. They are also called 'holy ones', because they are not infected with human filthiness. We are full of many faults, not only because we dwell on earth but because from our first parent we contract the disease that corrupts all the parts of body and mind. Hence Nebuchadnezzar wished by this name to distinguish angels from mortals. For although God sanctifies his elect here and now, yet so long as they live in the prison of their flesh, they never attain angelic holiness. So a difference is here marked out between

5. Mg., Ps. 103:20.

angels and men. Nebuchadnezzar was not able to grasp this by himself; but he was divinely instructed to understand that the fall of this tree was not from men but by the command of God.

Afterwards he adds that *"an angel cried with a great voice, 'Cut down the tree, strip off its leaves, break off its branches, scatter* [or, 'cast away'] *its fruit; and let the beast flee from its shade and the birds of heaven not live in its branches.'"* By this figure God wished to declare that King Nebuchadnezzar would for a time be like a beast. For we should not think it absurd, even if it is forced, that the tree is said to be despoiled of a human heart. We know that trees possess no other life than what is called 'vegetative'. Therefore the dignity or excellence of a tree cannot be diminished by being deprived of a human heart. For it never had a human heart. But although the expression is forced, it contains no absurdity, for Daniel now turns from his allegorical language. In fact, Nebuchadnezzar's allegorical dream was such that God intermingled with it something from which he could deduce that under the image of the tree something else was denoted. The angel therefore gives the command to strip or take away the human heart from the tree after it had been cut down and to strip and cast away its branches and fruit. Then he orders the heart of a beast to be given it, that its portion may be with the wild and savage beasts. But, as this will be repeated elsewhere, I pass over it lightly. The sum of it is that King Nebuchadnezzar would for a time be despoiled not only of his empire but also of human understanding, so that he would differ in nothing from the beasts, since he was unworthy to hold even a lowly place among the common people. Although in his own eyes he had seemed to tower above the whole human race, he was so cast down that he was not even the last among mortals.

Hereupon follows the nature of his punishment, when he adds, *'Let seven times pass over him';* and *'Do not cut through the bottom of its roots, but let it be watered still with the rain of heaven';* and *'Let its portion be with the beasts.'* Although this is a hard and terrible punishment, when Nebuchadnezzar was driven out from the society of men and made like the wild beasts, yet it is something that God did not utterly root him up but wished the root to remain, so that the tree might again arise and grow, even be put back in its own place and recover new vigour from its root. What is in Daniel's mind is that the punishment inflicted on King Nebuchadnezzar was one in which God nevertheless gave proof of his mercy. He did not completely destroy him but spared him, and part of the root was left.

Some here argue about the mitigation of punishments when God sees that those whom he had chastised with his rods repent; but I do not know whether it is appropriate. For, as was said earlier and as we shall see again more clearly, there was no true conversion in King Nebuchadnezzar. Therefore, the fact that God did not wish to press him harder ought to be ascribed to his mercy. Because even when he seems to punish men's sins without moderation and measure, he leaves some taste of his mercy in all temporal punishments, so that also the reprobate may remain inexcusable. For the assertion that punishments are not mitigated unless the guilt is remitted is false — as we see in the case of Ahab.[6] For God did not remit the guilt of that impious king but refrained from harsher punishment because he had seemed to show some signs of repentance. We may also see the same in King Nebuchadnezzar. God did not intend to root him out (and this refers to the metaphor of the tree), but he wished *'seven times to pass'*. Some understand it as seven weeks, but others seven years — but we will treat this more fully elsewhere.

Now finally it is also to be noted that even in the midst of the time when God's vengeance was seen to rage against the unhappy king, some blessings were still intermingled with it. This is indicated by the words *'Let his portion be with the beasts of the field'* (that is, let him eat some food, and so sustain his life) and *'let him be watered'*, or washed, *'with the rain of heaven.'* For God means that while he wished to punish King Nebuchadnezzar and to show that fearful instance of his wrath, he thought of what he could bear and so tempered the punishment that there might be hope for the future. Hence it comes to pass that he takes food with the beasts of the earth, and does not cease to be washed by the dew of heaven.

> *Grant, almighty God, since we see it is so difficult for us to bear prosperity without almost losing our senses and forgetting we are mortals, grant that our weakness may always be before our eyes and keep us humble, so that we may give you the glory and, taught by you, learn to proceed with care and fear and to subject ourselves to you, to behave modestly towards our brethren, so that none shall disdain or despise others but shall study to show obedience and duty in every way, until at last you gather us into that glory which was won for us by the blood of your only-begotten Son. Amen.*

6. Mg., 1 Ki. 21:29, i.e., 21:27-29.

Lecture 19

17   ‘“*The word in the decree* [or ‘edict’, for that could be a good translation] *of the watchmen and the plea in the word of the holy ones, that those living may know that the Most High* [is] *ruler in the kingdom of men and that he gives it to whom he will and that he raises the lowly* [or ‘meanest’] *of men* [that is, ‘among men’] *above him.”’*

In this verse God confirms what he had shown the Babylonian king in the dream. He says that the king had been taught something certain, for so it had been decided before God and the angels. The sum of it is that Nebuchadnezzar should learn that he could not escape the punishment, of which he had seen a figure in the dream. But there is some ambiguity in the words. Interpreters make heavy weather of the second clause. They say that the angels ask a question to which the reply is made that the King of Babylon is an example to future generations that the power of the one God is supreme. But to me this seems forced. As for the term פִּתְגָּמָא, *pithgama*, it means ‘word’ among the Chaldaeans. But in my view this is properly taken for ‘edict’, as in the first chapter of Esther.[1] And this sense fits in best; the edict was promulgated in a decree, so that it might not be a passing word or an empty vision, but God wanted to show the king what was already settled and decided in heaven. We now grasp the prophet’s intention.

But there is yet another question. It seems absurd to attribute right and power to the angels, for in this way they seem to be made God’s equals. We know that God is the only Judge and that therefore it is his proper office to decide what seems good to him. To the extent that this is transferred to the angels it seems to

---

1. Est. 1:19.

detract from God's supreme power; for to admit associates to his majesty is not fitting. But we know that it is not unusual in Scripture for God to join the angels with himself, not as equals, but as his ministers; yet ministers to whom he ascribes the great honour of deeming them worthy to be summoned to his counsel. Angels are therefore often called counsellors of God. Hence, in this place also they are said to decree along with God, not of their own will or of themselves, as they say; but because they subscribe to God's judgment.

Meanwhile we must note that a twofold role is given them here. For in the first clause Daniel makes them subscribers to God in the decree, and afterwards he says *"they plead"*. And this also fits in well, because the angels desire and pray that all mortals may be humbled, that God alone may be exalted, and thus whatever obscures his glory put in its proper place. It is right that the angels should plead. For them, as we know, there was nothing better than to adore God and to have all mortals as their companions. But when they see the pride and arrogance of men violating God's dominion, without doubt they plead that God will force all the proud and defiant to submit to his yoke.

So now we see why Daniel says *"this was made an edict in the decree of the watchmen and a plea in their word"*; as if he would say, 'You have all the angels against you. With one consent, with one voice, they accuse you before God of obscuring his glory so far as you can; and God assents to their verdicts and determines to cast you down and make you contemptible and ignominious before the whole world.' And this decree is attested by all the angels as if it were the joint decision of God and themselves. For their agreement or consensus could be powerful confirmation with the heathen king. There is no doubt that God, after his usual manner, accommodated the vision to the grasp of this particular man, a man who had never been instructed in the Law but was only imbued with such a confused awareness of a deity that he did not distinguish between God and the angels. Nevertheless, it is a true statement that the edict was promulgated by the common decree of the whole heavenly host and at the same time by their plea. For such is the madness of men that they want to snatch and appropriate what is peculiar and proper to God alone, and the angels are grieved to the heart at any detraction from God's glory. This seems to be the genuine sense.

What follows leads on very well, *"that mortals may know that God is the ruler in the kingdom of men"*. For Daniel marks the end of the plea, that the angels wish God to keep his right unimpaired and undiminished by human ingratitude. But men cannot ascribe even the least trifle to themselves without despoiling God of the praise that belongs to him alone. The angels therefore beg God to cast down all the proud and not to let himself be defrauded of his own right but that he may keep all power perfect and unbroken in his possession.

This also is to be carefully noticed, *"that mortals may know that the Most High is the ruler in the kingdom of men"*. Even the worst men confess that God has supreme power (for they do not dare with their blasphemies to drag him from his heavenly throne), but yet they imagine that by their own industry or resources or other means they are able both to attain and also to preserve their kingdoms in the world. Unbelievers would therefore gladly shut God up in heaven, just as Epicurus invented a god that enjoyed his delights in idleness. Therefore Daniel shows that God is despoiled of his right unless 'he is known to rule in the kingdom of men', that is, on the earth, to humble whom he will. Thus also in the Psalm it is said, 'Not from the east, nor from the west, but from heaven is power.'[2] And elsewhere, 'It is God that raises up the poor from the dung-hill.'[3] Also in the canticle of the holy Virgin, 'He puts down the proud from their seat, and exalts the humble and lowly.'[4] All confess this, but hardly one in a hundred will really think that God rules on earth in such a way that none is able to exalt himself or remain in a high position, but that this is the unique blessing of God.

Since it is difficult to convince men of this, Daniel expressly says here that *"the Most High is the ruler in the kingdom of men";* that is, he does not exert his power only in heaven but also governs the human race and assigns to each his rank or place. *"And to whom he will he gives it."* He speaks of the various empires in the singular, but it is as if he said that some are exalted by the will of God and others cast down, and that all that happens as it pleases God. The sum of it is that to each his condition is divinely ascribed. Neither their own ambition, nor ingenuity, nor wisdom, nor resources, nor outside help is any good to those who aspire to some high state, unless God raises them, as it were, with outstretched hand. Paul teaches the same thing in different words: 'There is no power but of God.'[5] Later Daniel often repeats the same statement.

He adds, *"he will lift up the humble among men above him"*. In such a clear-cut change the power of God shines brighter; for he raises from the dung-hill those who had been obscure and despised and sets them above even kings. When this happens, infidels say that God is playing a game and men are tossed up by his hand like balls; now they go up high, now they are thrown down on the ground. But they do not consider the cause. It is because God wishes to show by plain proofs that we are under his will, so that our state depends on him. Because we do not grasp this of ourselves, examples have to be set before us, in which we are forced to see what we nearly all like to be ignorant of. Now we have the prophet's statement as a whole; the angels beg God by incessant prayers to declare his power to mortals and to bring down the proud who think that they excel by their own virtue and industry, or by chance, or by human help. That God may drive away irreligious pride, the angels ask that he will cast them down and so show that he is king and ruler, not only of heaven, but also of earth.

2. Mg., Ps. 75:7, i.e., 75:6-7.
3. Mg., Ps. 113:6, i.e., 113:7.
4. Mg., Lk. 1:52.
5. Mg., Rom. 13:1.

Now this did not happen only to one king; tor we know that the histories are full of such instances. For from what background, from what rank, were kings often made? And as there was not in the world a greater pride than in the Roman Empire, we may see what happened there. For God produced a certain monstrosity, that such a spectacle might stupefy the Greeks and all the Orientals and the Spaniards and the Italians and the French. For nothing was more monstrous than some of the emperors. Their origin was so infamous and shameful that God could not have shown more plainly that empires are not transferred by the will of men nor acquired by their power, purpose, and large armies; but that they are under his hand, to put in command whomever he would.

Let us go on:

18 *"'I, King Nebuchadnezzar, saw this dream; and you, Belteshazzar, tell* [literally, 'say'] *its interpretation; for all the wise men of my kingdom are unable to reveal its interpretation to me. But you can, because the spirit of the holy gods is in you."'*

Here Nebuchadnezzar repeats what he had said before — that he was seeking the interpretation of his dream. He knew that he had been shown something figurative, but he could not understand God's purpose, nor even determine its drift. He therefore sought Daniel's competence in this. He asserts that he saw a dream, so that Daniel may give all his thought to its interpretation.

And for the same reason he adds that *"all the wise men of his kingdom had been unable to explain the dream";* where he acknowledges, at least partly, that all the astrologers and diviners and the rest of that tribe who professed to know everything had been worthless and false. Some were augurs, some soothsayers, some interpreters of dreams, some astrologers (not only those who investigated the course and order and distances of the stars and their properties, but such also as wanted to presage the future from the course of stars). Although they claimed so magniloquently supreme knowledge in all things, Nebuchadnezzar admits that they were impostors. For he credits Daniel with being endowed with a divine spirit. Therefore, he excludes all the wise men of Babylon from possessing such a gift; for he had learned by experience that they were without the Spirit of God. He does not say precisely this, but from his words it can easily be elicited that he had found all the Chaldaean wise men to be hollow.

In the second clause he excepts Daniel from their number and at the same time indicates the reason — that he was distinguished by a divine spirit. Nebuchadnezzar therefore here ascribes to God what belongs to him and also acknowledges that Daniel is his prophet and minister.

That he calls the angels *"holy gods"* should not, as we said elsewhere, seem strange in a heathen who had not been trained in the true doctrine of godliness but had only tasted some elements. But we know that in the common opinion angels were confused with the one God. Nebuchadnezzar was therefore speaking in the common and accepted sense when he says that the spirit of the holy gods dwelt in Daniel.

Now he goes on:

19 *Then Daniel, whose name was Belteshazzar, was stupefied for about one hour, and his thoughts troubled him. The king replied and said, 'Belteshazzar, do not let the dream and* [its] *interpretation trouble you* ["terrify you"].' *Belteshazzar answered and said, 'My lord, may the dream* [be] *to your enemies and its interpretation to your foes.'*

Here Daniel relates that he was, in a certain measure, thunderstruck. And this I refer to the grief that the holy prophet conceived from the fearful punishment which God had shown under the figure. It should not seem strange that Daniel was touched with sorrow over the disaster of the King of Babylon. For although Nebuchadnezzar was a cruel tyrant, had brutally harassed the Church of God, almost destroyed it, yet it behoved Daniel as his subject to pray for him. For God through Jeremiah expressly commanded the Jews to do this: 'Pray for the prosperity of Babylon; for in its peace shall be your peace.'[6] After the end of seventy years it was right for the devout servants of God to seek freedom. But until that time (which also had been predetermined by the mouth of the prophet) it was not right either to hate the king or to pray for God's vengeance. For they knew that God's just punishment had been inflicted; they knew also that this man had been set over them and was to be regarded as holding the place of a lawful king. Since, then, Daniel had been treated humanely by the king and had, moreover, been taken into exile in accordance with the laws of war, it was his duty to be loyal to his king, even though he had exercised tyranny against God's people. This alone was why he became sorrowful at the unhappy oracle. Some think it was 'inspiration'. But this seems to fit better, because he does not simply say that he was stupefied, but also that he was disturbed or terrified in his thoughts.

Meanwhile we must note that the prophets had mixed feelings when God denounced his imminent judgments through them. So often, then, as God appointed the prophets as heralds of severe disasters, they had an equivocal feeling. On the one hand they sympathized with the unhappy men whose destruction they saw to be nigh. Yet on the other, they boldly proclaimed what had been divinely commanded; and sadness never hindered them from discharging their duty readily and steadfastly. Here we can see both feelings in Daniel. It was a right affection to sympathize with his king, so that he was almost silent for nearly an hour. But that the king here tells him to be of good courage and not to

6. Mg., Je. 29:7.

171

be worried illustrates the security of those who have never comprehended God's vengeance. The prophet is terrified; yet he is not in any danger. God has not threatened him. The very punishment that he sees prepared for the king even gave him some hope of future liberation. Why then was he frightened? Even believers, when God spares them and shows himself merciful and gracious to them, still cannot feel his judgments without fear. For they know that they themselves are liable to the same punishments unless God treats them indulgently. Again, they never put off their human feelings, and mercifulness constrains them when they see the ungodly destroyed or, at least, vengeance hanging over them. So for these two reasons they become sad and sorrowful. But the ungodly, even if God openly indicts them and sets their punishment before them, are quite unmoved; they remain stupid or openly mock at his power, and until they are seriously pressed they take his threats as fables.

Just such an example the prophet shows us in the King of Babylon. *'Belteshazzar'*, he says, *'do not let your thoughts trouble you; do not let the dream and its interpretation frighten you.'* But Daniel was afraid on his account. Nevertheless, as I have already said, believers fear, although they feel God is gracious to them; but the ungodly, so long as they are asleep in their security, are unmoved, untroubled, by any threats.

Daniel adds the reason for his sorrow. *'My lord'*, he says, *'may this dream be to your enemies, and its interpretation to your foes.'* Here Daniel explains why he was so confounded; that is, because he desired to avert such a fearful punishment from the king's person. For although he might deservedly have detested him, he revered the power divinely delivered to him. We learn, therefore, from the prophet's example, to pray for our enemies, who wish us to be ruined; and especially to pray for tyrants, if it should please God to subject us to their passions. For although they are unworthy to receive any obligations of kindness, yet, because they rule only by God's will, let us bear their yoke meekly — and that, as Paul says, not only for wrath, but for conscience' sake.[7] Otherwise we are rebels, not only against them but also against God himself. But on the other hand, Daniel shows that he is not weakened by any feeling of mercy, nor even softened, from going on resolutely in his vocation.

For he says:

20 *'The tree which you saw, which* [was] *large and strong, and whose greatness reached to heaven and the sight of it to the whole earth;*
21 *And its foliage* [was] *beautiful* [that is, "its leaves were beautiful"] *and its fruit abundant; and in which* [literally, "and in it"] *food for all; under which lived beasts of the field and in whose branches the birds of heaven rested;*
22 *You yourself, O King,* [are]*, who have multiplied and strengthened* [that

7. Mg., Rom. 13:5.

is, "who have become great and strong"], *so that your greatness has been multiplied and reached the heavens and your power to the ends of the earth.'*

Here we see what I have touched on, that Daniel carried out his duty to the king in such a way that he was still mindful of his prophetic office and was not feeble in prosecuting God's commandment. We must take note of a distinction. Nothing is more difficult for ministers of the Word than to keep to this middle way. In their zeal some are always thundering and forgetting that they themselves are men; they show no sign of goodwill but croak unadulterated acrimony. The result is that they have no authority and all their admonitions are odious. They expose God's Word to distaste and reproaches when, without any sign either of sorrow or of συμπάθεια [*sympatheia*],[8] they so inhumanely frighten those who are sinners. Others are lazy, worse, are faithless flatterers, burying the most serious crimes. They always plead that neither the prophets nor the apostles were so fervent that their zeal lacked human affection. Thus it is that they paint such a picture with their flatteries as to destroy unhappy creatures. But our prophet, like all the others, here shows a middle course, which is to be kept by all God's ministers. Thus Jeremiah was sorrowful and bitter over his antagonistic prophecies;[9] but he did not swerve from his freedom of reproach, nor even from the harshest of threats: both were from God. All the others are the same — for this repeatedly happens in the prophets. Daniel, therefore, here on the one hand sympathizes with the king; but on the other, knowing that he is the herald of God's vengeance, he is undeterred by the danger of telling the king about the punishment which he had treated lightly.

Hence also we gather that he was not overcome by fear of the tyrant — many dare not utter a word when the embassy committed to them is very unpleasant and might stir the ungodly and unbelievers to madness. Daniel, then, was not overcome by such fear — but only because he had asked God to deal mercifully with his king. For here he says, *'You yourself, O King, are.'* He does not speak doubtfully or ambiguously or with dark hints or even using many excuses, but boldly and plainly declares that King Nebuchadnezzar is signified by the tree which he had seen. Hence, *'the tree which you saw large and strong, under whose branches lived the beasts of the field, in whose branches nested the birds, you'*, he says, *'O King, are.'* Why? *'You have become great'*, he says, *'and strong; your greatness reaches to the heavens and your power to the ends of the earth.'*

Now what follows?

23 *'And that the king saw a watchman and a holy one descend from heaven who said* [literally, "and said", but the copula should be resolved into a relative

8. συμπάθεια: fellow-feeling.
9. Mg., Je. 9:1.

pronoun], *"Cut down the tree and scatter it; but leave the bottom of its roots in the earth, and* [let it be] *in a band of iron and bronze in the grass of the field, and let it be watered by the dew of heaven, and its portion with the beasts of the field, until seven times pass over it."*

24 *This is the interpretation, O King, and the decree of the Most High which relates to my lord the king.'*

Daniel pursues the same theme with unabated steadfastness — the imminent destruction of the Babylonian king. It is true he calls him 'lord', and that sincerely; but, as the ambassador of the Most High King, he does not hesitate to exalt the Word commanded him even more highly. For it is common to all the prophets, that they rise up against mountains and hills, as it is put in Jeremiah. This statement is also noteworthy, 'I set you above kingdoms and peoples, that you should pluck up and plant, build up and pull down.'[10] God wishes to claim such reverence for his Word that there may be nothing either magnificent or splendid in the world that will not give way. Daniel confessed that, humanly speaking and by political order, the king was his lord; but he still persisted in the embassy committed to him.

'That you, O King', he says, *'saw a watcher descend from heaven'* — he is still speaking of an angel. And we said why Scripture calls the angels 'watchers' — because they are at hand to carry out the commands of God. And we know that God executes by their hands what he has decreed; and this, I said, the angels are always at hand to do. Again, they are also on watch to act on behalf of believers. But here the word 'watcher' is general and refers to that promptitude with which angels are endowed, so that whatever God commands they at once perform with the utmost speed.

So *'you saw one descend from heaven who said, "Cut down the tree and scatter it, etc."'* He repeats what had already been said, that the time of punishment is here limited; for God could wipe out the King of Babylon and all memory of him, but he wished to soften the punishment. He therefore adds the limitation, *'until seven times pass'.* I have said nothing as yet about these 'times'. But the view is probable of those who think the number is indefinite — that is, 'until a long time pass'. Some think it means 'months', others 'years'. But I very readily incline to the first interpretation, that God did not mean to punish King Nebuchadnezzar for only a short time, lest this should seem his usual custom; but since it was his intention to give a remarkable example to all ages, he meant to prolong his punishment over a long period. This therefore relates to the number of seven years. And we know that the number seven signifies a long time in Scripture, as denoting perfection.

10. Mg., Je. 1:10.

Grant, almighty God, so often as you set our sins before us and at the same time declare yourself the judge, that we may not misuse your tolerance and lay up for ourselves a store of greater vengeance by our indolence and dullness; but let us fear in good time and take good heed to ourselves, and be so frightened by your threats that, drawn also by your sweetness, we may freely submit ourselves to you and seek nothing more than to consecrate ourselves entirely to your obedience, so that your name may be glorified by us in Christ our Lord. Amen.

Lecture 20

25 *'And they will drive you out from men and your habitation shall be with the beasts of the field, and they will feed you with grass like cattle and wash you with the dew of heaven; and seven times will pass over you until you know that the Most High* [is] *ruler in the kingdom of men and that he gives it to whom he will.'*

Daniel continues his explanation of the dream. The previous verse, which I expounded yesterday, treated of the fact that the dream was about King Nebuchadnezzar. But it had to be expressed, because the tidings were sad and bitter to the king. And we know how disgraceful kings think it not only to be put in their place but also to be summoned before God's judgment throne, there to be covered with shame and disgrace. For we know that prosperity goes to the head of even common people. What, then, can it do to kings except make them forget their human condition and think they are free from all difficulties and trouble? For they do not reckon themselves to be of the common order of humanity. So because Nebuchadnezzar was hardly able to bear this message, the prophet told him in few words that the felling of the tree was a figure of the ruin which was threatening him.

This he now continues at length, and says, *'They will cast you out from men; your habitation shall be with the beasts of the field.'* When previously Daniel had spoken of the four monarchies there can be no doubt that the king was at first exasperated. But it was much harder and less tolerable to the king that he should be compared with wild beasts, that he should be cut off from the number of men; again, that he should be banished to the fields and woods to be pastured along with the beasts. Had Daniel said only that he would be despoiled of his royal dignities it would have lessened the gravity of the

176

offence. But when he was placed in such ignominy he without doubt raged within himself. But God restrained his fury so that he should not want to avenge what he thought was an insult. For we see from the later context that he had not repented. Always nurturing the same pride in his mind, he was doubtless also cruel. For these two vices are conjoined. But the Lord checked his madness, so that he spared the holy prophet.

Meanwhile, the constancy of God's minister is worthy of notice. He did not indirectly hint to the king what was going to happen but clearly and with many words related what a disgraceful and shameful condition awaited him. *'They will cast you out'*, he says, *'from men.'* If he had said, 'You will be like one of the human herd, differing nothing from the rabble', it would already have been very hard. But when the king is cast out from human society so that not a single corner is left for him and he is not allowed to live even with cowherds and swineherds, anyone can imagine how detestable it was to him. Yet Daniel does not hesitate to declare such a judgment.

And the words that follow have the same or a similar weight. *'Your habitation'*, he says, *'will be with the beasts of the field; they will feed you with grass.'* The plural should be taken as indefinite and it can well be translated, 'You will feed on grass; you will be watered with the dew of heaven; your habitation will be with the wild beasts.' For I do not like the clever way that some philosophize and supply the word 'angels'. Of course, I admit it is true; but the prophet is simply telling of the imminent punishment of the King of Babylon, that he will be reduced to the utmost shame, differing nothing from the brute beasts. This freedom of speech, as I said, is worthy of note, that we may learn that God's servants who are given the office of teaching cannot faithfully fulfil their duty unless they shut out of sight and despise all the loftiness of the world.

Next, let us also learn from the king's example not to be refractory and stubborn when God threatens us. For although King Nebuchadnezzar did not repent, as was said and as will appear again from the context, yet we see that he allowed himself to be threatened with a horrible judgment. If therefore we, who beside him are almost rubbish, cannot bear God's threats when they are laid before us, he will be our witness and judge who possessed such great power yet dared do nothing against the prophet.

Now at the end of the verse the statement is repeated which has already been explained: *'until you know'*, he says, *'that the Most High is the ruler in the kingdom of men, and to whom he will he gives it'*. This place again teaches how difficult it is for us to ascribe supreme power to God. By tongue we are indeed great heralds of God's glory. But yet there is no-one who does not restrict his power, either by usurping some of it for himself or transferring it to something else. In particular, when God exalts us to some degree of honour we forget that we are men and snatch God's honour from him and want to put ourselves into his place. This disease is hard to cure and the punishment which God inflicted on the King of Babylon is a warning to us. For a light chastening would have been enough had this madness not stuck, as it were, in his entrails and marrow — the madness of men claiming for themselves what is proper to God. Therefore a really violent medicine is needed to teach them modesty and humility.

Today monarchs claim in their titles that they are kings and dukes and counts 'by the grace of God'.[1] But how many falsely claim God's patronage in order to assert their supreme power? For what is often the worth of 'by the grace of God' in the titles of kings and princes? Merely that they may not acknowledge any superior, as they say. Yet God (the shield behind which they hide) will be pleased to tread them under foot. So far are they from earnestly considering that it is by his blessing that they reign. Therefore it is sheer pretence for them to boast that they enjoy their dominions *'Dei gratia'*. Since this is so, we can easily judge how proudly heathen kings despise God, even when they do not falsely use his name as a defence, like these worthless characters who openly mock at God and so profane the word *'gratia.'*

Now he goes on:

26 *'And what they spoke about leaving the root of the trunk of the tree: your kingdom will stand for you from when you know that* [there is] *a power of heaven* [or, "that there is dominion in heaven"].'

Here Daniel ends the interpretation of the dream and teaches King Nebuchadnezzar that God will not deal so severely with him as to not allow room for his mercy. He therefore softens the extreme rigour of the punishment so that Nebuchadnezzar may apprehend a hope of pardon and call upon God and repent — a clearer exhortation will afterwards follow. But Daniel already prepares him for repentance when he says that *'the kingdom will stand for him'*. God could drive him out of human society so as to remain with the wild beasts always. He could even cast him out of the world at once. But it is a sign of mercifulness that he wishes to restore him not only to some middling position but to his own dignity, as if it had always remained whole and entire. So we see that the dream was profitable to King Nebuchadnezzar so long as he did not despise the prophet's holy admonition — more, so long as he was not ungrateful to God. For Daniel not only foretold the imminent disaster but at the same time brought a message of reconciliation. So God's teaching would have been profitable had he not been unteachable and stubborn, like most people. But from this we may gather a general doctrine: when God sets a term to his chastisements he is inviting us to repentance. For God offers a taste of

---

1. *Dei gratia:* part of the title of some European monarchs, including the French king. It is still to be seen on some British coins as *Dei gratia Reg. or D.G.R.*

his mercy so that we can hope he will be entreated by us if we go to him for help heartily and sincerely.

But we must notice what Daniel adds in the second part of the verse: *'from when you know that there is a power of heaven'*. For under these words there is a promise of spiritual grace, that God will not only punish the Babylonian king in order to humble him, but also he will work inwardly and change his mind, just as in the end, late as it was, he did. Therefore, 'from when you know', he says, 'that there is a power of heaven'. I have said that here the grace of the Spirit was promised; for we know how little profit men gain, even if God repeats the stroke a hundred times. For such is the hardness and stubbornness of our hearts that we grow harder and harder while God is calling us to repentance. And without doubt Nebuchadnezzar would have been like Pharaoh unless God had not only humbled him with outward punishments but had also added the inward impulse of his Spirit, so that he let himself be taught and subjected himself to the heavenly judgment and power. This, then, is what Daniel intended when he said, 'from when you know'. For Nebuchadnezzar would never of his own will have come to such knowledge without being touched by the secret moving of the Spirit.

He adds, that *'there is a power of heaven'*; that is, that God governs the world and holds supreme rule. For here he opposes heaven to earth, that is, to all mortals. For if kings see everything quiet in their realm and there is none to frighten them, they think they are outside all chance of danger, as they say; and when they want their state to be sure, they keep an eye on everything — but they never raise their eyes to heaven; as if the preservation of their kingdoms had nothing to do with God, as if he would not raise up whom he would or cast down all the proud. So, as if it were outside God's sphere of operation, the princes of this world never consider that 'there is a power of heaven'; but, as I said, they look to the right and to the left and to the front and to the back. This is why Daniel says that there is a heavenly power. For as I have mentioned, there is a tacit antithesis between God and all mortals; as if he were saying, 'that you may know that God rules, as you saw before'.

He goes on:

27 *'Moreover, O King, let my counsel please you* [שפר, *saphar,* signifies "to be beautiful"; but metaphorically it is transferred to "approving" or what is commonly called "complacence". Therefore, "let my counsel please you"], *and* [that is, "in order that"; for ו, *vau,* should be resolved in this way] *you may redeem your sins by righteousness* [so they translate it; we shall speak of this word "redeem" later] *and your iniquity in mercy toward the poor; behold* [the Greeks translate it, "if perchance"], *there shall be a prolonging of your peace* [or, "a medicine for your error"].'

Because there is no agreement among interpreters on the meaning of the words, and the substance of the teaching partly depends on it, we must first notice that מלכי, *milchi,* is here equivalent to 'my counsel'. Some translate it 'King, my king'. Both words are derived from the same root, מלך, *malach,* which means 'to reign'. But this word sometimes signifies 'counsel', and there is no doubt that that is how it should be taken in this verse. Therefore 'may my counsel please you and may you redeem your sins'.

The word פרוק, *peruk,* they here translate 'redeem'. But it often signifies either 'to break off', or 'to separate', or 'to crush'. Therefore in this place it can well be rendered 'separate (or, break off) your sins by mercy and humaneness'; as if he were saying, 'So make an end to sinning that you may set off on a new course, that your cruelty may be changed to kindness and your tyrannical violence to mercifulness.' But it is not really important, for the word often means 'to liberate' or 'to save'. This place will not admit of 'save'; and it would also be harsh if we were to say, 'Liberate your sins by righteousness.' Therefore, I readily embrace the sense that Daniel is exhorting the King of Babylon to change his life, to break off the sins in which he had already lived for too long.

Now, what follows at the end of the verse, *'Behold, there will be a healing for your error',* as I have said, the Greeks render 'If perchance there may be a healing'. But the other sense seems to flow better; as if he were saying 'This is the proper and real medicine.' Others translate it, 'prolonging', since ארך, *arach,* means 'to lead forward'. At the same time they change the signification of the other word. They say, 'There will be a prolonging of your peace, or rest.' That sense might be tolerable, but the other agrees better with rules of grammar. It is also more generally received: 'this is the proper medicine for error'. A different sense could even be elicited, although, so far as the words go, nothing would be changed: 'there will be' (that is, 'let there be') a medicine in your errors', that is, 'you will learn by your errors to be healed'. For daily indulgence increases an evil, as is well known. Thus, this last part can be taken as Daniel continuing with his exhortation, as if he were saying, 'It is time for you to leave off from your errors. Hitherto you have lacked all sense, when you have given yourself unbridled licence. Let there be, then, some moderation of your ignorance; open your eyes and at last understand that you must repent.'

Now I return to the substance of the teaching. *'May my counsel please you',* he says. Here Daniel deals more gently with the heathen king than if he had been preaching to his own people. For then he would have exercised his prophetic authority. But he knew the king did not hold the first rudiments of piety, and therefore takes only the role of a counsellor, for he was not a *doctor ordinarius.*[2] Nebuchadnezzar's summons was not a daily event for him; nor was

---

2. *Doctor ordinarius:* in medieval universities a regular, as opposed to occasional, lecturer in his subject.

he called because the king wanted to subject himself to his teaching. Daniel therefore remembered with whom he was dealing and what sort of man he was and tempered his words by saying, *'may my counsel be approved by you'*.

Afterwards he explains his counsel in a few words: *'Break off'* (or, 'throw away'), he says, *'your sins by righteousness and your iniquities by mercy towards the poor.'* There is no doubt that Daniel intended to exhort the king to repent; but he touches on only one aspect of it, as we know is quite usual with the prophets. When they recall the people to the right way, they do not always fully describe what repentance is or define it in general, but indicate it by synecdoche[3] or the external duties of repentance or some part of them. Daniel now follows this custom. If it is asked what repentance is, it is the conversion of a person to God from whom he had been alienated. But is this conversion only in the hands and feet and tongue? Rather, it begins in the mind, next in the heart, and afterwards passes to the external activities. True repentance, therefore, has its beginning in a person's mind; so that someone who wanted to prize himself too highly will renounce his own shrewdness or will reject his foolish trust in his own reason; next that he will subdue his depraved affections and subject them to God; finally will follow the outward life. But the works are only testimonies of repentance. For repentance, as I said, is too excellent a thing for its root to be visible to human eyes. Only by its fruits do we declare our repentance. But because the duties of the second table [of the Law] in a way lay open a person's mind, the prophets often, in enforcing repentance, put forward only the duty of love, as Daniel does here.

Therefore *'redeem* (or, "break off", or, "cast away") *your sins',* he says. How? *'By righteousness'.* There is no doubt that the word 'righteousness' means the same as 'grace' or 'mercy'. But those who here render 'grace' into 'faith' twist the prophet's words very violently. For we know that nothing is more frequent in Hebrew than to say one and the same thing in two different expressions. Since, therefore, Daniel here speaks of sins and iniquities in the same sense, we also infer that righteousness and mercy should not be differentiated. The second word better expresses what he understood by righteousness. When people see that their lives ought to be changed, they invent many 'obsequies'[4] (a name they do not deserve) because they do not look at what pleases God nor at what he commands in his Word; they rashly thrust their own whims on God — as we see happening in the papacy. What is righteous and holy living there? Just traipsing to and fro, undertaking votive pilgrimages; putting up a statue; founding masses, as they call them; fasting on this day or

3. Synecdoche: rhetorical term denoting the indicating of a whole entity by one of its parts.

4. Obsequies (Latin *obsequia*): in the sense of solemn, sometimes ceremonial, acts of obedience. See *A New English Dictionary,* ed. J. A. H. Murray, *s.v.* 'Obsequy'.

that; and heaping up those nonsenses about which God has not uttered one syllable. So, because men go so greatly astray on the knowledge of true righteousness, the prophet here adds 'mercy' in explanation; as if he were saying, 'Do not think you will please God by those external pomps which delight those who are carnal and given to earthly things and measure God by their own minds and thus incorrectly. Do not let this falsehood deceive you, but learn that true righteousness lies in mercy towards the poor.'

In this second clause there is also a synecdoche. True righteousness is not restricted simply to this word but embraces all the offices of love. Therefore we should act faithfully towards men and defraud neither rich nor poor; not to oppress anyone; to render to each his right. But this way of speaking should be familiar to us if we are even only moderately versed in the teaching of the prophets. However that may be, Daniel wanted briefly to show the King of Babylon what it is to live righteously — to cherish faith and integrity among men; yet not to neglect the first table of the Law. For the service of God is more precious than all human righteousness, that is, which men cultivate among themselves. But true righteousness is known by external testimonies, as I have already said. And he speaks of the second table rather than of the first because while hypocrites pretend that they serve God with their many ceremonies, they allow themselves any savagery, any plundering, any fraud, so that there is among them no law of right living with their neighbours. Because hypocrites hide their malice behind this pretence, God gives us a touchstone, as they say, when he calls us to the duties of love.

Now as for the end of the verse, we have said that a twofold sense is drawn from it. If we keep the future tense, *'Behold, there will be a medicine'*, it will be confirmation of the previous teaching; as if he were saying that it is not to be done by lengthy and roundabout methods; this is the only medicine. Or, if you prefer a word of exhortation, it will also fit in well: 'Let this be the medicine for your errors', that is, 'From now on do not indulge yourself as you have done hitherto, but open your eyes and see how wretchedly and wickedly you have lived, and so take pains to heal your errors.'

That the papists abuse this passage to prove that God is pleased by satisfactions is too frivolous, even ridiculous if we look carefully at their doctrine. When they define satisfactions they call them 'works of supererogation'. If anyone performs what God has commanded in his Law, he will not be able to make satisfaction for his sins. This the papists are forced to admit. What remains then? That we offer God more than he commands. This they call 'works not owed'. But Daniel is not demanding from King Nebuchadnez-zar some work of supererogation; he is demanding righteousness; and he afterwards shows that a person's life is only rightly ordered when kindness is strong and flourishes among us, and especially when we are merciful to the poor. There is certainly no supererogation here! For what is the point of the

Law? So it follows that this cannot be dragged into 'satisfaction', and the papists are both stupid and disgusting.

But even if we grant it to them, it still does not follow that sins are redeemed before God, as if works made compensation for the guilt, or 'the penalty', in their phraseology. They do not assert that the guilt is redeemed by satisfactions; that is one thing. But as for 'the penalty', they say this is redeemed. But we must see whether this agrees with the prophet's intention. I am not now arguing over a word. I grant them it can be taken for 'redeem' — 'redeem your sins'. But we must see whether this redeeming takes place within the judgment of God or among men. And it is certain that Daniel is thinking of how wickedly and inhumanely Nebuchadnezzar had behaved, how tyrannically he had harassed his subjects, how arrogantly he had despised the poor and miserable. It is because he had completely thrown himself into iniquity that Daniel shows the remedy. And if this 'remedy' is put for 'redemption' or 'liberation', it will not be absurd, because we redeem our sins among men when we give them satisfaction. I 'redeem' sins with my neighbour if, after having injured him, I try to be reconciled to him; I acknowledge that I have sinned, and in this way I 'redeem' my sin. But it does not follow that the sins are expiated before God's judgment, as if the beneficence I show is some kind of compensation. And so we see that the papists are inept and foolish when they steal the prophet's words for their own use.

Now finally it is asked to what end Daniel exhorted King Nebuchadnezzar 'to break off, or redeem, his sins'. For either the exhortation came by accident (which would be an absurdity) or it was a heavenly decree (just as the king's dream was the promulgation of an edict, as we saw earlier). If this was determined before God, it could not be changed in any way. It would therefore be useless to wish to redeem sins. If we follow the other explanation, no difficulty will remain. But even if we confess that the prophet was here speaking of the redeeming of sins, his exhortation is not useless. For although King Nebuchadnezzar had to prepare himself to bear God's chastising, yet it would be a great help to him to be aware that God is merciful. And he was also able to shorten the time which his obstinate malice had prolonged. Not that God will change his decree, but because he often declared by way of threatening, so that he may deal more kindly with men and temper the rigour of his vengeance, as appears from many other examples. This, therefore, would not have been useless with someone teachable, nor was Daniel's exhortation to King Nebuchadnezzar to redeem his sins fruitless. He could expect some pardon even if he had suffered punishment. Again, although not a day was taken off the seven years, it was a great step if the king should humble himself before God in time, so that he might be capable of obtaining the promised pardon. For in that a definite time had been fixed, or at least a time had been indicated by the prophet, it was a great help to the king in wishing to entreat his judge if he had already prepared himself to obtain pardon.

Hence, this teaching is useful in every way, since the same thing is true for us. Although we must be prepared for God's chastisements, yet there is no little or common alleviation in miseries when we so subject ourselves to God that we are convinced that he will on the contrary be favourable to us because he sees our displeasure, because he sees that we detest our sins from our hearts.

Grant, almighty God, that we may learn to bear all adversities patiently and know that, so often as we are afflicted in this world, you are exercising the office of judge against us, so that in this way we may forestall your vengeance and condemn ourselves with true humility and, trusting in your mercy, may always flee to you, relying on the Mediator whom you have given to us, your only-begotten Son, and thus we may seek pardon from you, yet so that we practise true penitence, not in empty and useless inventions but in true and serious proofs — that we may cherish true love and faithfulness among us and in this way bear witness also to the fear of your name, so that you may truly be glorified in us by the same Christ our Lord. Amen.

Lecture 21

28 *All this was fulfilled* [or, 'lighted'] *upon King Nebuchadnezzar.*
29 *At the end of twelve months* [that is, 'After twelve months'] *he was walking in the royal palace which is in Babylon.*
30 *The king spoke and said, 'Is not this the great Babylon, which I have built into the home of the kingdom* [that is, "that it may be the royal seat"] *in the strength of my power, and in the worth* [or, "excellence"] *of my glory?'*
31 *The word* [was] *still on the lips of the king* [that is, 'When the word was still on the lips of the king'] *a voice fell from heaven* [that is, 'came down', or 'fell down'], *'They say to you, King Nebuchadnezzar,* [your] *kingdom has removed* [or, "departed"] *from you.*
32 *And they shall cast you out from men, and your dwelling with the beasts of the field; they will make you taste grass like cattle* [or, "they will feed you with grass like cattle"]. *And seven times shall pass over you until you learn that the Most High* [is] *the ruler in the kingdom of men, and that he gives it to whom he will.'*

After Nebuchadnezzar declared that Daniel was the messenger of God's imminent judgment, he further says in what way God would execute the judgment he had threatened through the prophet. He speaks in the third person, but we know that change of person occurs very frequently in the Hebrew and Chaldaean languages. Then, the king does not tell Daniel all he had said but only gives a summary. Thus it is that as he now introduces the king as the speaker, he goes on to speak in his own person. There is nothing to worry us in this diversification, for the meaning is not obscure. In the first verse Nebuchadnezzar says that the dream which Daniel had explained had not been in vain. So he shows from its accomplishment that it was a heavenly oracle; for dreams vanish away, as we know. But because God fulfilled in his own time what he had shown the King of Babylon by a dream, it makes it plain that it was not an extravagant nightmare but a sure revelation of the future punishment which threatened the king.

He also expresses the manner of it. Daniel says that when a year had passed and the king was walking in his palace, he boasted of his greatness; and at that moment a voice fell down from heaven which repeated what he had already heard in the dream. Afterwards he relates how he would be expelled from human society and live for a long time with the brute beasts, so as to differ nothing from them.

As for the words: because מהלך, *mehallech,* is put here, some reckon that he was walking on the roof of his palace, which gave him a view over all the parts of the city. For we know that Orientals walk on the roofs of their dwellings. But I do not interpret it so subtly, for the prophet seems to mean nothing more than that the king was then at leisure and was enjoying delightful thoughts of his greatness. In the rest of the passage there is no obscurity.

Now I come to the substance of it. Some think that Nebuchadnezzar was touched with repentance when he had been taught about God's wrath, and that therefore the time of punishment was deferred. But this does not seem probable to me. I rather incline to another view, that God withheld his hand until the end of a year so that the king's pride might be the more inexcusable. For he had to be as frightened by the voice of the prophet as if God himself had thundered from heaven — nay, had struck him like lightning. He does not show any change at all. Of course, I do not deny that he might have been terrified at the first announcement; that I leave undecided. However that may be, I do not think that God spared him for a time because he gave some sign of repentance. He sometimes indulges the reprobate, I admit, if he sees them humbled.

A remarkable enough example is set before us in King Ahab. He never repented from his heart; but when he pardoned the king, ungodly and obstinate in his malice as he was, God was wanting to show how greatly penitence pleases him.[1] The same could be said of Nebuchadnezzar if Scripture had conveyed it. But, so far as we can gather from the prophet's words, Nebuchadnezzar persisted in his pride until his carelessness reached its full measure. For it was intolerable that, after God had threatened him, the king should still be so proud; it is a monstrous insensibility that he could be unconcerned even had he lived for a hundred years after hearing the threatening. In short, I think that although Nebuchadnezzar already understood that an awful and horrifying punishment was imminent, yet, in spite of being terrified at the time, he did not lay aside the pride and haughtiness of his mind. Meanwhile that prediction

1. Mg., 1 Ki. 21:29, i.e., 21:27-29.

could seem empty; and it is probable that over a long time what he had heard vanished from the king's memory, because he thought he had escaped — the ungodly are wont to abuse God's tolerance, and so heap up to themselves a store of heavier vengeance, as Paul says in Romans 2.[2] Therefore it could be that he made light of the prediction and so became more and more hardened.

However that may be, nothing else can be gathered from the context than that the prophet's warning was in vain at this time; worse, that the oracle by which Nebuchadnezzar had been called to repentance was in vain. If there had been the slightest trace of sanity in him, he would surely have fled to the mercy of God; he would have pondered how he had provoked God's anger in so many ways; he would have devoted himself entirely to the services of love; as he had exercised oppressive tyranny towards all, so he would show zeal in benevolence, according to the prophet's exhortation. This he is so far from doing that he goes on disgorging those empty boasts that show that his mind was swelling with pride and at the same time with contempt for God.

A certain space of time is noted here. From this it is apparent that God suspends his judgments in case those who seem to be completely incurable may perhaps repent; but reprobates abuse God's kindness and indulgence because they become even more determined when they think that God has retired from his office of judge when he takes no notice for a time.

At the end of twelve months, therefore, *the king was walking in his palace. He spoke and said.* This double expression signifies that the king spoke from, so to say, premeditated pride. For the prophet could simply have said, 'The king said'; but in fact he says, 'He spoke and said'. I know that it was customary for the Hebrew and Chaldaean languages to join these words together, but in this place I think the repetition is emphatic, that the king then, as it were, vomited forth what he had already taken and, so to say, digested in his mind.

'Is not this the great Babylon which I have built as a royal palace, and that in the strength of my power? and which I have built for the excellence of my splendour?' In these words we do not see any open blasphemy which would be so offensive to God. But we must consider that the king spoke like this to claim everything for himself as if he were in the place of God. And this can also be inferred from the words: *'Is not this',* he says, *'great Babylon?'* He boasts of the greatness of his city, as if like the Giants he wanted to set it in opposition to heaven. *'Which I',* he says. The pronoun here seems to me to be emphatic — *'which I have built, and that in the strength of my power',* he says. We see how he despoils God of all honour and claims it all for himself.

Yet before I go any further we must see why he says that Babylon was built by him. For all the historians agree that the city was built by Semiramis. Now, much later, Nebuchadnezzar sings his own praise as the builder of the

2. Rom. 2:4-5.

city. But the solution is easy. For we know that earthly kings use any way they can to undermine the glory of others, so that they may alone be pre-eminent and acquire an undying name. In particular, when they make some change in buildings or palaces or cities, they want to appear as the initial builders and so blot out the memory of those by whom the foundations had been laid. Thus it is likely that Babylon had been improved and elaborated by King Nebuchadnezzar; and so he transferred all the glory to himself, whereas the larger part should have been ascribed to Semiramis, or Ninus. This is the way tyrants talk, that is, the way tyrants often and commonly use, when they steal the praise that belongs to others.

'*I built*', he says, '*in the strength of my hand.*' Now it is easy to see why God was displeased at this boasting of the King of Babylon — that is, at this sacrilegious boldness in saying that the city had been built by his strength. But God shows that the praise belonged to him; and deservedly, for, 'Except the Lord build the city, the watchman watches but in vain.'[3] Although, therefore, men labour strenuously in the building of their cities, it is no good unless God himself is in charge of the work. So when Nebuchadnezzar exalted himself and opposed the force of his strength against God and his grace, it was a quite intolerable bragging. And this is why God was so inflamed against him.

Therefore let us know that this example proves what Scripture so often insists on, that God resists the proud, humbles their loftiness, and cannot bear their arrogance.[4] That God everywhere proclaims that he is the enemy of all the proud is confirmed to us by the present example, as if God were showing us an image of his judgment in a mirror. That is one thing.

And we must also note the reason why God declares war on all the proud — because we are not able to raise our heads on high, however slightly, without declaring war on God. For his is the rule, the power; in his hand is our life; we are nothing and can do nothing apart from him. Whoever, then, assumes this or that for himself, to that extent detracts from God. It is therefore not surprising if God should declare that he cannot bear the lofty haughtinesses of men, because they freely challenge him when they usurp even the least thing to themselves. It is true, of course, that they build cities by hard work and that kings who build cities or improve them deserve praise — but let God's praise remain undiminished. But when men elevate themselves and want their own strength to attract attention, they bury, so far as they can, the blessing of God. So it is necessary that God should summon their sacrilegious audacity to judgment, as we have already said.

Also the king's vanity is betrayed when he says, '*I have constructed it as a royal palace and for the excellence of my splendour*'. In these words he

3. Mg., Ps. 127:1.
4. Mg., Ps. 18:28 (i.e., 18:27); Jas. 4:6; 1 Pet. 5:5.

does not hide the fact that in all his building activity he had been thinking of his own glory, so that his fame might be declared to future generations. In sum, he wants to be famous in the world both in his own age and after death, so that beside him God may be nothing — as I have already said, all the proud aim at usurping God's place.

Now he goes on: *The word was still in the king's mouth when a voice fell down from heaven, 'They say to you, King Nebuchadnezzar, that your kingdom has departed from you.'* At this point God does not warn the King of Babylon either by the prophet's mouth or by the dream of the night, but he himself sends forth a voice from heaven. Because he had not tamed the king's swollen pride either by the oracle or by the prophet's explanation, a voice is now heard from heaven which will strike him with more terror. God is accustomed to deal thus with hardened and inflexible people. He denounces imminent punishment upon them by his prophets; but when he sees they are not touched or affected, he doubles the terror until the final execution follows — just as happened to this tyrant.

So, *the word was still in the king's mouth when a voice was heard.* We see that in one moment God checks the madness of those who inordinately exalt themselves. But it is not surprising that the voice was heard so suddenly, since King Nebuchadnezzar had been given time for repentance. In the form of the expression, *'They say to you'*, we should not be worried about who 'they' are. Some restrict it to angels; but I do not like this. It seems rather to be taken from the common idiom 'They say to you', that is, 'It is said to you', as if it were confirmed by public consent.

Therefore, *'They say to you, King Nebuchadnezzar'*. God does not simply call him by his name but prefixes the word 'King'; not for the sake of honour but in mockery and also to root out of the king all the flatteries he deceived himself with. 'You have been made drunk by your present splendour, with everyone worshipping you, and you have forgotten your frailty. But this royal majesty and power will not prevent God from laying you even with the ground. Because you were not willing to humble yourself freely, the kingdom is departed from you.' This was quite unbelievable, for the quiet possession of the kingdom lay in Nebuchadnezzar's hands. None was betraying any hostility; he had tamed all his neighbours; his monarchy was a terror to all nations. Yet now God declares, *'the kingdom is departed from you'*. And this strengthens the certainty of the oracle, so that Nebuchadnezzar may know that the time is already fulfilled and the punishment can no longer be delayed; for he had been trifling with God's indulgence.

He goes on, *'And you will be driven out from men, and your dwelling will be with the beasts of the field* (or, "wild beasts"); *they will make you taste grass like the cattle.'* Some think that Nebuchadnezzar was changed into an animal, but that is too harsh and absurd. So we are not to imagine some metamorphosis. But he was so rejected from human society that, save for his human shape, he differed nothing from the brute beasts; more, such a deformity took place in that banishment that he became a horrible sight — as we shall see later, all the hairs of his body increased so much that they grew like the feathers of an eagle, and his nails were like birds' claws. This is what he had in likeness to the animals; for the rest he kept his human shape.

It is uncertain whether God smote the king with madness so that he took flight and hid himself for a time, or whether he was cast out by an uprising and conspiracy of the nobles or even by the consent of the whole people. This is doubtful, because the history of those times is unknown to us. But either Nebuchadnezzar was seized by insanity, or while he was mad he left human society, or he was ejected, as often happens to tyrants. It was a memorable example, that he lived with the beasts for a time. And yet it is probable that he was quite stupefied; God left him his human shape but took away his reason, as will better appear from the context.

Therefore *'they will cast you out from the society of men; your dwelling will be with the wild beasts';* and also, *'they will make you taste grass like the cattle'.* That is, 'deprived of all pleasures, even of common and cheap food, you will find no other food than what cattle eat. You will therefore eat grass as if you were a brute beast.'

And *'seven times will pass over you'.* I spoke a little earlier of the 'seven times'. Some restrict it to days, but this is quite out of the bounds, not only of all reason, but also of likelihood. Nor do I expound it as months, for that would be too short a space. Therefore the opinion of those who extend it to seven years is more probable; for if Nebuchadnezzar had been banished through an uprising, he would not have been recalled so quickly. Moreover, since God wished to show in his person an example which should be remembered for ever, there is no doubt that he was driven out from community life for a long time. For if the punishment had been only seven months, we see that God's judgments would be ignored in the world. Therefore, that God might engrave this punishment more deeply in the hearts of all, he wished to protract it — not, I say, just for seven years (for I have earlier explained that a certain number is put for an uncertain) but for a very long time.

'Seven years shall pass over you', he says, *'until you know that the Most High rules in the kingdom of men.'* This is the purpose of the punishment, as we said before. For I will not repeat what I have said before. Yet it is to be borne in mind that God softens the harshness of the punishment, making it temporary. Moreover, it had a definite purpose, that Nebuchadnezzar might at last repent, for he could not without a taste of the rod — as the old proverb says about fools, they are never recalled to sanity except by harsh dealing. So to subject himself to God, King Nebuchadnezzar had to undergo the stripes, since he had received no profit from the holy warnings and even the heavenly

oracle. God does not deal like this with everyone. Therefore we have a special example of his kindness in making the punishment he inflicted on King Nebuchadnezzar useful and profitable. For the reprobate are more and more hardened against God; they are even carried away and excited to rage. That Nebuchadnezzar was chastened by God's hand for a time only, and that he repented at last and learned that God holds sway in all the earth, was by special grace.

He says, that *'God is the ruler in the kingdom of men'*. Nothing is harder than for tyrants to convince themselves that they are under God's power. Of course, they confess in the one word that they reign 'by his grace', but yet they reckon they received their realm either by power or by fortune, and that they keep it by their own defences, plans, resources. So far as they can, they reject God from the government of the world while they are puffed up with the false conviction that they keep their position by their own power or counsel. It was therefore no ordinary progress, when Nebuchadnezzar began to think that *'God is the ruler in the kingdom of men'*. Kings want to place him half-way, as it were, between themselves and the masses. They admit that the masses are lower than God, but they think they themselves are outside the common order and, for the sake of their caprices, invent the privilege for themselves of not being under the hand and rule of God. So this was, as I said, something uncommon that at last Nebuchadnezzar learned that *'God reigns on earth'*. Mostly tyrants shut him up in heaven and think he is satisfied enough with his own happiness without involving himself in human affairs. Therefore, *'that you may know he is the ruler'*.

Afterwards he adds the quality of that dominion — that *'God exalts whomsoever he pleases and casts down others'*. God is the ruler, not only in that by his universal providence he sustains the world, but because none can, save by his will, obtain rule. On some he girds the girdle, others he ungirds, as is said in the book of Job.[5] We should not therefore imagine a power of God which is idle, but we should join it with 'present action', as they say. Whether tyrants or godly and righteous kings obtain power is all governed by the secret counsel of God. Otherwise he would not be the King of the world.

He goes on:

33 *In that hour the word was fulfilled on King Nebuchadnezzar and he was cast out from men and ate grass like the cattle, and his body was washed with the dew of heaven, until his hair grew like an eagle's, and his nails as a bird's.*

The prophet concludes what he had said, that as soon as the voice came from heaven, Nebuchadnezzar was cast out from men. It could be that some

5. Mg., Jb. 12:18.

191

occurrence was the cause of the expulsion. But because that would be a dubious conjecture, I prefer to leave undecided what the Holy Spirit did not reveal. I only wanted briefly to suggest that when he boasted that Babylon had been built by the strength of his might, it could be that the nobles were disgusted at such an arrogant outburst. Or he may have spoken like this thinking that he was being plotted against or that an uprising was afoot. However that may be, God sent out his Word and at the same moment expelled King Nebuchadnezzar from human society. Therefore he says, *In that hour the word was fulfilled.* If a long time had intervened, the cause might have been ascribed to fortune or other inferior means. But when the voice and its effect were connected like that, the judgment is too plain for it to be obscured by men's malignity.

He says that *he was cast out and was fed with grasses,* so that he was no different from cattle. *His body was washed with rain,* because, of course, he lay out under the sky. We are also often wet with rain and no one can escape that in the open air; and often soaked travellers are called in to shelter themselves. But here the prophet is speaking of God's continual judgment, that he had no roof to withdraw under but slept in the fields. So he says, *he was washed with the dew of heaven.*

Until, he says, *his nails and hair grew like eagles' and birds'.* This place further confirms what has been said, that the seven times are to be explained as a long time; for his hair would not have grown so much in seven months nor would he have become so deformed. Hence the change the prophet describes shows clearly enough that King Nebuchadnezzar suffered for a long time. Nor could he have been humbled so quickly; for pride is untameable even in a man of the middle classes; how much more in a great monarch?

Afterwards he goes on:

34 *'And at the end of the days* [that is, "when that time was past"] *I, Nebuchadnezzar, raised my eyes to heaven and my understanding returned to me, and I blessed the Most High, and praised and glorified him who lives* [in] *the ages, because his power is the power of ages* [that is, "eternal"] *and his kingdom with age and age* [that is, "of perpetual duration"].'

Now the prophet again shows King Nebuchadnezzar speaking. He says that *'after that time had passed he raised his eyes to heaven'.* There is no doubt that he means the seven years. From the fact that he only then began to raise his eyes to heaven it is apparent how long the cure was for his disease, that is, pride. Just as the remedy is difficult and lengthy when some vital part is corrupt, almost wasted away, so, because pride is deeply infixed in men's hearts and invades their innermost being and infects everything within the soul, it is not easily eradicated — and this is important to note. We are also taught that God so worked within King Nebuchadnezzar by his Word that he did not produce the open effect of his grace at once. It was good for Nebuchadnezzar to be treated ignominiously for seven years (or the like time) and banished from human society. But he could not see this until God had opened his eyes. God often chastises us like this and little by little invites us and even prepares us for repentance; but we are not immediately aware of his grace.

But I am being too prolix, and I will defer the rest until tomorrow.

Grant, almighty God, since, even if we are nothing, we do not cease to please ourselves and are so blinded by vain confidence in ourselves and emptily boast of our power (which is nothing) — grant that we may learn to put off this perverted disposition and be so subjected to you that we may depend on your grace alone and learn that we stand and are upheld only by your power. And let us learn so to glorify your name that we may not only obey your Word with true and pure humility but also incessantly implore your aid and, with no trust in ourselves, may rest on the grace which is our sole support, until at last you shall gather us into your heavenly kingdom where we may enjoy that blessed eternity which you have gained for us by your only-begotten Son. Amen.

Lecture 22

I will now go on with the sentence that was interrupted yesterday.

Nebuchadnezzar says that *'he raised his eyes to heaven and his understanding returned to him'*. From this we gather that he was for a time out of his mind. Yet in my judgment he was not so senseless that he could not feel his evils, but was chafing at the bit and was like a madman. Others would have him a complete maniac. I will not argue about this; for me it is sufficient that he was out of his mind, so that he had something of the beast in him. But to me it is probable that there were some remnants of intelligence, so that he should feel some torment from his ruin. Yet he did not raise his eyes to heaven until God had caused him to come to himself. For God's chastisements do us no good unless he works inwardly by his Spirit, as was said yesterday. The expression is equivalent to saying that he began to think that God was a just judge. Although his disgrace tortured him for a time, he did not look at the hand smiting him, as is said elsewhere.[1] So he began to acknowledge that God is the avenger of pride, after that prefixed time of which we spoke had elapsed. But they raise their eyes to heaven who at the same time lower their eyes to earth. Nebuchadnezzar ought to have been, as it were, stirred up from his lethargy to rise to the God he had forgotten. He ought also at the same time to have prostrated himself on the earth, because he had now received the wages of his pride. He had dared to lift up his head above the human condition when he snatched to himself what belonged to God alone. He did not 'raise his eyes to heaven' in vain confidence, as he did earlier when he was drunk with the splendour of his monarchy, but he so regarded God that he was cast down and prostrate in mind.

1. Mg., Is. 9:13.

194

Afterwards he adds, *'and I blessed the Most High, and praised and glorified the one who lives for ever'*. This change shows that the chief cause of the punishment inflicted on King Nebuchadnezzar was that he despoiled God of his rightful honour. For here he describes the fruit of his repentance. If this attitude of blessing God flowed from repentance, it follows that Nebuchadnezzar was sacrilegious before in robbing God of his legitimate honour and wanting to exalt himself into his place, as also has been said.

And from this we must learn what it is truly to praise God; that is, when we are reduced to nothing and acknowledge and are convinced that all things lie in his will and that (as we shall see later) he is the governor of heaven and earth, so that his will stands as law and as reason and as the complete rule of righteousness. For we might sing the praises of God at the top of our voices; but it will be mere pretence. For none praises him sincerely and from the heart save he who ascribes to him all the things which we shall see afterwards.

And first Nebuchadnezzar says, *'Because his power is eternal power'*, he says, *'and his kingdom with age and with age'*. In the first place he here confesses that God is the eternal King, because he is great. For to this perpetuity he contrasts the frailty which is in human beings. Sometimes even the highest, the monarchs with the greatest power, have no stability. Not only are they liable to changes of fortune (as the profane commonly call them), or rather, dependent on the will of God, but also they just melt away in their vanity. We see the whole world tossed about, so to say, like a rough sea. If there is peace in one part or in many, yet some new and unexpected change can happen in a moment, something quite unlooked for. As a storm can at once blow up in a calm and serene sky, so also we see the like happening in human affairs. Since this is so, there is no firm condition on earth; monarchies especially are shaken by violent agitations. What is here declared by King Nebuchadnezzar is therefore perpetual; that God is αὐτοκράτωρ[2] *[autokratōr]* and by himself holds his rule, which is therefore out of all danger of change. This is the first thing.

Now he goes on:

35 *'And all the inhabitants of the earth are counted as nothing, and he does according to his will in the host of heaven and* [in] *the inhabitants of the earth; and there is none that may check his hand* [or, "that may abolish". מחא, *meha*, signifies both "to wipe out" and "to check"], *and may say to him, "What have you done?"* [or, "Why have you acted thus?"].'

Now the opposite clause is added, to complete the antithesis. For although it follows that there is nothing firm or solid in men when that principle

---

2. αὐτοκράτωρ: absolute ruler.

is active (namely, that God is the eternal King), yet few reason like this. All will say they agree that God has a firm and perpetual state. Yet they do not descend into themselves, to consider their frailty seriously. Unmindful of their position, they defy God himself. The added explanation is necessary — after Nebuchadnezzar has praised God that his power is eternal, he adds on the other side *'all the inhabitants of the earth are counted as nothing'*. כלה, *kela,* some think to be a unique word and take it for something finished, for כלה, *kala,* is 'to finish' or 'to complete'; it also sometimes means 'to consume'; from this they think the word is taken — that men are reckoned according to their measure, but God is immeasurable. But that is harsh. The more accepted opinion is that ה, *he,* is put here for א, *aleph;* so that Nebuchadnezzar is saying that men are reckoned as nothing, that is, before God. Now we see how well these two clauses fit together — God is the eternal King; but men are nothing. For if anything is ascribed separately to them, it is to that extent taken away from the supreme power and rule of God. It therefore follows that God's right will not be maintained until all mortals have been reduced to nothing. Although men make themselves very important, Nebuchadnezzar here declares, by the moving of the Spirit, that they are nothing — that is, before God. The only reason why they so highly exalt themselves is that they are blind in their darkness. But when they are dragged to the light they feel their own οὐδένειαν [*oudeneian*], that is, that they are completely 'nothing'. But whatever we are depends on God's grace, which moment by moment sustains us and adds new strength. Therefore, our part is to do nothing but subsist in God. For at the same time that he should withdraw his hand and the power of his Spirit, we vanish away. Therefore we are something — but in God. In ourselves we are nothing.

Now he goes on, *'God does according to his will in the host of heaven and the inhabitants of the earth.'* It might seem absurd that God is said to act according to his will, as if there were no moderation or fairness or rule of righteousness in him. But we must hold what I have said elsewhere, that men are ruled by laws because their will is perverted and is carried without moderation hither and thither by its desires. But God is the law for himself, because his will is most perfect righteousness. Therefore, so often as Scripture sets before us God's power and bids us be content with it, it is not attributing a tyrannical rule to God, as the ungodly slanderously say. But we never cease to oppose God and set our reason against his secret counsels and so bring a case against him, as if his actions which we do not approve of were not just and wise. Therefore, that his Holy Spirit may check this audacity, God declares that he does all things according to his will. Let us therefore remember when mention is made of God, that nothing perverted or unrighteous can have any place in him. His will is not carried away by desires but is supreme righteousness. Since this is so, let us also remember how great and how unbridled and stubborn is our boldness in daring to burst out and make this or that objection against God. From this it follows that this doctrine which bridles us with modesty is necessary — the doctrine that God does all things according to his will; as also it is said in the Psalm, 'Our God is in heaven; he does whatever he will.'[3]

Now from this statement we gather that nothing happens by chance but whatever happens in the world depends on the secret providence of God. Nor at this point should that disgusting distinction between God's permission and God's will be admitted. For we see that the Holy Spirit, who is the best master in the art of speaking, here expressly states two things: that God acts, and that he acts according to his will. But those vain speculators say that permission differs from will, as if God reluctantly yields what he wished not to do! Nothing is more ridiculous than to pin such weakness on God. Then he adds the efficacy of the acting. Therefore, *'God does what he will'*, says Nebuchadnezzar. And he is not speaking from carnal sense but by the moving of the Spirit, as was said. He is therefore to be listened to as if he were a prophet sent from heaven.

Now, therefore, let us hold this fast — the world is so administered by the secret providence of God that nothing happens but what he has commanded and decreed, and that he should deservedly be reckoned the author of all things. Some object that this seems absurd and that God is the author of sin if nothing happens save by his will, more, if it is his own work. But this calumny is easily refuted, because God works in a different way from men. For when someone sins, God is at work there in his own way; but that is far different from that person's way; because God is executing his judgment (as he is said to blind and to harden). When, therefore, God commands the reprobate or the devil he sentences them to be cast into every kind of licence. When God acts like that, he is executing his judgment. But the one who sins is deservedly guilty; nor can he implicate God as an accomplice in his crime. Why? Because God has nothing in common with him, so far as the reason for sinning is concerned. So we see that what many think are contradictions agree very well: God governs by his will whatever takes place on earth; yet he is not the author of sin. Why? Because he so uses the devil and all the reprobate as always to be the just Judge. The cause may not always be apparent to us; but the principle must be held that supreme power is in God's hands, and therefore it is not right to argue against his judgments, even if they have an appearance of incongruity.

Hence it goes on consistently, *'there is none that may check his hand or that may say to him, "Why have you done this?"'* When Nebuchadnezzar says that none can check God's hand, he is deriding the madness of those who do not hesitate to rise up against God. If they could, they would lift up their finger

3. Mg., Ps. 115:3.

to check his hand; and even when they are convinced of their weakness they continue in their fury. Nebuchadnezzar rightly shows how ridiculous their madness is when they exalt themselves inordinately and want to check God or to enclose him within their own limits, or forge chains to bind him. When men break out like this in sacrilegious passion, they are deservedly laughed at. And this is the drift of the words that we read here in Daniel.

Afterwards he adds that *'none says, "Why have you done this?"'* We know how free tongues are with their utter impudence, for hardly one in a hundred will keep himself in the modest course of ascribing glory to God and confessing that he is just in his works. But here Nebuchadnezzar is not considering what usually happens among men but what is right. He says therefore that God cannot be corrected (justly, that is), since, however the reprobate may prate, their futile arguing falls of itself, because it is supported by no reason, it has not even any colour of truth. The sum is that God's will stands as our law, because we quarrel against him in vain; and because, if we permit ourselves so much licence, and if our madness bursts out into wanting to contend with God, we shall be unsuccessful. For God is justified in his judgments, and so every human mouth will be stopped.[4] This is the sum.

But we must note this insertion: *'God's will shall be done in the host of heaven and in the inhabitants of the earth.'* By 'the host of heaven' I do not understand, as in some places in Scripture, sun, moon, and stars, but the angels, and even devils (who can be called heavenly without absurdity in respect of their origin; and we also know they are princes of the air). Therefore Daniel means that angels, as well as devils and men, are governed by the will of God; and although the ungodly rush on intemperately, they are held back by a secret bridle and cannot follow the dictates of their desire. God is therefore said 'to do both in the host of heaven and in men whatever he wishes', because he has the angels obedient to him (namely, the elect angels), but devils are forced to obey his will even if they strive to do the opposite. Of course, we know that devils are adversaries in every way; but they are at length forced to yield obedience to God, not voluntary, but coerced.

As God acts in angels and demons, so also in the inhabitants of the earth. He governs some by his Spirit; that is, the elect, who afterwards are regenerated by his Spirit, are so led by him that his righteousness truly shines in all their actions. He also acts in the reprobate, but in another manner. For he drags them headlong by the hand of the devil; he also drives them by his secret power, strikes them with a spirit of giddiness, blinds them and casts them into a reprobate mind, and hardens their hearts to obstinacy. See how God does all things according to his will in men and angels!

Now there is also a difference in the mode of acting so far as external

4. Mg., Ps. 51:6, i.e., 51:4.

condition goes. For God raises this one on high buts casts down that. So we see the rich suddenly become poor. He raises others from the dung-hill and they ascend to the highest ranks of honour.[5] The irreligious call it a game of fortune. But the government of God's providence, although incomprehensible, is completely fair. God therefore so acts according to his will in men and angels. But the interior action is put first, as we have said.

Now he goes on:

36 *'And in that time* [although זמנא, *zimna,* is properly a prefixed and determined time] *my understanding returned to me and to the excellence of my kingdom* [namely, "I returned". It is a defective locution]. *My glory and my dignity returned to me, and my counsellors and my nobles sought me out; and I was confirmed in my kingdom, and my dignity was the more increased* ["added"] *to me.'*

Here Nebuchadnezzar explains at greater length what he had already briefly touched on — that he had recovered his sanity — and so he commends God's mercy in being content with a moderate and temporary chastisement, and that he had at last stretched out his hand to him and from beast formed him again into man. (Not that he had been changed into a beast, as was said, but because he had been cast into the ignominy of being like the wild beasts and feeding with them. That deformity was so horrifying that his restitution could well be called a new creation. And so Nebuchadnezzar had good reason so highly to celebrate this grace of God.)

'In that time my understanding returned to me.' He had said this once; but intelligence and reason is such an inestimable benefit of God that Nebuchadnezzar emphasizes his words, confessing that he had experienced a singular grace of God, in being restored to sanity.

At the same time he adds that *'when he was returned to the glory and excellence of his kingdom, he was sought out by his counsellors and nobles'.* The full story is not known; the memorial of those times is buried. But it is probable that in the end the princes of the kingdom were turned towards clemency and wished to receive again their banished king. We do not say that they did this on purpose; for God made use of them in such a way that they did not know that they were carrying out what he had determined. They had heard the voice from heaven, *'It is said to you, King Nebuchadnezzar, "Behold, your kingdom is taken from you, etc."'* This ought to have been commonly known and acclaimed everywhere. But we know how easily forgetfulness creeps over people, when God has spoken. So although the princes did not know they were employed on God's work, they summoned their king back

5. Mg., Ps. 113:7.

199

again. In this way he returned to the dignity of his kingdom; in fact, a greater dignity than before was added to him.

Finally he goes on:

37 *'Now I, Nebuchadnezzar, praise and extol and glorify the King of heaven; for all his works are truth and his ways judgment, and he can humble those who walk in pride* [that is, "he is powerful to humble the proud"].'

This is the close of the statement. Nebuchadnezzar joins a frank confession of his guilt with the praises of God. For what he says of the proud he is without doubt applying especially to himself, as if he were saying, 'God wanted to set me up as a remarkable proof for all to know that the proud are humbled by his hand. I was swollen with pride; God corrected it with such a terrible punishment that my example ought now to profit everyone.' I said that King Nebuchadnezzar does not here simply thank God but at the same time confesses he was guilty and had undergone such harshness deservedly, because his pride could not have been corrected by a lighter remedy.

But first he says, *'I praise, extol, and glorify the King of heaven.'* This accumulating of words proceeded no doubt from his strong emotion. At the same time an antithesis is to be supplied from the principle which we saw before, that God is never praised aright but when men's disgrace is uncovered; God is never extolled aright but when their loftiness is cast down; God is never glorified but when men lie prostrate, as if overwhelmed by their shame. So in this place, when Nebuchadnezzar 'praises, extols, and glorifies God', he at the same time confesses, as before, that he and all other mortals are nothing, merit no praise, but are worthy of all shame.

Afterwards he adds, *'because all his works are truth'.* Here קשוט, *kesot,* is taken for 'uprightness' or 'integrity'. For דיני אמץ, *dine emez,* are called 'true judgments'; but here it refers to equity. So *'all the works of God are truth',* that is, 'are integrity'; as if he were saying that there is nothing blameworthy in God's works. Then follows the explanation: *'all his ways are judgment'.* Hence we see that here perfect righteousness is praised in God. But this should be referred to the person of Nebuchadnezzar, as if he were saying, 'God did not deal with me over-strictly; I have no quarrel with him, or grumble at him for being too severe with me. I confess that whatever punishment I undergo has been my due.' Why? *'Because all the ways of the Lord are judgment';* that is, supreme rectitude is in them. Then, *'all his works are truth';* that is, no unfairness is found in them, nothing underhanded; everywhere supreme righteousness shines. So we see that in these words Nebuchadnezzar condemns himself with his own mouth when he declares God's righteousness in all his works. This generalization (as they call it) does not prevent Nebuchadnezzar from openly and freely presenting himself as guilty at God's judgment seat;

but the expression has more force when he is admonished by his own example to confess in general that God is just and right and true, whatever he does.

And this is noteworthy, because it is not so hard for many to celebrate God's righteousness and rectitude when they are treated as they would wish; but if God begins to deal with them more harshly they spew out their venom and start quarrelling with God and make him out to be unjust or cruel. When Nebuchadnezzar here without reservation confesses, even after being so severely chastened, that God is righteous and true in all his works, his confession is not feigned. What he said had to come from the bottom of his heart, for he had experienced the rigour of the divine judgment.

At the end he adds, *'he can humble those who walk in pride'*. Here Nebuchadnezzar lays his disgrace open even more; for, with the punishment known to all, he was not ashamed to acknowledge his guilt before all the world. Just as God had wished his madness to be hateful everywhere when he published such a horrifying example of punishment in him, so now Nebuchadnezzar comes forward and declares that he had deserved that severe punishment because he had been too proud. And here we see that God's power is joined with righteousness, as was said earlier. He is not attributing to God any lawless tyranny. For after Nebuchadnezzar had confessed that all the ways of God are judgment he at once adds that he himself had been proud. Therefore without doubt he was exposing his shame before men that he might glorify God.

And this is the true way of praising God, not only when we confess that we are nothing but also when we reckon up our faults. Not only do we inwardly acknowledge that we are completely guilty before him, but also, when there is need, we declare the same among mortals. And when he uses the word 'humble', it should be referred to external humiliation. For Nebuchadnezzar was humbled when God cast him out into the woods to lead a life in common with the wild beasts. But he was humbled also in another respect, that is, as one of the sons of God. So there is a twofold humbling; but Nebuchadnezzar is here referring to the former sort, that God prostrates and casts down the proud. This is one way of humbling; but such humbling will do no good unless God afterwards controls us in a spirit of mildness. And so here Nebuchadnezzar is not including the grace of God, even though it deserved extraordinary record and proclamation; nor does he put down in this edict everything that could be demanded of a godly man who had been educated in the school of God; but by ascribing supreme power to God, he shows that he had greatly profited under his chastisements; he also praises his righteousness and rectitude and also confesses his own guilt and testifies that his divinely imposed punishment had been just.

Grant, almighty God, since the disease of pride, by which we were corrupted in our father Adam, is so infixed in us all, grant, I say,

201

that we may learn to examine ourselves inwardly and be duly displeased with ourselves; also, that we may feel that there is no wisdom, no uprightness save from you alone, so that we may flee to your mercy, first admitting that we are adjudged to eternal death, but then, relying on your goodness which you condescend to offer us through your gospel, relying also on the Mediator whom you have given to us, we may not hesitate to flee to you and to call upon you as Father, that, regenerate by your Spirit, we may walk in true humility and modesty, until at last you raise us to that heavenly kingdom which you have prepared for us by the blood of your only-begotten Son. Amen.

Lecture 23

CHAPTER 5

1 *Belshazzar the king made a great feast for a thousand of his nobles and drank wine before the thousand.*

Daniel here relates the story of what happened when Babylon was captured. But meanwhile he leaves it to his readers to consider God's judgment, which the prophets had foretold even before the people had gone into exile. Here he is not using a prophetic style, as we shall see presently, but is satisfied with a straightforward narration. But the usefulness of the story can be learned from what follows; and so it is our task now to reflect on the value of the story for the edification of faith and the fear of God.

In the first place, we must notice the time when Belshazzar celebrated this feast. Seventy years had now passed since Daniel and his friends had been carried into exile. For although afterwards Nebuchadnezzar is called the father of Belshazzar, yet it is certain enough that Evil-Merodach was between them. But Evil-Merodach reigned for twenty-three years. Some even reckon two kings before Belshazzar; they put in Regassar and afterwards Labassardach besides. These two make up eight years. Metasthenes[1] is the authority for this and many follow him. But it is certain that Nebuchadnezzar the Great (who led away Daniel and who was the son of Nebuchadnezzar the First) reigned for forty-five years. Some transfer two of these years to the reign of his father. However that may be, he held royal power for forty-five years. Now add on twenty-three years for Evil-Merodach, and it comes to sixty-eight years.

1. See p. 20, n. 5.

Belshazzar reigned for eight years. So we see that seventy-two years had passed from the time when Daniel was taken into captivity. Metasthenes allows thirty years for the reign of Evil-Merodach; then the eight years are added to him. Thus it would be more than eighty years. And this is quite probable. Yet Metasthenes seems incorrect in differentiating kings when only the names were different. For Herodotus[2] does not call the king we are talking about Belshazzar. He calls his father Labynetus and gives the same name to Belshazzar. It would therefore seem that Metasthenes was deceived about the names. But so far as the reckoning of the time goes, I freely accept what he says — that Evil-Merodach reigned for thirty years.

When we are dealing with the seventy years which Jeremiah signified, we ought not to begin at Daniel's exile, nor yet from the fall of the city, but with the calamities between the first victory of King Nebuchadnezzar (which he won while his father was alive), and the burning and destruction of the temple and city. For, as we have said elsewhere, he returned to his own land lest some uprising should occur in his absence. So, to get the seventy years in which God willed to end the captivity of his people, we shall have to make the reign of Evil-Merodach longer than twenty-three years. Yet there is little difference in actual fact. For soon after Nebuchadnezzar returned he carried off the king, although the city was still unharmed. But although the temple was yet standing, God inflicted on the people a very heavy punishment; it was like an ultimate disaster, or at least not far short of it. However that may be, we see that Belshazzar celebrated this feast when already the time of liberation was imminent.

And here we must consider God's providence, which governs every second of time, that the ungodly may, when the time of their ruin is ripe, freely run headlong into ruin. Thus it happened to this ungodly king. It showed amazing stupidity that he should prepare a splendid supper, full of delights, even when the city was besieged. For Cyrus had a long time before begun to besiege the city with a great army. The unhappy place was already half captured. And yet as if in contempt of God, he put on a sumptuous feast for a thousand guests. From this we may rightly guess how noisy it was and how extravagant the repast. For if one has only ten or twenty guests, there will be a lot of organizing and turmoil — if one is going to do it in style. But with all the royal preparations and a thousand nobles, the king's wife and his concubines — with such a huge crowd gathered together, he would have needed to seek the food and delicacies from far and wide. This could seem unbelievable. But Xenophon,[3] although he romances about many things and does not pay heed to seriousness or historical reliability, because, as Cyrus's public orator,

2. Mg., Herodotus, 1, i.e., *History* 1:74, 77, 188.
3. Xenophon, *Cyropaedia* 7:5:13.

he wants to sing his praises — although he trifles in many things, yet in this matter he had no reason or occasion for lying, and he says that they had a corn supply that could last the siege of Babylon for ten or many more years. And he also rightly compares Babylon to a region in itself. For the size of the town was so great as to be unbelievable. Of course, it was also very heavily populated; but since they brought the corn supply from the whole of Asia, it is not surprising if the Babylonians had a store of food that could sustain them for a long time, even if they were cut off.

Nevertheless, there is something abnormal and terrible in this feast. That the king, who ought to have been on guard himself, or at least to have posted sentries lest the city should be surprised, should at that time have given his mind to feasting, as if he enjoyed a settled peace with no danger from external enemies! Yet he was at war with as energetic a man as ever lived. Cyrus both possessed remarkable intelligence and also far surpassed all others in speed of action. When Belshazzar was being attacked so fiercely, his indolence in celebrating a feast is astounding. Xenophon says that that was a feast-day.[4] The Jews' view that the Chaldaeans were victorious over the Persians is worthless. For Xenophon, who is reliable in this respect (that is, when he is not telling lies on behalf of Cyrus, he is a most serious author and worthy of credit; but when he wants to praise Cyrus, he knows no bounds) — but in this respect he is a good historian, when he says that the Babylonians held it as an annual solemn feast-day.

He also tells how Babylon was captured — by his generals Gobryas and Gabatha. For Belshazzar had castrated the one to humiliate him and had killed the son of the other while the father was still living.[5] Hence the one burned with desire for revenge for the death of his son, the other for his ignominy; and they conspired together. So it happened that Cyrus diverted many streams of the Euphrates and Babylon was unexpectedly captured.

But we must note that it was captured twice; for otherwise the prophecies cannot be believed. When the prophets threaten Babylon with the vengeance of God, they say that its enemies will be very fierce, not looking for gold or silver but with an appetite for human blood; they also recount the most dreadful outrages, which are wont to be perpetrated in war.[6] But nothing of this sort happened when Babylon was taken by Cyrus. When, however, the Babylonians shook off his yoke and freed themselves from Persian rule, Darius recovered the city through the actions of Zopyrus, who mutilated his body and pretended he had been so cruelly used by the king that he would betray the city. It is on that occasion, we gather, that the Babylonians were treated so harshly; three thousand nobles were crucified. And what became of the common folk, when

4. *Cyropaedia* 7:5:15.
5. *Cyropaedia* 4:6:2-7; 5:2:28.
6. Mg., Je. 50:42, i.e., 50:41–51:35.

no less than three thousand nobles were eliminated, all strung up on gallows, even crucified? So it is quite apparent that the punishment on the Babylonians was temporarily delayed, although they were in the meanwhile subject to foreign rule and were treated badly and insolently by the Persians, reduced, in fact, to slave labour. The use of arms was prohibited and they were taught from the first day to serve Cyrus and dared not take to the sword.

It is necessary briefly to mention these things, so as to learn that human affairs are governed by God's hidden judgment, that he casts down the reprobate when their punishment is ready. Of this we have a clear example here in King Belshazzar. The time of liberation foretold by Jeremiah was come,[7] the seventy years were over, Babylon was besieged. Now the Jews could lift up their heads with good hope, for Cyrus's coming had happened beyond all belief. Suddenly he had irrupted from the mountains of Persia, at that time a backward nation. So when Cyrus had suddenly come like a whirlwind, the change could give some hope to the Jews; but when he had so long laid low, so to say, while the city was being besieged, they could have been cast down. Now, when Belshazzar is feasting with his nobles, it seems as if Cyrus could cast him out as easily as playing games, as they say. But in the meanwhile the Lord was not sitting idly in heaven. He blinded the mind of this ungodly king, so that he gave himself up to punishment of his own will. None betrays him; he offers himself. How did this happen, save because God had given him to his enemy? And that according to the decree which Jeremiah had proclaimed.[8] Although, therefore, Daniel tells a story, it is our task (as I said) to reflect on far greater things — that God, who had promised freedom to his people, now stretches out his hand from his secret place and fulfils what had been foretold by the prophets.

Now he goes on, that *King Belshazzar was drinking wine before the thousand.* Some of the rabbis say that he was competing with his thousand nobles to equal them all in intemperance in drinking. But this is quite ridiculous. When he says *he drank wine before the thousand,* it refers to the custom of the land. For it was rare for Chaldaean kings to hold feasts. They usually banqueted alone, like the kings of Europe nowadays. For they think that it enhances their dignity, if the table is prepared for only one. The Chaldaean kings had a similar arrogance. So when it is said *Belshazzar drank wine before the thousand,* something unusual is indicated: this solemn feast was outside the daily routine, and moreover, he held his nobles in such honour that he received them as his table companions. For the conjecture of some is rather weak that he drank wine openly because he usually got drunk without any witnesses. But *before* is to be taken as implying fellowship or society.

Let us go on:

7. Mg., Je. 25:11.
8. Mg., Je. 25:26.

2 *Belshazzar commanded* [literally, 'he said'. But here it means 'to command'], *in the taste* [or, 'savour'] *of wine, that they should bring the vessels of gold and silver* ['golden and silver'][9] *which Nebuchadnezzar his father had carried away* [or, 'taken out'] *from the temple which* [is] *in Jerusalem; that the king, his nobles, his wives, and his concubines might drink in them* [some translate it 'wife', because there was one chief wife, who was the sole companion of the king, and had the name of 'queen' given to her, as we shall see later].

Here King Belshazzar hastens his punishment. He furiously provokes God's wrath against himself as if he had grown bored with God's deferring his judgment. This is what I said, that when ruin threatens the house, the ungodly exalt the doors and gates, as Solomon says.[10] When, therefore, God intends to execute his judgment, he drives the ungodly on by a secret impulse so that they run to meet it as if of their own accord and bring themselves a swift destruction. This is what Belshazzar did. Carelessness was a sign of insensibility; and this in its turn was a sign of God's anger, to take time off for pleasures in all his troubles and in the midst of danger. But this blinding shows God's vengeance even more clearly; not satisfied with his own intemperance and his ill-timed pleasures, he openly declared war on God.

He commanded the golden and silver vessels which Nebuchadnezzar had removed to be brought to him. It seems that the vessels were stored in the treasury. Hence Nebuchadnezzar had never abused the vessels like this as long as he lived. Nor do we read that Evil-Merodach had done such a thing. But now Belshazzar sets out deliberately to insult God. For there is no doubt that he commanded the vessels to be brought for sport, to re-enact a triumph over the true God, as we shall see presently.

The prophet calls Nebuchadnezzar the father of Belshazzar, but we have already explained in what sense this is to be understood. It is common enough in all languages to call grandfathers and great-grandfathers and even great-great-grandfathers 'fathers'. So Belshazzar is called King Nebuchadnezzar's 'son' because he was sprung from his seed and was of his lineage. And we shall look at this later.

There are some who think it was Evil-Merodach who was smitten with that terrible malady that was recounted in the last chapter. And it could be that he also was called Nebuchadnezzar. But we are not compelled to accept their view. For it was too silly, when the word 'father' occurred, to jump immediately to that conjecture.

The prophet says *Belshazzar commanded this in the savour of wine.* טעם,

9. See on 2:32, above.
10. Mg., Pr. 17:16, i.e., 17:19.

taam, means 'to taste'; so there is no doubt he is talking about tasting. But, as this is metaphorically transferred to the understanding, some explain it that the wine drove him on and drunkenness usurped the place of reason and judgment. 'Night, and love, and wine', says one, 'are immoderate persuaders.'[11] But that exposition seems to me to be too forced. I simply take it that when Belshazzar was heated with wine, he ordered the vessels to be brought. And this is the commoner view.

When therefore the savour of wine prevailed — that is, when the wine had overcome the king's senses — *then he commanded the vessels to be brought.* And it is important to notice this, so as to learn to beware of all intemperance in drinking. We are only too prone to undertake and discharge all sorts of things as soon as the savour of wine disturbs our sense. Therefore, wine must be used soberly, that it may invigorate not only our body but also our mind and all our senses; and not that it may debilitate and weaken our bodies, far less that it may stupefy our senses. And this is more than usual, as it is declared in common proverbs — 'pride is born of drunkenness'.[12] Hence also the poets sang of a crowned Bacchus — for intemperate drinkers are uplifted and even the meanest think they are kings. So what will it be like with real kings, when they forget themselves and dream that they are not only kings of kings but even gods? This therefore is the vice the prophet meant to indicate when he said, *Belshazzar commanded in the savour of wine the vessels to be brought to him.*

Now he goes on:

3 *Then they brought the gold vessels* [he puts only 'gold', for it is probable that the most precious vessels were brought. It could be that silver vessels were also brought, but what the prophet expressed was more splendid] *which they had taken out* [he does not now say 'which Nebuchadnezzar had taken out', or, 'carried away', but transfers it to all the Babylonians in general. They had won the victory under this king's command and he had taken the spoils for himself. But in that all the Babylonians had been victorious, the prophet is now referring to them] *from the temple of the house of God, which* [was, or, 'which temple was'] *in Jerusalem.* [Here he expresses more than he had done a little before. He does not now say 'out of Jerusalem' but 'out of the temple of the house of God'.] *And the king drank in them, and his nobles and his wife* [or, 'wives' in the plural] *and his concubines.*
4 *They drank wine, and praised the gold and silver, bronze, iron, wood, and stone gods.*

11. Mg., Ovid, 1 *Amores Elegeia* 6, i.e., *Amores* 1:6:59.
12. Cf. Erasmus, *Adages* III.vii.53.

a. Reading *coronatum* ('crowned') for *cornutum* ('horned'). Bacchus was described variously as 'crowned' and 'horned'. The context here renders 'crowned' more probable.

Here the prophet shows more clearly and distinctly that the king insulted the true and only God when he ordered the vessels to be brought. For when they were brought, *they praised,* he said, *all their gold and silver gods.* That is, as an insult against the true God they praised their false gods as if they were giving them the thanks — just as Habakkuk also says,[13] as if without doubt they were sacrificing to their own industry, their own strength, as the prophet also says in the same place. But they covered the glory of the true God and praised their own gods. And this is also why the prophet expressly mentions that the vessels were taken *from the temple of the house of God.* For here he stresses the ungodliness of the king and his nobles in raising their horns against the God of Israel. An antithesis is therefore to be observed between the God who had commanded a temple to be built to him and sacrifices to be offered in Jerusalem, and the false gods. And when Belshazzar deliberately rose up against God he in fact fell sheer down into punishment. He not only tyrannously and cruelly oppressed the unhappy Jews, but he also enacted a triumph over their God, that is, over the Creator of heaven and earth. This madness hastened his final destruction. But this took place because the time of liberation was at hand. This is why I said that he was drawn by a secret impulse of God to a madness that would hasten the vengeance.

He says, *they drank wine and praised their gods.* The prophet is not ascribing their praising the gods to drunkenness, although he indirectly says that their impudence was increased by the wine. For if anyone had been at home and sober he would not so shamelessly have arisen against God. But since their hearts were dominated by ungodliness, their intemperance in drinking was an accessory, fanning it, as it were. This is therefore what the prophet seems to me to signify when he repeats that *they drank.* For he had said, *the king and the nobles drank, his wife and concubines.* Now a second time he emphasizes the same thing in almost the same words — *they drank.* But he adds, *they drank wine.* As if he were saying that their madness was the more kindled when they were roused by the heat of wine.

Then they praised the gods of silver, etc. The prophet here in a tone of insult speaks of *gold, silver, and bronze, and wood, and stone gods;* for we know that God has no affinity with gold or silver. Therefore his true likeness cannot be expressed in corruptible materials. This is why the prophet here says that all the gods worshipped by the Babylonians were *of gold, silver, bronze, and wood and stone.* It is, of course, quite true that the heathen were never so mad as to think God's essence was of gold or silver or stone; they call them only images of the gods. But because in their opinion the power and majesty of God was always enclosed under the stone and wood and gold and silver, it was right for the prophet to condemn their stupidity out of hand; for we know

13. Mg., Hab. 1:16.

209

how earnestly they think out subterfuges for their idolatry. And today the papacy is clear proof that the superstitious never lack a camouflage when they want to excuse their errors. So here the prophet does not allow those vain excuses by which the Babylonians and their like colour over their wickedness.

But he says that *their gods were gold and silver.* Why? Because although they confessed in word that the gods reign in heaven (for they received such a multitude and crowd of gods that the supreme deity was, so to say, wrapped up in darkness) — although, therefore, the Babylonians confessed that the gods live in heaven, yet they had recourse to statues and pictures. Therefore the prophet quite deservedly blames them because they worshipped gold and silver gods.

But when he says *then the vessels were brought,* it is apparent that this tyrant's servants obeyed even his worst commands; for without delay the vessels were produced from the treasury. Thus Daniel suggests that all the servants were ready for the king's will — to please a drunken man, almost a brute.

But at the same time he also shows how brief was the drunken exultation; for he says:

5 *In that hour the fingers of a man's hand came out and wrote opposite the lamp* [or, 'candelabra'. Some expound it as 'window'], *on the plaster of the wall* [others 'on the face'. But some prefer to take it as 'the whitewash', which is also probable. Therefore, 'on the plaster of the wall'] *of the king's palace; and the king saw the palm* [some call it 'knuckles'] *of the hand that wrote.*

Here Daniel begins to relate how things were quite reversed. In that very moment the king realized that something grievous and disastrous was imminent. Yet he did not immediately know what it was; only that God was showing some sign like a sinister omen, as the heathen were then wont to put it. God therefore gave a prelude in this way when he saw the king so inflamed in mad debauchery with his nobles.

So, *a man's hand appeared,* says the prophet. He calls it a man's hand from its likeness or shape. For it is certain it was not the hand of a man; but in that it had that form, he calls it a man's hand. And Scripture often uses this manner of speaking, especially in reference to external symbols. This is therefore a sacramental expression, so to say. For God himself wrote by his power, but he shows King Belshazzar a figure as of a man writing on the wall.

There came forth, therefore, *the fingers of a hand.* When he says that fingers came forth it greatly confirms the certainty of the miracle. For unless Belshazzar had seen this initial stage he might have imagined that the hand was put there by some trick. But when the wall was completely blank before and then suddenly a hand came into sight, it was easy to infer that the hand was a heavenly sign by which God wished to show something momentous to the king.

There came forth the fingers of a hand, he says, *and wrote opposite the candelabra,* or lamp. It is certain that this feast was held at night; and Babylon was captured in the middle of the night. Nor is it surprising that the feasting went on for a long time. For the intemperate keep no moderation and they are used to revelling. I admit that they did not feast in the middle of the night usually; but when they were celebrating some splendid and sumptuous feast they did not think daytime plenty sufficient unless they ate themselves nearly putrid (so to say).

Thus, *a hand appeared opposite the candelabra;* so it was the more conspicuous. And, says the prophet, 'the hand wrote on the plaster of the wall in the palace'. If anyone had told the king that the likeness of a hand had appeared, it could have been doubtful; but he says the king was an eyewitness. For God wished to terrify him, as we shall see soon. Therefore he set this spectacle before him.

The king perceived; the nobles perhaps not. Later we shall see that the king alone was struck with terror, although some began to share his trepidation. For when they saw his face changed and overcast with sadness, they also began to fear — although they all tried to cling to some comfort. God wanted somehow to summon the ungodly king to his judgment seat when the man's hand appeared in his sight. What he wrote — well, what he wrote we shall see in its place.

> *Grant, almighty God, since we are so prone to forgetfulness that we indulge ourselves too eagerly in fleshly pleasures, grant, I say, that each of us may forthwith recall himself to thoughts of your judgments, so that we may walk carefully as in your sight and may be frightened by your just judgments and not provoke you by our stubbornness and other faults, but that we may so subject ourselves to you that, raised and supported by your hand, we may go on in the course of your holy calling until at last you raise us to the heavenly kingdom which you have won for us by the blood of your only-begotten Son. Amen.*

Lecture 24

6 *Then the king's countenance was changed* [literally, 'form' or 'figure'. So, 'the king's countenance was changed'] *and his thoughts terrified him and the bands of his loins were loosened* [the Hebrews, and the Chaldaeans also, say 'hips' periphrastically] *and his knees knocked together.*

Here Daniel shows that the king was stricken with fear; nor should we think he was frightened for nothing. By many details he expresses that the king was disturbed, so that it is easy to see the case was serious. For he had to be so beaten that all should understand that God was, as it were, on his judgment seat and arraigned him as guilty. We said before (and Daniel also shows it) how overweening was the king's pride, and his carelessness was clear proof of his guilt. For when he should daily have been attending to the siege he was celebrating a solemn feast, as if at complete peace. From this it is apparent that a certain intoxication of the spirit had seized him, so that he did not even feel his evil. This is why God arouses him, more, why he shakes him in his drowsiness, because he could not return and be recalled to a sane mind in any ordinary way. But that he was so frightened could seem a good preparation for repentance. Yet he shows us the same thing in his person that was in Esau, who was not only a little sad when he saw himself disinherited, but with great weeping and lamentation sought a blessing from his father.[1] But it was too late. The same is now related of King Belshazzar.

But the details must be noted in order: Daniel says *the king's countenance was changed;* next, *the bands of his loins were loosed and he was disturbed,* or terrified, *by his thoughts;* finally he adds, *his knees knocked together.* (For

1. Mg., Gn. 27:34.

the word strictly means 'to strike against'.) The prophet shows the reality from the signs: King Belshazzar was terribly frightened at the vision which has been recounted. There is no doubt, as I said earlier, that this terror came by the impulse of God. For we know that the reprobate, even when God openly shows that he is taking his judgment seat, still remain senseless, unmoved by any fear. But God wished to affect the mind of this ungodly king, so that he could not plead ignorance as an excuse.

And it is to be observed, that God touches men's hearts in various ways — I speak not only of the reprobate but also of the elect. For we see some of the best of men slow and sluggish when God summons them to judgment. So that it is necessary to drive them with beating; for they will never come to God of their own accord. He could, of course, move their minds without violence; but he wishes to set before us as in a mirror what our slowness and sluggishness is like, for we shall never submit to his Word except reluctantly. Therefore he tames even his children with beatings when they do not profit by his Word alone. As for the reprobate, he often uncovers their obstinacy by sweetly inviting them before he undertakes the office of judge. And when this does no good, he threatens; when even threats are useless and quite ineffectual, he summons them to his judgment seat.

As for the Babylonian king, God had suffered Daniel to be silent. For the ingratitude or pride of the king had shut the door, and Daniel was not able to undertake and perform his duty of teaching, as he had been ready to do. Hence the King of Babylon was without a teacher. But God suddenly appeared as judge in the writing — of which something has already been briefly spoken, but there are still many things to be said in their place. However that may be, we see that King Belshazzar was not only warned by an outward sign of his imminent destruction, but also he was inwardly shaken up, so that he might realize that he had to do with God. For the reprobate often treat it all as a joke, as I have said, although God shows that he is their Judge. But he acted differently with King Belshazzar. He wanted him to be smitten with terror so as to be the more attentive to reading the writing. This terror was, as I said before, a preparation for repentance. But he fails in mid-course — something that we see happen with many who tremble at God's voice or at the signs of vengeance, as soon as he warns them, but die away soon after and fail to get the clear teaching that they need.

And Esau was a similar example.[2] He despised God's grace when he heard he was deprived (and that by God) of the promised inheritance. He regarded the blessing as a fairy-story until he felt that it was all too serious; then he began to lament, but to no purpose. King Belshazzar was troubled in the same way. Even at the end, as we shall see, when Daniel explained the

2. Mg., Gn. 25:33, i.e., 25:33-34.

writing to him, he was unmoved by the actual situation, but simply honoured Daniel with royal insignia. But it was useful for another purpose — God demonstrated his glory when the nobles were affected and the matter was revealed; and Darius, who captured the city along with Cyrus his son-in-law, understood that he had not won the victory by his own industry and power nor even because he was helped by the two satraps, Gobryas and Gabatha, but that the whole event was brought about by the power of God. So God shows as in a mirror that he is the avenger of his people, as he had promised seventy years before.

Now he goes on:

7 *The king shouted loudly that the magi, Chaldaeans, and astrologers should be brought in* [on these words we have spoken elsewhere]; *and the king spoke and said to the wise men of Babylon, 'Whoever shall read this writing and tell me its interpretation shall be clothed in purple and a chain of gold* [that is, "golden"] *upon his neck, and he shall rule as third in the kingdom.'*

The prophet relates that King Belshazzar sought a remedy for his anxiety. And from this we again infer that his mind was so deeply pierced that he felt he was unable to escape from God's hand. Otherwise he would not have so suddenly summoned the wise men in the middle of the feast. Again the prophet also says that *he shouted loudly;* and from this it is clear he was so amazed that he forgot he was a king; for to shout so loudly at table was not consonant with his dignity. But God had beaten all the pride out of him. He was forced to break out shouting as if he were a madman.

But now it will be right to ponder what his remedy was. He commands *the Chaldaeans, magi, and astrologers to be called.* From this we gather how prone men are to vanity, and lying, and deceit. Daniel ought to have been first among the Chaldaeans. His response had been memorable when he had predicted to King Belshazzar's grandfather that he would be like the wild beasts. Since this prophecy was proved by the outcome, his authority ought surely to have flourished for over a thousand years. He was daily in the king's sight, yet he was passed over; and the king summoned all the Chaldaeans and astrologers and diviners and magi. It is, of course, true that the magi and astrologers and Chaldaeans were at that time so prized as deservedly eclipsing Daniel's reputation. They thought it a disgrace that a captive should be preferred to their own doctors, for they were aware that their fame was pre-eminent among all the nations, because they alone were wise. Since, then, they wanted to keep that estimation of being almost advisers to God, it was not surprising for them to despise a foreigner. But this has no weight with God.

For what can be said in defence of the ungodly king? His grandfather had been a memorable example of the vengeance of God, when he was cast out from

214

human company and lived with the brutes, even with wild beasts. And this could not be seen as fortuitous, for God had warned him by a dream and then had given the prophet as his interpreter of the oracle and vision. As I have already said, the fame of this thing ought to have been lasting among the Chaldaeans. But the grandson of King Nebuchadnezzar forgot this example, insulted the God of Israel, profaned the vessels of his temple, and enacted a triumph with his idols. Yet when God put forth the sign of his judgment, he called together the magi and Chaldaeans and overlooked Daniel. How could there be any excuse for this? Therefore we see, as I have said, that men's hearts are too ready for Satan's impostures; and the proverb is true, 'The world wants to be deceived.'[3]

And this is noteworthy, because today many would gladly cover and shield their ignorance when there are disturbances. But the reply is easy; they voluntarily blind themselves, more, they shut their eyes to the manifest light. For if God made King Belshazzar inexcusable when once the prophet had been brought to him, of what use will it be for us today to shelter behind such excuses as 'Oh! I, if I can only be sure what God's will is, I will at once subject myself?' For God daily cries openly and invites us, shows us the way. But there is none that responds to him or follows — at least, very few.

Therefore we must diligently consider the example of the King of Babylon when we see he is assiduous enough, yet does not seek God as he should. Why? He wandered through winding ways. He sees himself hemmed in; he cannot flee from God's judgment. But yet he seeks relief from the magi and Chaldaeans, that is, from impostors. For they had already once been found out, and twice, as we saw. This should have been famous enough and known to everybody. So we see that King Belshazzar was blind. He closed his eyes to the offered light — just as today nearly all the world is blind; it does not, indeed, wander in the darkness, but when light is offered it closes its eyes as if it rejected God's grace and wanted deliberately to rush into danger. And this is all too common.

Now the prophet says that *the king had promised the wise men that whoever should read the writing, there would be given him a golden chain;* and then, *he should be clothed in purple; he should be the third in the kingdom.* From this it is clear that he was not sincerely touched by any fear of God. And this contradiction can be seen in reprobates. They shudder at God's judgment, yet their inward pride is not corrected but breaks out, as we see in this king. For *his knees knocked together,* and *the bands of his loins were loosed;* in short, there was no part of his body which was not trembling. The king was almost dead with terror; the dread of God pervaded all his senses. Yet we see that there was still a hidden pride in his mind, and at last it broke out with his promise that *'whoever should interpret the writing should be third in the*

3. Of unknown origin, found in Sebastian Brant's *Ship of Fools* (1494), Luther (e.g., *Werke* [Weimarer Ausgabe], vol. 29, p. 40), and Sebastian Franck's *Paradoxa* (1554).

kingdom'. God had already deposed him from his royal dignity; yet he wants to exalt others, as if in contradiction to God. What did he mean by this? We see that so often as the reprobate are frightened they still nurse a hidden stubbornness within them so that God may never subject them. Of course, they show many signs of penitence; but if anyone thoughtfully weighs up all their deeds and words, he will find what the prophet here relates of King Belshazzar — they rage against God and are neither docile nor compliant, even though they are stunned. We have seen it partly in this verse and shall see it still clearer at the close of the chapter.

As for the end of this verse, when he says *'he shall rule as third in the kingdom'*, it is uncertain whether he is promising him a third part of the kingdom or says that he will actually be the third. For many think that the queen, whom he at once mentions, was the wife of King Nebuchadnezzar and the grandmother of King Belshazzar.[4]

He goes on:

8 *Then came in all the king's wise men, and could not read the writing and reveal* [its] *interpretation to the king.*
9 *Then King Belshazzar was much frightened and his countenance was changed upon him* ['in him'], *and his princes* [were] *stunned* [or, 'anxious'].

Here Daniel relates that the king was cheated in his belief when he hoped for an interpretation of the writing from the magi and astrologers and Chaldaeans and genethliacs. None of them could read it. Therefore he suffers for his own ingratitude in holding the prophet of God as worthless, although he knew that what had been foretold to his grandfather had happened and that Daniel had always excelled in wisdom. So there were many firm enough proofs of his calling. Because Belshazzar so despised the incomparable blessing of God he is left without counsel and sees that he has called all the Chaldaeans and astrologers in vain.

But Daniel says that *there were none that could read the writing or reveal its interpretation to the king.* Since this seems absurd, the rabbis devote much work to it. Some think the letters have been transposed; others conjecture that the letters were altered so that they might be of equal value; yet others suppose the pointing [*characteres*] has been changed. But we have said elsewhere that the Jews were audacious in their guesses whenever a sure reason did not occur to them. But we have no need of these conjectures, for it is probable either that the writing was set in front of the king and hidden from all the Chaldaeans, or that they were so blinded that seeing they did not see — as God often denounces similar stupidity in the Jews. We see what he declares through Isaiah, 'The Law

4. Calvin's argument seems to be that, if the queen were Belshazzar's wife, she would be second in the kingdom and Daniel could then be the third.

will be to you like a closed book. If it shall be said to any, "Read this", "The book is sealed", he will say, "I cannot." Or the book will be opened, but you will all be as blind, even those who now seem to be the most acute of all will say that they are unlearned and not lettered men.'[5] God made this threat to the Jews, and we know it was fulfilled in them and is still being fulfilled today, because the veil is cast before their eyes, as Paul says, so that they are blind in the clearest light.[6] What is surprising in the same thing happening to the Chaldaeans, so that they could not read the writing? So what need is there to hazard guesses about transposed letters or things written in a different order or putting one for another, so that the word תקל, *tekel,* can come first, and מנא מנא, *mene, mene,* after? This is too frivolous. It is certain that God intended to tell the king of his approaching downfall; then, that he was troubled, not to repentance, but so that his sloth might be inexcusable; and so, whether he would or not, he sought assistance, for he knew he was dealing with God.

Now as for the writing; God would not be free unless according to his will he could address on one occasion one man alone, on another many. Therefore, he wanted King Belshazzar to be aware of the writing. But all the magi, as if blind, could not read the writing. As for the interpretation, it is not surprising if they were perplexed. For God spoke as in a riddle when he said, 'MENE, MENE', then 'TEKEL' (that is, 'weighed'), 'PERES' ('it is divided'). If the magi had read these four words a hundred times they could neither have guessed nor reasoned out what they meant. For it was an allegorical prediction until an interpreter had been divinely appointed. But as for the actual letters, we should not be surprised that the eyes of the magi were made dull, because this was God's will, who wished to summon the king to his judgment seat, as we have already said.

The prophet says that *the king was frightened, his countenance was altered in him; the princes also were disturbed.* The sense that this was God's judgment had to be increased lest the matter should be hidden. For, as we shall see later, that same night King Belshazzar was killed. Cyrus broke in while the Babylonians were feasting and carelessly enjoying their pleasures. In the drunkenness this remarkable proof of God's judgment might have been buried at once unless it had been made clear by many circumstances. Daniel therefore repeats that *the king was disturbed,* that is, after he had seen that there was no counsel or help in his magi and astrologers. He says also that *his princes were stunned;* for not only the king but the whole court had to be troubled, so that the report of it should flow out not only throughout the city but also to foreign nations. For there is no doubt that Cyrus was afterwards taught by this prediction. Daniel would not have been so favoured and treated so honourably unless the matter had been known.

5. Mg., Is. 29:10, i.e., 29:11-12.
6. Mg., 2 Cor. 3:14.

Afterwards he goes on:

10 *On account of the words of the king and the nobles, the queen entered into the banqueting house* [for so it should be translated; the word is derived from שׁתה, *sathah*, 'he drinks'] *and spoke and said, 'O King, live for ever! Do not let your thoughts terrify you and do not let your countenance be changed.*
11 *There is a man in your kingdom in whom* [is] *the spirit of the holy gods; and in the days of your father understanding* [literally, "light", but here it is taken metaphorically] *and learning and wisdom, as it were the wisdom of the gods, was found in him. And King Nebuchadnezzar your father appointed him master of the magi* [I will not linger over the words], *astrologers, Chaldaeans, soothsayers — your father the king,* [I say].'

Here Daniel relates that he was brought before the king, to read and interpret the writing. He says that the queen was responsible. There is doubt whether this was the wife of King Belshazzar or his grandmother. It is probable she was an elderly woman, who could tell about the times of King Nebuchadnezzar. Yet that conjecture is perhaps not strong enough. I prefer here to suspend judgment rather than assert something imprudently; although we saw earlier that his wife was at the same time seated at table.

But what we can certainly gather from the prophet's words must be carefully noted, that the king is rebuked for his ingratitude in not admitting Daniel among the magi, Chaldaeans, and astrologers. Of course, the holy man did not wish to be numbered in that order, and he would have deserved God to strip him of the prophetic spirit if he had mixed himself up with the impostors. So it is quite clear that he was separated from them. King Nebuchadnezzar had made him chief of all the magi; he did not wish to use this honour; because, as I was just saying, he would have divested himself of his unique prophetic gift. For we must look at what is right for us. We know that we are altogether too prone to be led by the world's enticements. In particular, ambition blinds us and disturbs all our senses. There is no worse pest; for when anyone sees he can acquire either esteem or honour he does not look at what is right or what God permits, but is carried away as by a blind frenzy. The same could have happened to Daniel had he not been kept back by a genuine attitude of godliness; but he repudiated the honour offered him by King Nebuchadnezzar. So he never wanted to be reckoned among the soothsayers and astrologers and the similar impostors who deceived that nation with their tricks.

This is how it happened that the queen now said that 'there was a certain Daniel'. But this was no excuse for the king, because (as has already been said) Daniel had been very famous for a very long time; God had been pleased to distinguish him with an indisputable mark, so that everyone should have their minds fixed on him as if he were a heavenly angel. The fact that King Belshazzar is ignorant that such a prophet is in his kingdom is wicked and brutish sloth. God therefore intended to rebuke King Belshazzar through a woman when she says *'Do not let your thoughts trouble you.'* Seeing that he is terrified, she soothes him sweetly. Yet she shows him that he is erring grossly, wandering in twisting paths; but he can at once get on to the way, for God had put a torch in his prophet's hand which would have given light if King Belshazzar had not freely wished to wander in darkness, as all the reprobate do. In short, we may discern in this king a fault common to the whole human race — none runs off the road save he who either gives himself up to his ignorance or even wishes all light to be put out.

Now the queen says that *'the spirit of the holy gods is in Daniel';* and we have explained elsewhere what she meant. For it is not surprising that the heathen spoke like this, for they could not distinguish between the unique God and angels, and indiscriminately called gods whatever was divine and heavenly. Hence it is that the queen calls angels 'holy gods' and puts God among the host. But it is for us so to acknowledge the unique God that he may alone be on high, and even the angels themselves be forced into their rank, and no excellence on earth or in heaven obscure the glory of the one God. For Scripture insists that God be put in the supreme position, and that nothing shall be so lofty as not to yield to his majesty. But here we see how very necessary it is for us to be taught about the unique being of God; for from the first beginning of the world men have always been convinced that there was a supreme deity. But afterwards their thinking all dissolved and God slipped from them. Next they mixed him in with the angels, so that there was a complete confusion. So when we see this, let us know that we need Scripture as our leader and master and our bright light, so that we may think nothing about God save so far as he invites us to himself and freely reveals himself.

Grant, almighty God, since you unremittingly address us by your prophets, and do not let us wander in the darkness of errors; grant, I say, that we may be attentive to your voice, and show ourselves teachable and compliant to you; especially when you give us masters who possess all the treasures of wisdom and learning; grant, I say, that we may so subject ourselves to your only-begotten Son that we may hold the right course of our holy calling and always keep right on to the goal to which you call us, until all the struggles of this world are overcome and we at last arrive at that blessed rest which you have won for us by the blood of the same your Son. Amen.

219

Lecture 25

Yesterday we began to expound the place where Daniel relates that King Belshazzar was advised by the queen to summon him. And we said that this was enough and more than enough to convict the king of ingratitude in letting such an excellent prophet of God lie neglected when that memorable prediction that we saw must have been well known and on every tongue, so that the holy man should have had an enduring authority.

Now, Daniel says that *the queen entered into the banqueting house;* and from this the probable conjecture can be drawn that she was not the king's wife but his grandmother. I have said I do not wish to argue about this; for in things doubtful anyone can enjoy his free judgment. But the two things are inconsistent, that the king was feasting with his wife and concubines, and then that the queen entered into the dining chamber. So we gather that 'queen' was a courtesy title and she still possessed, if not the power, at least authority and esteem. And this is confirmed by the testimony of Herodotus,[1] who praises the wife of King Nebuchadnezzar (whom he calls Labynetus); he praises her for her remarkable good sense (and calls her Nitocris). It is therefore consistent that this lady should be absent from the feast; it was quite foreign to her age and gravity to eat with those who were intent on excess. So she entered the dining chamber and advised the king about Daniel.

And now she adds why Daniel was set in command of all the magi and arioles and diviners and Chaldaeans:

12 *'Moreover, because an excellent spirit and understanding and knowledge, the interpretation of dreams and revelation of secrets and the solving of*

1. Mg., Herodotus, 1, i.e., *History* 1:185.

220

difficulties [that is, "he solved difficulties". Thus I read it in a single construction, although here a noun is put, there a verb. But I want it to flow easily, so that it may not be ambiguous] *is found* [namely, prudence and knowledge, as he had said at first] *in him,* [namely] *in Daniel, to whom the king gave the name Belteshazzar. And now let Daniel be called and let him reveal the interpretation.'*

The queen here gives the reason why Daniel obtained the dignity of being regarded as chief and master of all the wise men — because, as she says, *'an excellence of spirit was found in him, because he interpreted dreams, revealed secrets, solved difficulties'.* She enumerates those gifts that Daniel possessed and so proves that he excelled among all the magi, in that there was none to compare with him. Of course, the magi boasted that they were interpreters of dreams, that they could solve all difficulties and explain riddles. But their vanity and senseless boasting had already twice been caught out. So the queen rightly claims these three gifts for Daniel, to show that he surpassed all the rest. Then she gives authority for her reasoning, by saying that it was the king who had given him his name. On the name 'Belteshazzar' we have spoken elsewhere; but in this advice the queen now says that this name had been given to him so that Belshazzar might know that he had been held in the highest esteem and honour by his grandfather. She uses the word 'father' here because she knew that Belshazzar despised outsiders, whereas reason demanded that he should defer to the judgment of his grandfather, whom everyone knew to have been a very great man, even if God had humbled him for a season, as we saw and as Daniel now repeats.

Let us go on:

13 *Then Daniel was led before the king. The king spoke and said to Daniel, '[Are] you that Daniel?* [if we read it as a question; or "You are that Daniel"] *who of the children of the captivity of Judah, whom the king my father brought from Judah.*

14 *And I have heard of you, that the spirit of the gods is in you and understanding* [or "perspicacity". We said yesterday that this word, although properly it means "light", is metaphorically taken for "perspicacity" or "ingenuity"] *and knowledge, and excellent* [or "uncommon"] *wisdom is found in you.*

15 *And now the wise men, the arioles* [or "genethliacs" — I will not dwell on these words, as I said before], *were brought before me, who might read this writing and reveal its interpretation to me; and they could not show the interpretation of the saying.*

16 *And I heard of you, that you can solve difficulties and explain secrets. Now if you can read the writing and reveal its interpretation to me, you shall be clothed in purple and a chain of gold on your neck and shall rule as third in the kingdom.'*

Here the king does not acknowledge his negligence but interrogates Daniel without shame — and interrogates him as if he were a prisoner: *'You are Daniel, of the captives of Judah, whom my father led away?'* He seems to speak contemptuously, to put Daniel in the position of servile submission. Yet we can read this sentence as if Belshazzar were inquiring admiringly: *'Are you really that Daniel! I have heard about you.'* He had heard long since and thought it was nothing. But now, when extreme necessity presses him, he pays Daniel some respect. So, *'I have heard that the spirit of the gods is in you, that you can solve difficulties and reveal secrets'*.

As for 'the spirit of the gods', we have already said that King Belshazzar followed the normal usage of all nations in promiscuously mixing up angels with God; for those poor souls could not exalt God as was right, with the angels, as it were, under his feet. Yet this statement shows that men have never been so brutish as not to ascribe everything excellent to God. For we see that even heathen writers call whatever is useful to men or has any excellence and worth 'the benefits of the gods'. Thus the Chaldaeans called the gift of understanding or a rare and outstanding penetration 'the spirit of the gods'. For they knew that men do not acquire or attain the prophetic office by their own industry but that it is a heavenly gift. Hence they are forced to ascribe praise to God; but, because the true God was unknown to them, they spoke from perplexity. So, as I said, they called the angels 'gods', because in the darkness of their ignorance they could not distinguish who was the true God.

However that may be, Belshazzar shows in what esteem he holds Daniel. But he says that he has all this only from the accounts of others. Once again his negligence is betrayed. He ought to have known the prophet by use and experience. But he was content with simple rumour, and it is clear how arrogantly he neglected what the teacher offered him; yet he does not even think of that and is unwilling to confess his shame. But God often extorts from the ungodly a confession in which they condemn themselves, even if this is what they are trying their hardest to escape.

This is also the tenor of what he says: *'All the wise men and the genethliacs — or arioles — were brought before me, who might read this writing to me and reveal its interpretation. And they could not'*, he says. For God punished him when in his extreme necessity he showed that the Chaldaeans and all the arioles could do nothing for him, although he had favoured them. When he was so disappointed in his hope, he acknowledged he had been deceived in supporting the magi and arioles and thinking they were equipped to advise him so long as he kept them at his side. Meanwhile, that the holy prophet was rejected was intolerable to God and rightly so. This fact Belshazzar confesses without meaning to. That is why I said it was not a sincere or voluntary confession, but extorted forcefully by the secret impulse of God.

He also promises Daniel what he had promised to the magi: *'You shall be clothed'*, he says, *'with purple, if you will read this writing, and there shall be a golden chain on your neck and you shall reign as third in the kingdom.'* At that moment the end of his kingdom was at hand — and yet unconcernedly he offered this dignity to Daniel. From this it is clear that the terror with which God had struck his mind was transitory — such madmen are greatly agitated and disquieted; they have no solidity and in the midst of their fears are so enthusiastic that they want to ascend — or even fly — to heaven. So, although this tyrant trembled at the judgment of God, he kept a hidden stubbornness in his heart and imagined he would be king for ever when he promised others wealth and all sorts of gifts.

Now he goes on:

17 *Then Daniel replied and said before the king, 'May your gifts be to yourself* [that is, "May they remain with you"]; *and give your presents to another. Yet I will read the writing for the king and reveal* [its] *interpretation to him.'*

Here in the first place Daniel rejected the offered gifts. We do not read that this was done earlier; in fact, we saw that King Nebuchadnezzar's gift had been accepted. The reason for this difference is sought. For it is improbable that the prophet changed either his mind or his purpose or his attitude. What then does he mean by earlier accepting honours from King Nebuchadnezzar but now refusing the offered dignity? Then another question arises: at the end of the chapter we shall see that he is clothed in purple and that a herald proclaims the edict that he shall rule as the third. It seems, then, either that the prophet forgot himself in receiving the purple he had so loftily refused, or it is asked why he spoke like this and then did not refuse to be adorned with royal insignia.

As for the first question, I have no doubt that he meant to speak roughly to the ungodly Belshazzar, a man beyond hope; but because there had been still some uprightness left in King Nebuchadnezzar and he had good hopes of him, he had treated him more gently. As for King Belshazzar, he had to be taken up more harshly because things had come to an end with him. I do not doubt this was the reason for the difference; the prophet had kept on evenly in his path, but his office made him distinguish between different persons. So because King Belshazzar was more stubborn and obstinate, he showed him less deference than his grandfather. Moreover, the time of subjection was soon to be ended and with it the need to honour the Chaldaean monarch.

In regard to the contradiction between his reply and the event that we shall see later, it should not seem absurd if the prophet will at first declare that he would have nothing to do with the king's gifts, would even flee from them, and yet that he will not contend too vehemently, in case it should be thought that he was acting craftily in order to escape danger. Therefore he wished to show his unconquerable courage in both respects — that at first he declared the king's gifts were nothing to him (for he knew that the kingdom's time was short) and then that he accepted the purple and the other insignia. Because he would have been blamed if he had gone on refusing — a sign of cowardice that would have led him to be suspected of treachery. Hence the prophet shows how nobly he looks down on all the dignity offered by King Belshazzar, a man already almost half dead.

At the same time he shows himself fearless of any peril. For the destruction of the king was imminent, and in a few hours, perhaps in the self-same hour, the city was captured. Daniel, by not rejecting the purple, shows that he will if necessary not flee from death. For he would have been safer in his obscurity, companying with common people and not in the court; if he had been regarded as one of the slaves he could have been safe from danger. So when he does not hesitate to accept the purple he shows he was unafraid.

Meanwhile there is no doubt at all that by saying *'Your gifts be to yourself, and give your presents to another!* I care nothing for them'*, he meant to cast down the king's dull and stupid arrogance, which was still swelling. By despising the king's liberality so spiritedly, there is no doubt he wanted to correct the yet swelling pride, or at least to wound or prick his mind to feel God's judgment — of which a little later Daniel would be the herald and witness.

Now he goes on:

18 *'O King* [literally, "You the king"; but he is addressing him], *the Most High God gave the rule, and the greatness, and the excellence, and the splendour to your father Nebuchadnezzar.*
19 *And on account of the greatness that he gave him, all peoples, nations, and languages trembled and feared in his presence. Whom he would, he killed* [that is, "whom he wanted to kill, was killed"], *and whom he would* [strike], *he struck; and whom he would* [raise up], *he raised up; and whom he would* [cast down], *he cast down.*
20 *But when his heart was lifted up and his spirit was strengthened* [or, "hardened"] *to pride, he was cast down from the throne of his kingdom and his glory was taken from him.'*

Before Daniel recites the writing and gives its interpretation he warns King Belshazzar of the source of this wonder. For he would not have done well to start from the reading. If he had said *'Mene, mene'* (as we see at the end of the chapter) the king would not have profited from such abrupt speech. But here Daniel shows that there is nothing surprising if God puts forth his hand — or puts forth the appearance of a hand — which writes down the king's destruction, for the king had been unyielding in provoking his anger. We see then why Daniel begins with the statement that King Nebuchadnezzar had been the supreme monarch, that he had subjected all the world to himself, that all had trembled at the sight of him; and then that he had been cast down from the throne of his kingdom — all this that it might be the more plain that Belshazzar had not sinned in ignorance; for he ought to have behaved modestly with that remarkable and memorable example of his grandfather before him. As that family admonition had done no good, Daniel shows that the time is now ripe for God to declare his wrath publicly, and that by a terrifying portent. This is the sum.

But as for the words. First he says, *'To King Nebuchadnezzar was given the rule from God, and greatness and loftiness, and splendour';* as if he were saying, 'He was magnificently adorned to be supreme monarch of all the world.' We have said elsewhere, and Daniel repeats it in many places, that kingdoms do not come to men by chance but divinely — as also Paul declares, 'There is no power but of God.'[2] And God wishes his providence to be seen in a special way in kingdoms. For although he takes care of the whole world, and in the government of the human race what seem the minutest details are still ruled by his hand, yet his special providence shines forth in the kingdoms of this world. But as I have treated this subject more fully elsewhere and we are still meeting this doctrine frequently, it is enough for me to touch briefly on the chief point — that earthly kings are raised on high by God's hand and not by chance.

And to confirm this doctrine Daniel adds, *'on account of the greatness that God conferred on him, all mortals trembled at his sight'.* By which words he means that the glory of God is engraven on kings for as long as he wishes them to rule. This cannot be described precisely, but the reality sufficiently demonstrates that kings are divinely armed with authority to contain under their hand and will a huge multitude of people. Now, there is none who does not desire to be first among mortals. How then is it that, with ambition so fixed in the hearts of all, many thousands subject themselves to one and suffer themselves to be ruled, even to bear many indignities? What is the source of this, except that God arms with the sword and power those whom he wishes to be chief? Hence this reason must be carefully noticed, when the prophet says that *'all trembled at the sight of King Nebuchadnezzar,* because God had armed him with greatness', that is, he wished him to be pre-eminent in the world. But God has many causes, and often it is hidden from us why he raises up this man, and humbles that. Yet this should be beyond controversy with us, that no kings possess power unless God stretches forth his hand, and then

2. Mg., Rom. 13:1.

225

supports them. But when he wishes to put off their power from them, they fall of their own accord — not that there is anything fortuitous in the changes, but because God, as it is said in the book of Job, ungirds the sword from those whom he had previously girded.[3]

Now he goes on, *'Whom he wished to kill, he killed; whom he wished to smite, he smote'.* Some think the abuse of royal power is described here. I prefer to take the words simply, that Nebuchadnezzar at his will could cast down some and raise up others, that it was in his power to give life to some, to kill others. I therefore do not refer these words to tyrannical licence, as if Nebuchadnezzar slaughtered many innocent people and shed human blood without cause; that he despoiled many of their fortunes and enriched others either with honours or wealth. I take it only that it was in his will to kill or to give life, to raise some and to cast down others. In sum, it seems to me that Daniel is here describing how much power kings possess, that they can freely decide about their subjects — not because it is right, but because all are silent. For all are forced to approve whatever pleases the king, or at least, none dare object. Since the licence of kings is so great, Daniel here (to show that King Nebuchadnezzar was raised up, not by his own industry, not by his own counsel, not even by his own good fortune) says that he was armed with the supreme rule and was dreadful to all because God had given him the insignia of his own glory. Meanwhile it is for kings to look carefully at what is lawful for them and what God permits. For, as they possess the kingdom, so also they should consider that some time they will give account to the Most High King. From this we do not gather that kings are appointed by God without any condition, so that they can do whatever they like; but the prophet, as I said, is talking about royal power. And since kings possess the power of life and death, he says that the life of all was in the hand of King Nebuchadnezzar.

Now he adds *'when his heart was lifted up, then he was cast down'*, or 'exterminated', *'from the throne of the kingdom and they despoiled him of his excellence'.* He goes on with his narration. For he wants to show King Belshazzar that God for a time bears with the haughtiness of those who forget him when they have obtained supreme power. So he wants to show this. Therefore he says, 'King Nebuchadnezzar your grandfather was supreme monarch. He did not receive this from himself, nor did he hold rule except because he was upheld by the hand of God. Now, his change was a remarkable proof that the pride of those who are ungrateful to God and do not acknowledge that they rule by his benefit cannot be tolerated for ever.' Therefore, *'when his heart',* he says, *'was lifted up and his spirit strengthened in pride,* a sudden change took place. It behoves you and all your posterity to be taught by this, lest pride should further deceive you. Rather let the example of your father strike you'

3. Mg., Jb. 12:18.

(as we shall say later). 'Therefore this writing is set before you, so that you may understand that the destruction of you and your life and your kingdom is at hand.'

> Grant, almighty God, since to each one of us is assigned his position, that we may be content with our lot, and that when you humble us, we may freely submit ourselves to you and suffer ourselves to be ruled by you and not desire any height that will cast us down to destruction; and that we may each one modestly so behave in his vocation that always you may be pre-eminent among us; that we may determine nothing but to strive to devote our work to you and also to our brethren to whom we are bound, that so your name may be glorified in us all, through Jesus Christ our Lord. Amen.

Lecture 26

In the sentence that we began to expound yesterday we should notice the expression where Daniel says that *'the heart of King Nebuchadnezzar was strengthened to pride'*. He means that he was not suddenly elated by foolishness, as vain men are often puffed up without any cause, and even without any preliminary inward state of mind. He wanted to express something more; the pride had been fostered over a long period; as if he were saying that he had not been overtaken suddenly by some vanity but he had exercised his pride, so as to add obstinacy or hardness to it. Afterwards the number is changed in the verbs; some refer the plural to the angels, that they deprived him, but by God's command. But I think the verbs should be taken indefinitely, that his glory will have been taken away from him — we saw similar expressions earlier.

Now he goes on:

21 *'And he was exterminated from the sons of men, and his heart was put with the beasts* [literally, "he put"; and so some translate it, "He put his heart with the beasts", which is a tolerable sense. But others prefer to attribute it to God, that God put his heart with the beasts. And we know that the substantive is often lacking with the Hebrews and Chaldaeans. So let us read it literally, "Nebuchadnezzar himself placed his heart" — that is, he applied all his senses — "to the beasts, so that he differed nothing from them" — or, "God put his heart with the beasts", that is, "he made him so foolish that he was like the beasts". Others take the word שׁוִּי, *savvi*, absolutely. But it should rather be expounded actively], *and his habitation with the wild asses; they fed him with grass like bulls* [some translate it, "they made him to taste grass, like bulls"; others, "that grasses" — making a change of number — "fed him", which is unambiguous in sense; but if you like to read it, "that they fed him grass", it

228

will be indefinite, as we have had many similar expressions before. But if anyone prefers the change of number, the sense will also be fitting, that "grasses gave him taste", or, "pasture"], *and his body was washed with the dew of heaven until he should learn that the Most High God rules in the kingdom of men and whom he wills he places in it.'*

This verse does not demand a long explanation, for Daniel is only repeating what he had written elsewhere, that the king's grandfather, Nebuchadnezzar, although not changed into a beast, was yet deposed from the community of men and his whole body deformed; more, he himself became averse to human customs and preferred to live with the beasts. This was a horrible abnormality, especially in so great a monarch; and it was an example that deserved to be handed on from generation to generation, even for a thousand ages — if that monarchy should last so long. But his grandson's wicked negligence in so soon forgetting this evidence is deservedly rebuked. This, then, is why Daniel repeats the story.

'He was deposed', he says, *'from the sons of men; his heart was placed with the beasts'* — that is, for a time he lost his reason and judgment. And we know that the chief difference between men and the brute animals is that men understand and judge but brute animals are carried away by their senses. God therefore gave a memorable example in the king when he despoiled him of all reason and understanding.

'His habitation', he says, *'was with the wild asses',* he who had previously lived in a palace illustrious throughout the whole world, and to which all Orientals at that time looked for justice. Moreover, for one used to being worshipped as a god, it was a horrible judgment to go on to live with the wild beasts — for him who had enjoyed all pleasures and was used to treatment as rich as the wealth of his country would bear, *'to have his fodder in grasses like a bull';* especially since we know that Orientals are more pleasurably inclined than others and Babylon was the mother of all luxury. Since, then, the king's condition was changed like this, none could be ignorant that it had not happened by chance but by an exceptional and remarkable judgment of God.

Afterwards he adds what he had said before, that *'his body was washed with the rain of heaven until he should know that the Most High God rules in the kingdom of men'.* Here he again expresses the purpose of the punishment — that Nebuchadnezzar might feel that he was divinely created king and that all earthly kings stand only to the extent that God supports them by his hand and power. They think they are set above any chance accidents; and, although they boast in words that they reign 'by the grace of God', yet they despise all deity and transfer the glory of the deity to themselves. This madness afflicts all kings, as we gather from these words. For if King Nebuchadnezzar had been convinced that kings are appointed by God, depend on his will, and stand

229

and fall as he decrees, there had been no need of this punishment — the words expressly stated this. Therefore he banishes God from the government of the world. But this is common to all earthly kings, as I have just said. Of course, they will all profess the contrary, but the Holy Spirit cares nothing for those false protestations, as they are called. Therefore, in the person of King Nebuchadnezzar there is set before us as in a mirror the drunken confidence of all kings; they reckon they stand by their own strength and exempt themselves from God's control, as if he did not sit as Judge in heaven. So Nebuchadnezzar had to be humbled until he should learn that God rules on earth (because the common opinion is that he is shut up in heaven, as if he were content with doing nothing and had no care for the human race).

Finally he adds, *'and whom he wished, he appointed'*, or 'put in charge'. This better expresses what had been said obscurely — how Nebuchadnezzar, when he was tamed and subjugated by such a harsh punishment, would know that God reigns on earth. For when earthly kings see that they have good defences and possess great resources and can call up large armies at will, even when they see that they are a universal terror, they think God has no further rights and they cannot conceive that there can be any change — that is what it says in the Psalm about all the proud;[1] and Isaiah in the same sense says, 'Even if the scourge shall pass through or if the flood shall overspread the whole earth, the evil will not touch us.'[2] It is as if they were saying, 'Although God should thunder from heaven, yet we shall be safe and sound from all harm and danger.' This is what kings persuade themselves of. Therefore they only begin to admit that God is the king of the earth when they feel it is in his hand and power to cast down those whom he had exalted, and to raise up the humble and lowly, as we saw earlier. Hence the close of the verse is, as it were, an explanation of the previous statement.

Now he goes on:

22 *'And you, Belshazzar, his son, have not humbled your heart; wherefore* [literally; but it is equivalent to "seeing that"] *you knew all this.'*

Here Daniel shows why he related what we have previously heard of King Nebuchadnezzar's punishment. For Belshazzar should have been so affected by that warning in the family as to subject himself to God. For it may well be that his father Evil-Merodach had forgotten the punishment. Yet because he was not so impudent as to set himself against God or to abuse true and sincere piety, God spared him, a wretched enough tyrant but one who had some self-control. As for his grandson Belshazzar, however, he was quite intolerable. And therefore God stretched forth his hand.

1. Mg., Ps. 10:6.
2. Mg., Is. 28:15.

This the prophet now teaches: *'You are his son'*, he says. This circumstance should be the more compelling; he does not have to seek afar off for an example among foreign peoples, for he can learn at home all that is necessary and useful for him to know. And he magnifies the fault in another way. He says, *'Yet you knew all this.'* For men plead ignorance to extenuate the blame for their crimes. But those who sin knowingly and willingly lack any excuse. Therefore the prophet convicts the king of manifest contumacy; as if he were saying that he had deliberately provoked the wrath of God, in that he was not unaware that a great and horrible judgment awaits all the proud, for he had such a clear and notable testimony in his own grandfather, which he ought to have had continually before his eyes.

He goes on:

23 *'And against the Lord of heaven you have exalted yourself, and the vessels of his house* [that is, "his temple"] *you have brought out in your sight; and you, and your nobles, your wives* [or, "your wife"], *and your concubines have drunk wine in them, and you have praised gods of silver* [that is, "silver gods"], *and golden, bronze, iron, wooden, and stone, which do not see, and do not hear, and do not understand; and you have not honoured God, him in whose hand is your soul* [that is, "in whose hand is your life"] *and* [in] *whose* [power are] *all that are yours.'*

The prophet goes on with his assertion, confirming what I said — that King Belshazzar was unteachable and deliberately blinded himself to God's judgment. *'For you have exalted yourself'*, he says, *'against the Lord of heaven.'* If he had wantonly raised himself against men, the fault would already have deserved punishment. But when he deliberately provoked God, his arrogance was quite intolerable. So the prophet again intensifies the king's pride and says 'he was raised up against the King of heaven'. At the same time he expresses in what way: that *'he ordered the vessels of the temple to be brought into his sight and drank in them'*. Now, that was profanation and an unworthy sacrilege.

But Belshazzar was not satisfied with abusing the sacred vessels for his own luxury and foul drunkenness and prostituting them with his concubines and harlots. He added a more serious contempt against God in that he then *'praised the silver gods and the golden, the bronze, and the iron, and the wood, and the stone, which do not feel'*. This ['which do not feel', etc.] had not been said before; Daniel in his role as teacher reports not as briefly as before. When, near the beginning of this same chapter, he said that Belshazzar celebrated that infamous feast, he wrote as an historian. Now, however, as I have already said, he discharges his office of teacher. *'You'*, he says, *'have praised gods fabricated from corruptible materials, who neither see, nor hear, nor understand. But you have defrauded the living God of his honour, in whose hand is your life, on*

231

whom you depend and from whom you have whatever you boast as your own. Since, then, you so despise the living God who has been so kind to you, how disgraceful and shameful is your ingratitude!' We see, then, that the prophet is here severe and convicts the ungodly tyrant of sacrilege and insane reck- lessness and foul ingratitude against God.

Now he goes on (I pass over these things quickly because they were treated elsewhere):

24 *'Then from his sight* [was] *sent part of a hand* [some translate it "palm", but they mean a hand without a body; a portion of a hand, that is, a hand amputated as it were from the body was sent from the sight of God] *and this writing was written.'*

The adverb באדין, *bedain* ['then'], contains the momentous statement that God's vengeance or declaration of vengeance is at hand. Daniel shows that God had for long been patient towards King Belshazzar and had not at once taken up instruments to execute his punishment. But God began to show his judgment and to mount his throne when Belshazzar's pride was irrecover- able, his ungodliness quite intolerable. We see, then, that *bedain* should be read emphatically, as if he were saying, 'You cannot complain of the swiftness of the punishment, as if God had sent it before due time. You cannot say that God has been precipitate in this punishment. Just think and consider in how many ways and for how long a time you have provoked his anger. And as for this final crime, you had certainly reached the climax of ungodliness when that hand appeared to you. So God is now dragging you to punishment in time, or opportunely. Hitherto he has borne with you and your crimes. After such tolerance, what remains, when you vaunt yourself so proudly against him, save that he restrain you? — for you are utterly irreclaimable; there is no hope of your correction.'

He says 'from him', so that Belshazzar may no longer ask where the hand came from. *'From the sight of God',* he says; that is, 'this hand bears witness to the vengeance of heaven. Do not imagine it is some transient spectre, but learn that God shows by this figure that your crimes have displeased him and that now that you have reached the culmination, the punishment is matured and ready.' *'And this writing',* he says, *'is written';* as if he were saying that King Belshazzar's eyes were not deceived, this was the hand of God, that is, 'sent from his sight', as a sure witness of vengeance.

Afterwards he adds:

25 *'And this* [is] *the writing which* [is] *written* [or, "marked out"], *MENE, MENE* ["it is numbered, it is numbered"], *TEKEL* ["it is weighed". Some translate it, "number, number: weigh"], *UPHARSIN* ["and dividing"].

232

26 *This* [is] *the interpretation of the saying: MENE, God has numbered and fulfilled* [or, "finished"] *your kingdom.*
27 *TEKEL* ["weigh", or "it is weighed"], *you are weighed in the balance* [or, "scales"] *and are found wanting.*
28 *PERES* [for "upharsin"], *your kingdom is divided and given to the Medes and Persians.'*

Here Daniel explains the four words engraved on the wall. The king could not read them, either because of his dullness or because God had stupefied all his senses and, as it were, weakened his eyes, as was said earlier. And the same must be said of the magi and arioles. For they could have read had they not been blinded by God.

So in the first place Daniel recites the four words, *'Mene, Mene, Tekel, Upharsin'*. Then he gives the interpretation. One word, *'Mene'*, is spoken twice. Some make the distinction that the years of the king's life were numbered and then the time of his kingdom. But that does not seem strong enough to me. I think the word was put twice to strengthen it; as if the prophet were saying that the number was already completed. For slips are easy in adding up, as the common saying goes. Therefore, that King Belshazzar may understand that both his own life and his kingdom are finished, God confirms that the number is completed; as if he would say that not a moment of time could be added to the predetermined end. And this is how Daniel himself interprets it: *'God has numbered your kingdom'*, he says; that is, God has determined and appointed a definite end to your kingdom. So it must needs be that he accept the end; his time is completed.

Although God here addresses one particular king and it was before his eyes that the writing was set, yet we may deduce a general doctrine from it: God prefixes a definite time for all kingdoms. Scripture declares also the same thing about each of our lives.[3] If God prescribes his days to each individual, it is assuredly even more pertinent for whole empires, for their existence is more momentous. Let us know, then, that not only do kings live and die at God's will, but also their kingdoms are changed (as was said earlier) and they are established by him in such a way that he prescribes their certain end. We must seek comfort from this when we see tyrants rushing wildly ahead without any moderation in their licence and savagery. When they run riot, as if they would mix heaven and earth, let us remember this message: 'Their years are numbered.' God knows how long it is expedient that they should reign. He is not mistaken. For unless he knew it was useful for the Church and the elect that tyrants should run riot for a time, he would certainly soon restrain them. But because from the outset he has 'appointed the number', let us know that

3. Mg., Jb. 14:5.

233

the time of his vengeance is not yet ripe while he suffers them to misuse so unrestrainedly their own rule and power allowed them by God.

Now follows the explanation of the word *Tekel*. *'Tekel'*, he says, *'because you are weighed in the scales'* (or, 'in the balance'), *'and are found wanting.'* Here Daniel shows that God regulates his judgments as if he held scales in his hand. It is a similitude taken from a human custom. We know why scales are used, to make an assured distribution. So God is said to do all things in weight and measure,[4] because he does nothing confusedly but uses such moderation that we never find it more or less, as one commonly says. This is why Daniel says that Belshazzar *'was weighed in the balance';* God was not in a hurry to exact punishment, but justly punishes him according to his manner and perpetual rule — because, that is, he is *'found wanting';* that is, something vanishing, as if he were insubstantial. It is as if he were saying, 'You think your dignity should be spared. Because all pay you homage, you think you deserve honour. You are wrong', he says, 'God's judgment is quite otherwise. God does not use ordinary balances, but he has his balances, and there you are "found wanting", that is, you are found of no account, or, a man of nothing.' There is no doubt that at these words the tyrant must have been quite exasperated. But the final time was come, he had to bear with the voice of the herald. And no doubt God restrained his ferocity, so that he should not turn on Daniel.

Finally he adds פרס, *Peres,* for the word *Pharsin,* because *'his kingdom is divided'* — namely, *'by the Medes and Persians'*. Without doubt God signified by that word the imminent destruction of the monarchy. When, therefore, he says, *'Upharsin, and they will divide',* he signifies that the monarchy can stand no longer because he intends to tear it to pieces or break it up. But the prophet is alluding very appositely to the division that was made between the Medes and the Persians. And thus the reproach is increased, in that the Babylonians had to serve many masters. In itself it is serious and troublesome for a nation that has held sway far and wide to be forced to bear the yoke of a single overlord when conquered. But when there are two lords, it magnifies the indignity. So Daniel shows here that God would not simply be avenger by destroying the monarchy of Babylon, but there would be an added weight of punishment in the Medes and Persians ruling over them. Of course, it is true that the city was taken by the strength and activeness of Cyrus. But because Cyrus had given his father-in-law the honour of being admitted to a share in the rule, the Medes and Persians are said to have divided the kingdom, although, strictly speaking, there was no actual division of the kingdom. Afterwards Cyrus, seized by insatiable ambition and avarice, was drawn away to other expeditions. But Darius, who was more than sixty years old, as we shall

4. Mg., Wisd. 11:21, i.e., 11:20.

see, lived quietly at home. He was, as is well known, a Mede. If we are to believe the many histories, his sister, Cyrus's mother, had been, as it were, banished to Persia, since the oracle had been proclaimed about the greatness of Cyrus. His grandfather had exposed him; afterwards he took revenge for this injury, yet not so cruelly as to take his life. For he wanted him to remain in some dignity and made him a satrap. But afterwards his son reigned among the Medes, with Cyrus's consent; then Cyrus married his daughter; so that both on account of kinship and as thanks for this new relationship he wanted to have him as his associate in the kingdom. This is the background to Daniel saying that the monarchy was to be quickly divided, for the Medes and the Persians divided it between themselves.

He goes on:

29 *Then Belshazzar commanded and they clothed Daniel with purple and a golden chain* [was put] *upon his neck. And they cried before him that he should rule as third in the kingdom.*

It is strange that the king should command this when he had been so roughly treated by the prophet. It seems that he showed no irritation at this time. Previously he would have flared up a hundred times and sentenced God's holy prophet to a thousand deaths. How is it, then, that he commands him to be adorned with royal insignia? that he commands him to be proclaimed by his own herald as third in the kingdom? Some think this happened because royal laws were sacrosant with the Babylonians, even that their words were law, and they intended whatever they declared to be held as firm and inviolable. They think, therefore, that King Belshazzar was making a display that he kept his promises. But I consider that he was at first thunderstruck and although he heard what the prophet said, yet he was practically like a stock or a stone. I think further that he did this with an eye to himself and his own safety. For he could have been made contemptible to his nobles. So, to show he was unmoved, he commanded Daniel to be adorned with the insignia as if the threat had had no effect. He did not, indeed, despise what the prophet had said, but he wanted to persuade his satraps and all the guests that God had threatened him, not with the intention of carrying out such a severe punishment, but only to frighten him. And when kings are most terrified, they always take good care to give no sign of nervousness; otherwise, they think, their authority will be undermined. So, to keep some respect among his subjects, he resolves to seem particularly secure and unafraid. This, without doubt, was the tyrant's purpose in ordering Daniel to be clothed with purple and royal insignia.

Grant, almighty God, that what once you proclaimed as proof of your wrath against all the proud may be useful to us today; and, warned by the punishment of that one man, we may learn to behave humbly and modestly; not to desire a greatness that displeases you, but so to remain in our station that we may serve you and exalt and glorify your holy name; that nothing may separate us from you, but that we may so bear your yoke in this world and allow ourselves to be ruled by you that at last we may come to the blessed rest and lot of the heavenly kingdom which you have prepared for us and which was won for us by the blood of your only-begotten Son. Amen.

Lecture 27

30 *In that night Belshazzar king of the Chaldaeans* [was] *slain.*
31 *And Darius the Mede received the kingdom, when* [he was] *sixty-two years old.*

Here Daniel briefly relates that the prophecy was that night fulfilled. As we explained earlier, it was a festival-day that the Babylonians celebrated yearly and a solemn feast was being held. This was the occasion for the city to be betrayed by the two satraps Gobryas and Gabatha (for so Xenophon calls them).[1] On this passage the rabbis betray their shamelessness and ignorance in their usual way when they babble and brag about things they do not know. For they say this king was murdered because one of the keepers had heard the prophet's words and wished to put the heavenly judgment into effect — as if God's verdict should depend on the will of one heathen man! We ignore those childish trifles and must keep to the truth of the story; Belshazzar was seized during his licentious and liberal feast, when he had made himself and his nobles and concubines drunk.

Yet we must also here observe the wonderful grace of God towards the prophet. For he must needs have perished along with the others. He had put on the purple; scarcely an hour had passed before the Medes and Persians stormed the city; in the tumult he could hardly have escaped had God not covered him with the shadow of his hand. Thus we see that God takes care of his own and rescues them from the utmost perils as if he led them out of the sepulchre. There is no doubt that in the uproar the holy prophet was greatly troubled. For he was not a block of wood. But he had to be exercised, so as

1. Xenophon, *Cyropaedia* 7:5:24-32.

237

to know that God was the sure protector of his life and to prepare himself more readily to serve him; for he sees nothing better than to cast all his cares on him.

Daniel adds that *the kingdom was transferred to the King of the Medes,* whom he calls 'Darius', but Xenophon 'Cyaxares'. What is certain is that by Cyrus's industry and under his command Babylon was captured. For he was the strenuous warrior and possessed the supreme authority. But here there is no mention of him. But Xenophon relates that Cyaxares (who is here called Darius) was the father-in-law of Cyrus and also that he was held in the highest honour and esteem.[2] So it is not surprising if Daniel sets him before us as the king. Cyrus was content with the power and the praise and fame of victory; the title he readily yielded to his father-in-law, whom he saw to be an old man and rather lazy.

But it is not certain whether he might not have been the son of Astyages and thus Cyrus's uncle. For many historians agree that Astyages was Cyrus's grandfather and his daughter was allocated to Cambyses, for he had learned from the astrologers that from her would come a descendant who would possess power over the whole of Asia. And they add much also that he ordered the infant Cyrus to be killed. But because that is uncertain, I prefer to leave it undecided. To me it is probable that Darius was both the uncle and the father-in-law of Cyrus. Although, if Xenophon is to be believed, Cyrus was still unmarried at the time he captured Babylon.[3] For his father-in-law uncle had summoned him to bring reinforcements when he himself was unequal to the Babylonians and Assyrians. However that may be, what the prophet here relates is not inconsistent: Darius, the King of the Medes, held sway, because Cyrus, although the stronger and superior, granted him to be King of Babylon on a sort of leasehold. And so he ruled over the Chaldaeans only in title.

Now he goes on:

CHAPTER 6

1   *It pleased before Darius and he appointed over the kingdom one hundred and twenty rulers of the provinces, who were in the whole kingdom.*
2   *And over them* [there were; 'and that there might be over them'] *three satraps, of whom Daniel* [was] *one, and that the rulers of the provinces should render account to them and that the king might not suffer loss* [or, 'the king might not suffer trouble', as some translate it. But פֿוק, *nazac,* means 'to incur

2. *Cyropaedia* 8:5:19-20.
3. *Cyropaedia* 8:5:19-20, 28.

loss', and I readily take it in the sense that the king was not acting for the sake of his leisure or to escape work (although this could be, for he was an elderly man); but he wanted his affairs attended to, in case anything should go wrong among so many hands, and so entrusted the care to a triumvirate. For in a crowd there is always some confusion, as is well known. If there had been so many rulers of provinces, that is, one hundred and twenty, many inconveniences could have occurred and the king might have suffered loss in many ways. Hence he appointed three leaders over the one hundred and twenty.]

Here again we may perceive that the prophet was always under God's care, not so much for a private reason or in a private regard, as that the wretched exiles and captives might receive some alleviation of their lot through his activities and kindness. For God intended to reach out his hand to the Jews through Daniel. And we might deservedly call him 'the hand of God upholding the Jews'; for it is certain that the Persians, a barbarous race, would not have been merciful rulers by nature had God not interposed his servant Daniel to succour his people. It ought, then, to be noted in the context of the story that Daniel was chosen by Darius as one of the three supreme prefects. He had been third under King Belshazzar, although only briefly. Yet it could have stirred up ill-will with the new king that so much honour had been paid him. But it is probable that Darius had been told of the things that Daniel had earlier related — that a hand had appeared on the wall, that Daniel was the interpreter of the writing, and that he had been sent as from heaven as a herald to proclaim the destruction of King Belshazzar. For unless this had been reported to Darius, Daniel would never have received such authority from him. He had plenty of men in his own forces. And we know that a victorious general is surrounded by the hungry, all wanting a share in the booty. Hence Darius would never have taken up this foreigner and prisoner, to whom he gave so much honour and power, unless he realized that he had certainly been God's prophet and his herald in denouncing the destruction of the Babylonian monarchy. From this we gather that it was God's doing that he was among the first satraps and third in the kingdom; for he would become known to King Darius more quickly. For if Daniel had been abased by King Belshazzar, he would have hidden at home. But when the king sees him blazing with royal insignia, he asks who he is. He hears how he reached such honours; and so he knows that he is God's prophet and appoints him as one of the three prefects. Thus God's providence is again set before us; he not only kept his servant safe but provided for the safety of the whole Church, lest the Jews should be more and more oppressed through those changes.

But afterwards a temptation is added by which both that holy man and even the whole people could have been discouraged. For the prophet says:

3 *Then Daniel was the superior* [for נצח, *nazah,* means 'to surpass'. Therefore 'he was superior to', or, in a word, 'excelled'] *over the satraps and rulers of the provinces; moreover, because a fuller* [or, 'more excellent'] *spirit* [was] *in him; and the king was thinking to exalt him over the whole kingdom.*

4 *Then the satraps and rulers of the provinces sought to find occasion against Daniel from the part of the kingdom* [that is, 'in its administration'] *and all occasion* [that is, 'no occasion'] *and no blame could be found; for true* [or, 'faithful', or 'sound'], *he* [that is, 'because he was faithful']; *and no fault and no blame* [he repeats the word שחיתה, *sehithah;* therefore 'no blame'] *was found in him.*

5 *Then these men said, 'We shall not find in this Daniel any occasion, unless we find it in him on account of the law of his God.'*

Now, as I said, the prophet relates that there had suddenly arisen a temptation which could have dispirited both him and the elect people. For although only Daniel was cast into the den of lions, as we shall see later, yet, unless he had been set free, the state of the people would have been more hard and stormy. For we know that wicked men impudently harass the wretched and innocent when they see something adverse happen to them. If Daniel had been mauled by the lions there would have been a general uprising against the Jews. God, therefore, not only here exercises the faith and patience of his servant but also proves the Jews by the same trial. For in the person of one man they saw themselves about to suffer extremities unless God unexpectedly sent them help — as, in fact, he did.

First, Daniel says that *he excelled among all others because the spirit in him was richer,* or 'more excellent'. It does not always happen that those who possess wisdom or other gifts obtain also more authority and favour. In kings' courts we see the first places held by beasts. For, not to repeat old histories, kings today are nearly all fools and brutes; they are like horses and asses among the brute animals; so that the bolder and more shamelessly pushing anyone is, the more authority does he gain in courts. But when Daniel says that *he excelled,* he commends to us a twofold benefit of God: that he had been endowed with a greater spirit; and that Darius here acknowledged it and thus magnified it, when he saw the man was industrious and endowed with uncommon wisdom. Therefore, let us grasp what the prophet here intends to teach, that he had been divinely endowed with prudence and other gifts; and also that King Darius was a good judge, who could estimate his prudence and other virtues and so hold him in esteem.

So *because a fuller spirit was in him, he surpassed all others,* he says; *the king even thought to elevate him in the whole kingdom,* that is, to make him chief of the three satraps. But although this was a singular privilege, by which God at one and the same time honoured his people and the prophet, yet we must bemoan the negligence of kings nowadays, who arrogantly despise the gifts of God in the best of men, those who are well able to hold high positions of the greatest usefulness for the people. But they keep those who have gone foolish in their pleasures and are just like themselves, men given up to avarice and robbery, cruel and completely licentious. When we see no consideration in kings to discover those who are worthy of rule and power, the state of the world must really be deplored, for it is, as it were, a mirror for us of the divine vengeance when kings are so lacking in discrimination. At the last day King Darius alone will be sufficient to condemn them. He had so much discernment that he did not hesitate to appoint a foreigner and a captive over all the satraps. It was truly regal, more, an heroic virtue, for Darius to set a captive over all his own countrymen. But kings nowadays think of nothing else but to elevate their panderers or jesters, or whoever flatters them. They raise none but the worthless, whom God brands as ignominious. And although they are unworthy to be numbered among men, yet they themselves are 'kings of kings'! Kings today are not much better than slaves. And this happens through their laziness in getting out of all their duties. So they are forced to hand over the government to others and keep only the title. These things, as I said, are sure proofs of God's wrath; for the world is unworthy, towards which God today reaches out his hand as ruler.

Now, as for the envy of the nobles: we see that the vice has been rife in all ages, that those who aspire to greatness cannot abide virtue. Conscious of their own evil, they must needs be irritated by the virtue of others. Yet it should not seem strange that the Persians, who had undergone the hardest labours and encountered all sorts of dangers, could not bear a man obscure and unknown to be not merely included in their company but even made the chief, as if he were their superior. So their envy seems to have some cause or at least excuse. But for anyone to be devoted to his own advantage without considering the public good will always deservedly be condemned. Whoever aspires to power and thinks only of himself and not of the common state of the people, he must indeed be avaricious and grasping and cruel and faithless. In short, he forgets his duty. When, therefore, the nobles of the kingdom envy Daniel, they only betray their own malice, because they have no thought for the public good but desire to draw and snatch everything to themselves.

Now in this example we see where envy springs from. And we must note this carefully, because nothing is easier than to slip from one vice to another. He who envies loses all fairness and tries to turn everything to his adversary's loss. These nobles take it as a slur that Daniel is preferred above them. Even if they had stopped there, that vice, as I said, would still be a sign of a perverse nature. But they break out further and seek an occasion or fault in Daniel. And so we see that envy stirs them up to catching out a fault. Thus all the envious are, as it were, perpetually on the watch, observing those whose

241

fortune they envy so that they can oppress them for some reason. That is one thing. But when they do not find a fault, they trample on all fairness, and shamelessly, inhumanely, no less cruelly than treacherously, set out to destroy their enemy. Daniel relates this about their envy.

He says that in the beginning *they sought occasion and found none.* Then he adds that the occasion that they took was not from a just cause but was dishonest. For there is no doubt that they knew Daniel to be a good man and approved by God. Therefore, when they lay in wait for the holy prophet, it is as if they were waging war on God himself. But they were blinded by their perverse feeling of envy. But where does envy come from? Simply from ambition. So we see that ambition is the worst pest; from it envy is born; and from envy arise in their turn treachery and cruelty.

But by their example Daniel admonishes us also to devote ourselves to integrity, so that we may not give occasion for the malevolent and wicked to catch at. There will be no better defence for us against the envious and calumniators than to live uprightly and innocently. For although they will set traps for us on every side, they will not succeed, for our innocence will be like a shield to repel their malice.

Meanwhile we see that Daniel had not escaped altogether. They sought a pretext against him in something else — the service of God. But from this let us again learn that godliness and application to godliness should be more to us than our own life. Daniel was faithful and irreproachable in his business and carrying out his duties, so as to close the mouth of those hostile and malevolent to him. Therefore integrity, as I said, is the best shield.

Again, Daniel was in danger because he did not cease from his sincere service and profession of God. Therefore we ought boldly to undergo perils, whenever the service of God is at stake. For our fleeting life ought not to be more precious to us than the most holy matter of all — that God's honour may stand untarnished. So we see that from one point of view we are here being trained to nurture integrity, for we shall not be able to be more secure than when armed with a good conscience; as also Peter in his First Epistle[4] exhorts us in the same way. Now, whatever we may fear and whatever the outcome may be, even if a hundred deaths befall us, it is not right to defect from the pure service of God. Daniel did not hesitate to face death and enter the den of lions to profess that he worshipped the God of Israel.

Now, from the fact that the nobles broke out into this barbarous and cruel design of persecuting Daniel on the pretext of religion, we again infer how blind is the madness when ambition and envy possess men's minds. For it is nothing to them to fight against God. They did not attack Daniel as a man but rushed into a mad and sacrilegious battle with the aim of destroying the

---

4. Mg., 1 Pet. 3:16.

service of God, just to gratify their lust for power. This is why I said that we are warned by this example that we must beware of ambition and flee from it — and what envy also springs from it.

But the nature of this crime against the Law of God then follows:

6 *Then* [to him] *the satraps and rulers of the provinces assembled* [for רגשׁ, *ragas,* signifies strictly 'to join and associate oneself'] *with the king* [that is, a conspiracy having been made, they went to the king] *and spoke thus to him, 'King Darius, live for ever!*
7 *All the satraps of the kingdom, the nobles and rulers of provinces, the counsellors and leaders, have taken counsel that there be enacted a statute of the king* [that is, "a royal statute", or "from the king"] *and an edict confirmed, that whoever shall seek a petition from any god and man until* [those] *thirty days, apart from you, O King, shall be cast into the den of lions.'*

By this plot the nobles of the kingdom were aiming at overthrowing the holy prophet of God, namely, that he should be cast into the den of lions and perish, or else defect from the outward profession of the service of God. But they knew he was too stronghearted to buy his life with such impiety. Therefore they thought there was no hope for him. They thought themselves very clever; but God came in to oppose them and helped his servant, as we shall see.

Meanwhile, their seeking to destroy Daniel on this pretext showed a worse than detestable malice. Although they themselves did not worship the God of Israel, they knew that the prophet was godly and upright. Besides, they had experienced the power of this God who was unknown to them. They did not condemn Daniel on those grounds; they could not even make the religion he followed into a fault. Hence I said that they were so carried away into cruelty by hatred of the man that they struck against God. It could not be hidden from them that God ought to be worshipped. They themselves worshipped unknown gods and dared not condemn the service of the God of Israel. Hence, we see that the devil had bewitched them when they dared to fix this crime on the holy prophet.

But what occasion they took advantage of is unknown. Some conjecture that it happened because Darius could not bear the glory of his son-in-law. For he being old and the other in his prime, he thought he was despised. So some reckon that Darius himself was touched by a secret envy and so gave his nobles an opening for them to be able to deceive a wretched and too credulous old man and as it were dazzle his eyes. But this conjecture does not seem firm enough to me. But I am not much occupied about this; for it may be that at the start of this new kingdom they wanted to congratulate the king and thought of something new and unusual — a line that we see very often taken by flatterers of royalty. So they could have deceived this old man whose monarchy had lately increased. Hitherto he had ruled only the Medes. The Chaldaeans, the Assyrians, and many other nations had now come under his empire. Such an accession might well make him drunk with empty glory; and the nobles also thought they had a plausible cause for decreeing this divine honour. This reason alone, therefore, seems sufficient to me, and I do not enquire more carefully; for I embrace what is probable and what occurs to us of its own will, so to say.

The rest I will leave for tomorrow.

Grant, almighty God, just as you guided your servant Daniel, who, when honours came to him from every side and he was raised to the highest dignity, yet always applied himself to integrity and walked blamelessly amidst the great and general licence, grant, I say, that we may learn to keep ourselves in the moderate state within which you confine us, or that we may be content with our poverty and take the greater care to prove ourselves blameless to you, and also to those with whom we have to do, so that your name may be glorified in us, and that, protected by your help, we may keep vigorously on despite the malice of men, and although Satan besiege us on every side and the wicked lay traps and even attack us like savage beasts, that we may yet remain safe under your protection; and even if we have to undergo a hundred deaths we may learn to live and die to you so that your name may always be glorified in us through Christ our Lord. Amen.

Lecture 28

Yesterday I said that the nobles, who had hatched a plot against Daniel, were carried away by their wild fury and dared to dictate an edict to the king, which Daniel quotes. It was an intolerable sacrilege for the king to strip all the gods of their honour; yet he subscribed to the edict, as we shall see later — simply as a way to test the obedience of his people, whom he had recently subjugated by the hand of his son-in-law. For there is no doubt that he wanted to subdue the Chaldaeans, who up to this time had been predominant. And we know that power begets a ferocious boldness. Because the Chaldaeans had formerly ruled far and wide, they were difficult to tame and be brought to obedience; even more so now that they saw themselves the servants of those who had previously envied them. For we know that there had been many wars between them and the Medes. So, although they had been subjugated in war, their minds were still untamed. Darius therefore wanted to put their obedience to the test — that is, that was his motive. He was not deliberately provoking the wrath of the gods, but, in considering men, he forgot the deity and put himself in the place of the gods, as if it were in his power to make the power of heaven his own. This, as I said, was a horrible sacrilege. But if anyone could search into the hearts of kings, scarcely one in a hundred would be found who did not despise all divinity in the same way. For although they profess to reign 'by the grace of God', as was said yesterday, they want to be worshipped in his place. Now we see how easily flatterers persuade kings to do anything that seems to conduce to exalting their greatness.

He goes on:

8 *'Now, O King, enact an edict and seal a writing which is not to be changed* [that is, "which is immutable"] *according to the law of the Medes and Persians, which does not change.'*

9 *And so King Darius* [himself] *sealed the writing and the edict.*

From this, as I have said, it is more than apparent how prone the minds of kings are to deceit when they think they have a chance to thrive and to increase their dignity. For the king does not spend time discussing it with his nobles but just signs the edict — simply because he reckons it will be more advantageous to him and his successors to have the Chaldaeans so obedient that they are ready to deny all their gods rather than refuse his command.

As for the words, some translate אסרא, *esara,* as 'writing', and explain it as 'to inscribe'; for we know that laws were at one time inscribed on tables of bronze. But I interpret it more simply, that they ask the king for a sealing of the writing; that is, when the edict had been written down that he would seal it.

'Which will not change', they say — 'which is not to be changed'; that is, the edict was inviolable, *'according to the law of the Medes and Persians, which does not change',* that is, 'which does not pass away' (just as Christ also says, 'Heaven and earth shall pass away, but my words shall not pass away';[1] that is, 'they will never become of no effect').

They join the Medes with the Persians, and this shows what I said earlier, that Cyrus and Darius reigned jointly, as if colleagues. For although at the end of his life Darius was given the greater dignity, yet the power rested with Cyrus. Moreover, there can be no argument that his sons were heirs of each kingdom and of the eastern monarchy (except when they began to go to war with one another). Now, what they claim for the law of the Medes and Persians in saying that 'it is immutable' is certainly praiseworthy in laws — namely, that their authority is sacrosanct and that they stay in operation and continue to be effectual; for when laws start varying, many people will suffer injury; no individual rights will be safe unless the law is perpetual. Again, if laws are allowed to be chopped and changed about, caprice will take the place of equity. For if the very powerful are corrupted with bribes, they will promulgate now one edict, now another. Thus no equity can flourish when there is so much freedom in changing laws. And at the same time it is wise to remember, first, that no king may promulgate an edict or annul a law without grave and mature consideration; second, that kings should take care that they are not outwitted by cunning and indirect tricks, as often happens. So, constancy in kings and their edicts is to be approved and applauded, so long as prudence and equity come first. But we shall at once see that kings are foolish and like to be thought steadfast and thus completely pervert right by their stubbornness. But this we shall at once see in its place.

Now he goes on:

1. Mg., Mt. 24:35; Mk. 13:31.

10 *But Daniel, when he knew that the writing* [was] *sealed, came* [or 'entered'] *into his house (the windows* [were] *open in his chamber towards Jerusalem) and three times in the day* [that is, 'on three occasions in the day'; that is, 'daily on three occasions'] *he inclined himself on his knees* [the verb and the noun are from the same root, 'he kneeled upon his knees', or 'inclined himself'] *and prayed and confessed before his God as he had done from the first time* [that is, 'he had previously been accustomed to do'].

Now Daniel relates that God's Spirit had endued him with fortitude, so as to offer his life in sacrifice to God; for he knew no hope of pardon for him would be left if it was learned he had violated the king's edict. He also knew that the king would not be free to pardon him even if he wanted to — as was proved by the outcome. Therefore, with death before his eyes, the prophet preferred to meet it boldly rather than give up his duty of piety. It is to be noted that here it is not a question of the inward worship of God but of outward profession. If Daniel had been forbidden to pray, the fortitude with which he was endowed could have seemed really necessary. As it is, many might think he was running into danger and throwing his life away without serious cause, since he had been forbidden only the outward profession. But here Daniel is not trumpeting his own virtue; the Spirit is speaking by his mouth. So we must hold that this high courage in the holy prophet was pleasing to God. And his deliverance shows how greatly his piety was approved in preferring to give up his own life rather than change his usual way of worshipping God.

We know that the chief sacrifice demanded by God is invocation. For so we bear witness that he is the author of all our good; we also give proof of our faith when we turn to him and cast all our cares on his bosom and lay before him all our desires. Since, then, prayer has the primacy in the adoration and service of God, it was assuredly no light matter for the king to forbid anyone to pray to God. It was a manifest and altogether gross denial of piety.

Again, we gather from this how blind was the king's pride in subscribing to such an impious and detestable edict, and how great the passion of the nobles, who, to destroy Daniel, strove, so far as they could, to get rid of all piety and drag God down out of heaven. For what is left when men reckon they can do without God's help and carelessly forget him? We know that unless every moment he upheld us by his power we should be reduced to nothing. So when the king forbade any prayer to be made for a whole month, it was, as I said, to demand every individual to deny God. Hence Daniel could not obey the edict without injuring God severely and falling away from piety; for, as I said, this is the chief sacrifice that God demands. So it is not surprising that Daniel courageously opposed the sacrilegious edict.

Now, as for the profession, it was also necessary that he should testify before men that he was standing firm in the service of God. For if he changed

247

anything in his customs, it would be an indirect recantation. He would not have said openly that he was despising God for the sake of Darius, but the mere change would have been a sign of treacherous defection. And we know that God requires not only faith in the heart and inward affection but also the testimony and confession of our piety. Unless Daniel wanted to be the wickedest of apostates, he had to stand fast in the holy practice that was his habit.

But he was accustomed to pray to God with his windows open. He keeps to his course, lest anyone should object that he was temporarily gratifying an earthly king and degrading the worship of God. Would that this doctrine were engraven in the hearts of all nowadays as it should be! Yet many smile at the prophet's example; not, indeed, openly, but it is very clear that he seems to them too naive and thoughtless in encountering danger for nothing and needlessly. For they so separate faith from confession as to think that faith can remain sound even if it is buried, and for the sake of fleeing a hundred crosses desert from a pure and sincere profession.

And so let us understand that we must not only offer the sacrifice of prayer to God in our hearts but that an open profession is also required, so that at least it will be clear that we are true servants of God. I am not saying that we have got to publish all our sentiments and be haled off at once to death by the enemies of God and the gospel. But I do say that these two things are united — faith and confession; and they can in no way be separated. But confession is twofold. Either we declare openly and frankly what is in our minds; or, so far as is necessary, we so hold ourselves to the service of God that we give no sign of perverse and faithless pretence, as if we were renouncing all inclination to piety. As for the former, it is not always and everywhere necessary to profess our faith; but the latter should be perpetual. For it will never be right for us to simulate any defection or apostasy.

Daniel therefore did not blow a trumpet to summon the Chaldaeans when he wanted to pray, but formed his wishes and prayers in his chamber as usual. Yet he did not pretend that he had forgotten all about piety when he saw his faith tried, and when they tested him out, to see whether he would stand to it steadfastly. He expressly declares that *he came to his house* after he had learned about the sealed edict. Without doubt, had he been admitted to the council he would not have kept quiet. But the rest of the nobles were cunning and excluded him in case he should intervene, and they thought the redress would come too late — in fact, that there would be none; and he himself knew quite well that he must die. Therefore, if he had been admitted to the council by the king, he would have done his duty and boldly intervened. But as the edict was already sealed and the opportunity of warning the king removed, he went home.

This must be noted, so that we may learn that counsellors of kings can in no way be excused who deliberately and hastily make themselves scarce when they see it is dangerous to offer an opinion, and think that God is satisfied so long as they abstain. But such pusillanimity has nothing to be said for it. And they cannot shelter themselves behind Daniel's example, because, as was said, he had been excluded by the cunning and malice of the nobles from intervening and warning the king in time as he usually did.

Now he says that *the windows were open towards Jerusalem.* It is asked whether it was necessary for Daniel to open the windows. For someone could object this was done out of a very foolish notion; for if God fills heaven and earth, what is the point of opening windows towards Jerusalem? But there is no doubt that the prophet stimulated himself to ardent prayer by this assistance. For he was praying for the liberation of the people, and when he directed his eyes towards Jerusalem, the view as it were fanned his mind into a glow. The prophet, therefore, opened his windows, not in reference to God, as if God would hear him more easily if heaven were opened up between his house and Judaea; rather it was in reference to himself and he was thinking of his own infirmity. Now, if the holy prophet, who was constant in prayer, needed such a help, we must see whether our slothfulness nowadays has not need of even more stimuli. And so let us learn, when we feel we are too slow to pray, so cold in praying, that we should gather together all the helps that can stir up our zeal and correct the sluggishness of which we are aware. This, then, was the prophet's purpose *when he opened his windows towards Jerusalem.*

Moreover, by this symbol he wanted to demonstrate to himself and to his household that he was persevering in the hope and trust of the promised redemption. So when he was praying to God, he had Jerusalem in sight as it were. Not that his eyes could penetrate to such a far-off land; but he was directing his gaze towards Jerusalem, as if he were saying that he was a pilgrim among the Chaldaeans, even though there he was rich and had been given great power and one of the very highest positions. So he wanted everyone to know that his heart was in the promised inheritance, although for a time exiled from it. This was the second reason for his opening the windows.

But he says that *daily he prayed on three occasions.* And this also is noteworthy; for unless any of us set definite hours for prayer we shall easily forget. Therefore, although Daniel was constant and profuse in prayer, yet he laid on himself the solemn rite of prostrating himself before God three times a day. Thus, when we get up in the morning, it is too brutishly sluggish if we do not begin by calling upon God. So also when we go to bed. And also when we are about to take food; and at other hours, as each one sees is convenient for himself. God allows us this liberty; but each of us should feel his weakness and seek assistance. This is why Daniel was wont to pray three times a day.

And a sign of his earnestness is added when he says that *he prostrated himself on his knees.* Not that kneeling is in itself necessary when praying. But because we need stimuli, as was said, kneeling is quite important. First, because we are warned that we can only appear before God in humility and reverence. Second, so that our minds may be the better prepared for earnest prayer. And this symbol of worship is acceptable to God. It was therefore not superfluous that Daniel said that *he fell on his knees whenever he intended to pray to God.*

Now when he says that *he prayed and confessed before God,* or 'praised God', this also is to be carefully observed. For in their prayers many just grumble to God. Although they eagerly ask for this or that, they are carried away by an immoderate ardour and, as I said, scold God when they pray unless he at once obeys their wishes. This is why Daniel joins praises or thanks with prayers — as Paul also exhorts us to both: 'Let your requests be made known to God', he says, 'with thanksgiving';[2] as if he were saying that prayers and vows can only be rightly framed when we bless his holy name, even though he may not at once put us in possession of our desires.

And this quality is to be observed in Daniel: he had long been an exile and had lived through many and troublesome commotions; yet he celebrates God's praises. Which of us is trained in such patience to praise God if for three or four years we have been heavy laden with many troubles? No, scarcely a day passes without our desires over-heating, so that we break out in an attack against God. That Daniel could persevere in praising God when he was so oppressed with distresses and sorrows and troubles is a remarkable proof of an invincible patience. And without doubt it signifies a continuous action when he puts the demonstrative pronoun דְּנָה, *dena,* which refers to a regular practice, *even as he had done from the first time.* By indicating the time he denotes, as I said, perseverance; that he was accustomed thus to pray; not once or twice, but every day he steadily practised this godly duty.

Afterwards he goes on:

11 *Then those men joined together* [or 'met together', as others translate it] *and found Daniel praying and making intercession before his God.*

Here Darius's nobles betray their underhanded dealing, while they are watching Daniel; and they do so by mutual conspiracy. For their only motive in dictating the edict was to accomplish Daniel's death. Therefore they agree together, and they catch *Daniel praying and making intercession before his God.* Had Daniel prayed in secret, he would not have been exposed to their plots. But he did not hesitate to encounter death. For he knew the purpose of the edict, and he knew that the nobles would come. Therefore we see that he goes to meet death of his own free will; and that for no other reason than that he might keep the pure worship of God, even in outward profession. Away with those who want to cover their treachery with the pretext that one should not rashly run into danger, so that

2. Mg., Phil. 4:6.

when the wicked besiege them on every side they must be careful not to throw their life away rashly! According to them, Daniel was guilty of too great naivety and foolishness in encountering certain danger knowingly and willingly. But we have already said that this danger could not have been avoided without an indirect defection from God. For he would at once have met the accusation, 'Why have you left off your usual custom? Why have you closed the windows? Why do you not dare to pray to your God? It is quite clear that the king means more to you than the reverence and fear of God.' So, because he would have so reduced God's honour, Daniel willingly, as we have already seen, offered himself as a sacrifice for death.

We are also taught by this example that, however circumspectly they act and modestly they behave, traps are always being set for God's children. Yet their prudent behaviour should not extend to being too clever, too far-seeing. That is, they must take heed to their security in such a way that they do not forget what God demands and how precious his reputation is to him and how necessary the confession of faith — of course, in its right place and time.

Now he goes on:

12 *Then they came and said* ['and spoke'] *before the king upon the royal edict, 'Did not you seal an edict, that no man should seek from any god or man until* [these] *thirty days, apart from you, O King* [or, "that whatever" (thus rather it is to be translated) "man should seek from any god or man until these thirty days, apart from you, O King"] *should be cast into the den of lions?' The king replied and said, 'The word is firm according to the law of the Medes and Persians, which does not change.'*

Now Darius's nobles come in triumph to the king. But they approach him cunningly. For they do not speak straight out about Daniel, whom they knew the king loved. They just repeat what they had said, that the edict cannot be changed, because the law of the Medes and Persians was inviolable, and could not be made invalid. As far as they can, they again ratify the edict, so that afterwards the king might neither be free nor dare to retract what he had once commanded. This craftiness must be noted; they indirectly forestall the king and, as it were, enmesh him so that afterwards he shall not be free to change his word. Therefore *they come and make words about the royal edict,* he says. They keep quiet about Daniel and instead start off with the royal edict, so as to bind the king more and more tightly.

He goes on that *the king replied that the word was true.* Here we see how greedily kings love to be praised for constancy. But they do not distinguish between constancy and stubbornness. For kings should stand to their edicts to the extent that they are not ashamed to retract what they had promulgated rashly. Then, if anything thoughtless has slipped out, prudence and equity demand that they correct their mistake. But when all respect for justice is trodden under foot and they still want everything they commanded, however thoughtlessly, to stand firm, this is the height of foolishness. They should not pretend that their stubbornness is constancy, as we said.

But the rest for tomorrow.

Grant, almighty God, since you have won us by the precious blood of your Son, that we may not be our own masters but devoted to you in steadfast obedience, so that we may set our minds on consecrating ourselves entirely to you and so to offer body and soul in sacrifice that we are prepared to encounter a hundred deaths rather than defect from the true and sincere worship of your Godhead; and especially that we may so exercise ourselves in prayers that at every moment we may have recourse to you and cast ourselves on your fatherly care, so that you may govern us by your Spirit even to the end. Guard and uphold us until we are gathered into that heavenly kingdom which your only-begotten Son has won for us by his blood. Amen.

Lecture 29

We began yesterday to explain what Daniel related about the slander laid upon him before King Darius. The nobles of the kingdom, as we said, attacked the king cleverly. If they had made Daniel their starting point, the king might have cut them short. But they talk about royal edicts. They show how dangerous it would be if the authority of all royal edicts were not firm. And we see that by this subterfuge they got what they wanted. For the king confirms what they said, that it would be wrong for what was promulgated in a king's name to be made ineffective. For kings are pleased with their importance and want whatever is pleasing to them to be taken as an oracle. Darius's edict forbidding requests to God was ungodly and detestable. But he still wants it to stand firm, because his majesty would be undermined among his subjects. Yet he does not see the consequences. Therefore we are taught by this example that there is no virtue so rare in kings as moderation; and yet none is more necessary. For the greater the freedom, the more should they beware of giving rein to their desires. But they think that whatever they like to decide is lawful.

Now he goes on:

13   *Then they spoke and said before the king, 'Daniel, who* [is] *of the children of the captives of Judah, has not set his sense upon you, O King,* [or, "has not given his sense", or, "his mind, to you"] *nor to the edict which you sealed; and three times a day he prays his petition* [that is, "prays according to his custom", or, "as he was wont"].'

Now when the slanderers see that King Darius is no longer on safe ground for defending Daniel's cause, they open up more freely what they had

253

previously kept hidden. For if they had begun with Daniel, as we said, their accusation might at once have been refuted or weakened. But after the king had once declared his verdict that the statement was true that according to the law of the Persians and Medes royal edicts should continue to be effectual — when, then, this had been done, they come to the person himself.

'*Daniel*', they say, '*who is of the captives of Judah, did not give his mind to you, O King, or to the edict which you sealed.*' When they say Daniel was 'of the captivity of Judah', there is no doubt that they are making his crime more detestable. For if any of the Chaldaeans had dared to despise the king's edict, even his temerity would have been inexcusable. But when Daniel, who lately had been a slave and a captive among the Chaldaeans, dared to despise the authority of the king, who by right of war possessed all Chaldaea, it seems even less tolerable. It is just as if they were saying, 'This former captive was among your servants; you are the ruler, and the lords to whom he was subject are under your yoke because you defeated them. But this captive, this foreigner, this man of servile condition, is nevertheless lording it over you.' We see, then, that they were aiming to exacerbate the king's mind by this circumstance, when they say, '*he is one of the captives*'.

Now, their discourse is not at all straightforward. By every means they are trying to prick the king into action and inflame his anger against Daniel. '*He has not given his mind to you, O King*'; that is, 'he has not considered who you are'. Thus, 'your majesty has been despised by him'. Next, '*to the edict which you sealed*'. This is another amplification. '*Daniel has not set his mind either to you or to the edict. Will you put up with this?*' At last they recite the fact itself, that '*he prays three times a day*'. That was the simple story. 'Daniel did not obey your command, for he prays to his God.' But, as I said, they exaggerate the fault by accusing Daniel of pride and contempt and stubbornness. We see then by what devices Daniel was oppressed by his ill-wishers.

Now he goes on:

14 *Then the king, after he had heard the word, was very sad* [some translate it, 'troubled', others 'was greatly vexed, grieved greatly'; for באש, *bees,* signifies 'to grieve'] *in himself and set his heart to Daniel* [there is metathesis[1] in the letters, for בל, *bal,* is put for לב, *leb.* Therefore 'he set his heart'] *on saving him, and until sunset was anxious to rescue him* [or, 'set him free', that is, 'he was taking trouble to rescue him'].

15 *Then those men thronged together* [or, 'united together', as if in a solid body and in a crowd they assailed the king, to make him the more nervous. So 'they congregated themselves'] *to the king and said, 'You know, O King,*

1. Metathesis: transposition of letters.

that the law of the Medes and Persians [is] *that every edict and statute established by the king may not be changed.'*

In the first place Daniel relates that the king was troubled when he realized the malice of his nobles, something that formerly had escaped him. For what they were getting at or what they were after had never entered his mind. But now he saw that he had been deceived and trapped. So he was troubled. From this again we are taught how intensely suspicious kings should be of wicked advice. They are surrounded on all sides by treacherous people whose only purpose is either to get rich by false accusations or to oppress at one time their enemies, at another those whom they hope to despoil, and at another just to favour evil causes. Since kings are beset by so many snares, they should be the more careful to be suspicious of craftiness. For they will realize too late that they have been tricked, when no remedy is left, partly because they are afraid, partly because they want to look after their reputation. And they would rather offend God than incur a name for fickleness among men. It is because their reputation is so sacred to kings that they go on in evil begun, even if their conscience reproves them. And if equity itself is set before their eyes it is not a strong enough bridle to restrain them when ambition pulls them in the opposite direction and they do not want their fame among men to suffer.

Such an example is here set before us in Darius. First it is said that *he was sad at the word he heard and was anxious even until sunset how he might rescue Daniel from death.* He wanted to do this — if his fame could stand safe and sound, and, moreover, if he could also please the nobles. But on the one side he was afraid of danger if a conspiracy of the princes should raise a revolution; and on the other side he was moved by the foolish shame of not wanting to incur the ignominy of fickleness which he would encounter. Hence he was overcome and yielded to the desires of the wicked. Although he thought until sunset how to rescue Daniel, yet that perverse shame prevailed, as I said; and also the fear of danger.

For when we do not rest on God's help, we must of necessity always vacillate, even if we are otherwise well-affected. Pilate wanted to free Christ; but he was frightened by the threats of the people when they declared he had offended against Caesar.[2] And it is not surprising, for faith alone is the sure and firm support for us to rely on and do our duty fearlessly and overcome all fear. But when there is no faith, vacillation pushes us here and there, as I said. Thus it happened that Darius, fearing a conspiracy of his nobles, surrendered the innocent Daniel to their cruelty. Then came the shame, as I called it, that he did not want to seem a thoughtless man who would suddenly revoke his edict, it being a law of the Medes and Persians that whatever proceeded from kings was inviolable.

2. Mg., Jn 19:12.

And this Daniel next relates. For he says that *those men congregated themselves* when they saw the king wavering and, so to say, oscillating; they became overbearing and, as it were, attacked him. That they are said to meet together is equivalent to saying that they were going to frighten King Darius. *'Know, O King'*, they say. He did indeed know and they were teaching him nothing new. But they asserted menacingly, 'What? do you not see that the name of kings will henceforth have no authority if your edict is flouted unpunished? Will you let yourself be made a game of?' In short, they signify that he will not be king unless he takes vengeance on the injury offered him by Daniel, who had taken no notice of his authority. *'Know, O King, that with the Persians and Medes . . .'* He was King of the Medes. But it is just as if they said, 'What rumour will be spread through all your realms? You know that hitherto the rule has held among the Medes and Persians that the king shall not change his edicts. If you give such an example, will not all your subjects at once rise up against you? Will you not be contemptible to them?' So we see that here the satraps boldly opposed their king and deterred him from changing his mind. And, to move him the more, they joined the edict to the statute which the king had made, lest what he had ratified often and in the same words he would now allow to be treated as nothing.

He goes on:

16 *Then the king spoke* [that is 'ordained', or 'commanded'], *and they took Daniel and cast* [him] *into the den of lions. The king replied and said to Daniel, 'Your God, whom you serve continually* [the pronoun here is superfluous], *he will liberate you* [or, if we take it as a prayer, "May he liberate you!"].'

The king, as we said, was frightened by the announcement of the nobles and condemned Daniel to death. From this we infer that kings get the just reward for their pride by being forced to obey their sycophants. How was it that Darius was deceived by the cunning of his princes? Because he thought it would strengthen his authority if he tested everyone's obedience by commanding that none should pray to any god or man for a whole month. So he thought he would be superior both to gods and men if he experienced such obedience from all his subjects. Now we see how the princes rose against him impudently, how they warned him of his extreme danger if he did not obey them. Therefore, we see that when kings make themselves too lofty they are exposed to shame; they are the slaves of their own slaves.

And this is too common in earthly princes. Those who possess authority and favour with them applaud them in everything and worship them. There is no sort of adulation that they do not think of to curry favour. And meanwhile, what liberty do their idols possess? They are permitted no authority. They cannot even be familiar with their closest and most faithful friends while they are being watched by their guards. In short, compare them with wretches held in a close prison, and none that is shut up in the deepest dungeon, even if he has three of four jailers, but is more free than kings. But as I said, it is the just punishment of God; because, when they cannot confine themselves to the order and rank of men but want to pierce beyond the clouds and be equal with God, they must needs be held in ridicule. Hence it is that they serve all their servants, dare suggest nothing on their own account, have no real friend, dare not call up this or that man or entrust their wishes to anyone they choose. So, then, in earthly kingdoms they rule as slaves, because they do not reckon they are of the order of mortals.

This is what happened to King Darius; he arraigned Daniel and ordered him to be cast into the den of lions. This his nobles force from him and he unwillingly obeys. But we must observe the cause: he had recently forgotten he was mortal and wanted to snatch God's control from him as if he wanted to drag him out of heaven. For if God is in heaven, he must be prayed to. But Darius forbade anyone to frame a prayer. This was to annihilate God's power, so far as he could. Now he is forced to obey even his subjects, even if they should tyrannize over him almost contemptuously.

Now Daniel adds that *The king spoke thus with him, 'Your God, whom you continually serve'*, or, 'whom you worship continually', *'he will save you.'* This word can be read optatively, as was said. There is no doubt that Darius framed such a wish. But it can also be taken like this: 'Your God whom you serve will save you'; as if he were saying, 'I am not my own master. I am swept away as if by a tempest; the nobles are forcing me unwillingly to commit this crime. Therefore I now resign you and your life to God, since it is not in my power to save you' — as if in this excuse he were lessening his own fault by transferring the power to save Daniel to God. For this reason some praise King Darius's piety. But although I admit that this saying shows us his clemency and humaneness, yet it is certain there was not a trace of piety in him when he wanted to deck himself out with what he had stolen from God. For although the superstitious do not seriously fear God, they still retain some terror of him. But here he wants to annihilate all deity. What sort of piety was this? So we must praise the clemency in Darius, but his sacrilegious pride is in no way excusable.

Next, why did he treat Daniel so humanely? Because he had found him a faithful servant. It was therefore a love of his own that inclined him to clemency. He had not behaved in the same way with others. If a hundred or a thousand Jews had been dragged to judgment, he would quite carelessly have condemned the lot for not adapting their customs to the edict. With them he would have been rigid and ungodly and cruel. But he spared Daniel for the sake of his own convenience and also because he had taken him into his favour. Although his humaneness may be praised, no sign of godliness appears in him.

Yet he says, *'Your God whom you serve, he will save you'* — that is, he had earlier learned that Daniel had foretold the downfall of the Chaldaean monarchy. That convinced him that the God of Israel foreknew all things and that all things were under his will. But yet he does not serve him or allow others to serve him. For, so far as he can, he shuts God out of his rights. So although he here ascribes to God the power to save, he does not do it from his heart. Even if he does do so, his impiety is the worse when he deprives of his rights him whom he feels to be the true and only God and endowed with supreme power, and being only ashes and earth, dares to put himself in his place.

Now he goes on:

17 *And one stone was brought and placed upon the mouth of the cave; and the king sealed it with his ring and with the ring of his nobles, that the decision should not be changed in Daniel* [that is, 'in regard to Daniel'. Those who translate it 'against', as if the king might wish to oppose their violence deliberately, pervert the whole meaning. Without doubt it was done at their instigation, in case the king should take steps to have him stolen away.]

There is no doubt that it was done by the purpose of God that the nobles should seal with their rings the stone that blocked the mouth of the cave, so that the miracle should be the more conspicuous. For when next day the king came, the rings were intact, that is, the seals remained intact. From this it was clear that it was not by human contrivance that God's servant was unharmed, but by help from heaven. Yet we see how audaciously the nobles forced the king to assent to all their decisions. For he might have seemed to have done enough by delivering to them a man so dear and faithful to him and commanding him to be thrown into the den of lions. Yet they are still not content with the king's pliableness. They extort one more thing from him — to shut the mouth of the cave and also that all of them should seal the stone in case anyone should rescue Daniel.

We see that when once liberty has been stolen away, the flood-gates are open; especially when anyone by his fault has become a slave or given himself to the will of the wicked. For at first such slavery will not be so strong as to make a man who seems to be free do this and that, or whatever is commanded. But when he has given himself into slavery, as I have already said, he is forced to sin again, and again, and without end or moderation. For example, if anyone falls away from his duty through fear of men or flattery or any perverted disposition, he will make concessions here and there, not only on request but also at any rough command. But when once he has given up his freedom, as I have already said, he will be forced to do shameful things on the orders of anybody. It may be that a doctor or a pastor in a church is pliable out of ambition. He who got something out of him will come to him a second time. 'What! Do you dare deny me? Yesterday or the day before did I not get from you this or that?' Thus he is forced to sin a second time for the sake of the man he gave himself to; and a third time he will be forced to sin and so to the end, ad infinitum. So also if princes, who are not only free themselves but also rule others, allow themselves to be bound by a bad conscience, they renounce all their authority and are drawn in every direction at the desires of their subjects.

Thus the example is set before us of King Darius, who, after he had given Daniel over to unjust punishment, added also, that *the cave should be closed,* and that *the stone should be sealed.* To what end? *Lest the decision should be changed;* that is, lest he should dare do anything about Daniel. So we see that the king subjected himself to great shame, first, in that his honesty was impugned by the nobles, as if they said they could not trust him; even though he had ordered Daniel to be cast into the den of lions, they took precautions against his rescuing him. They were not going to let him try anything. So we see that they insolently detract from the credit of their king and, moreover, usurp power against him to stop him daring to remove the stone which had been sealed — unless, perhaps, he wanted to commit a fraud by breaking open a public seal, which would be equivalent to violating the public law-tables and being a swindler. This place therefore warns us not to sell ourselves into slavery to the desires of others. Let each serve his neighbours so far as love and usage demand; but let none allow himself to be deflected in any direction by a bad conscience; for when he ceases to be free, he is forced to bear many insults and to obey the most detestable orders — as we see happen with panderers and others who minister either to the avarice of princes or to their ambition or cruelty. For when once kings begin to be indebted, they are the most wretched slaves and cannot escape the ultimate compulsion of scurrilous service, a hundred times provoking both God and men to oppose them.

Now he goes on:

18 *Then the king went to his palace and spent the night in a fast* ['fasting'], *and musical instruments* [some translate it 'a supper' or 'a table'; but this does not fit; for first it says 'the king passed the night fasting'. The interpretation therefore fits better, that musical instruments] *were not brought before him* [and so there were no pleasures or delights] *and sleep* [also] *departed from him.*

Here Daniel tells of the king's too late repentance. Although he was very distressed, he did not correct his fault. And this happens with many who are not hardened in despising God and in depravity. They are dragged along by others and are displeased at their vices. Yet they go on. Would that the examples

259

of this evil were more rare! But they happen everywhere before our eyes. Darius is therefore here set before us as a sort of mean between the wicked and criminal and the upright and wise. Those who are thoroughly bad do not hesitate to challenge God to oppose them; they throw off all fear and shame and are unrestrained in their desires. But those who are ruled by the fear of God, even if they undergo hard contests with the flesh, put a bridle on themselves and restrain their perverse affections. There are other half-way men, who, as I said, are not yet hardened in their malice, even are not pleased with their vices, and yet they follow them as if they were on a string.

Such was Darius. For when, realizing that he was entrapped by the nobles, he should have firmly rejected their slanders and withstood them manfully, more, have accused them of abusing his compliance, he did nothing of the sort, but rather gave way to their onslaught. Meanwhile, he mourns in his palace, abstaining from food and all pleasures. So he shows that evil does not please him. Nevertheless, he engages in it.

Hence we see that when we sin it is not enough to be tortured by our conscience and to express some sorrow. We must go beyond that, so that our sorrow leads us to repentance, as also Paul teaches.[3] But Darius as it were sticks fast in the mire. When he mourned, he did not take pains to correct what he had done wrong. There was something of a beginning of repentance; but only a beginning. Therefore it is imperative that he who is conscious of his wrong shall impel himself to repentance; and when he feels some pricking of sorrow, that he shall excite it and not yield to any truce or to any peace. This is to be learnt from the present example, when Daniel relates that King Darius passed all that night in sorrow.

Afterwards he goes on:

19 *Then the king at dawn* [that is, 'early'] *rose when it became light and in hastiness* [that is, 'hastily'] *came to the den of lions.*
20 *And when he had drawn near to the den, he called to Daniel in a sad* [or 'mournful'] *voice. The king spoke and said to Daniel, 'Daniel, servant of the living God; your God whom you serve continually, has he been able to save you* [that is, "could he not save you"] *from the lions?'*

Here the king begins to behave a little more steadfastly, when he comes to the den. Formerly he had been so afraid that he had given way to the nobles and forgotten his royal dignity, as if he were committing himself to them as a slave. But now he does not fear their envy and wicked words. Therefore, *he came to the den of lions early,* he says, *at first light,* that is, before the sun was risen, just before dawn; *he came to the den, and hastily.* So we see that

3. Mg., 2 Cor. 7:10.

he was possessed by a bitter grief, which overcame all his previous fears. For he could still have been afraid and he had not forgotten the formidable threat, 'You will no longer possess power unless you vindicate this insult against your edict.' But, as I have already said, grief overcame fear. And yet we are unable to praise any piety in him, or even humaneness; because, although he had come to the den and called to Daniel with a mournful voice, he was not angry with his nobles before he saw the servant of God preserved safely. Then he conceived a better spirit, as we shall see. But he still persists in his weakness and is, as it were, in that middle degree between the perverse despisers and the hearty servants of God, who with an upright affection follow what they know to be right.

> *Grant, almighty God, since you show us in the example of your servant Daniel with what constancy we should persevere in the sincere worship of your Godhead, that we may go on to true courageousness, and so devote ourselves to you that we may not be turned hither and thither at the inordinate desires of men but may stand fast in your holy calling; and thus, having overcome all perils, we may at last arrive at the fruit of victory, the blessed immortality which is laid up for us in heaven, through Christ our Lord. Amen.*

Lecture 30

In our last lecture time forced me to break off the sentence where Daniel relates that the king drew near to the cave. Now he relates his words: *'Daniel, servant of the living God, your God whom you serve continually, was he not able to set you free?'* he says. Darius declares that the God of Israel is the living God. But if anyone is the living God, he excludes all imaginary gods, those whom men invent from their own ideas. For of necessity there is one Deity; and this principle holds good even among the heathen. Although afterwards each will fall back into his dreams, yet all confess that there are not many gods. They may divide God up, but they cannot deny that he is the unique God. Therefore, when Darius paid this tribute to the God of Israel, he was confessing that all other gods were mere inventions. But, as I said, this does not mean that the heathen keep to this principle, for afterwards it vanishes away from their thoughts. So this passage does not prove that King Darius was truly converted (as it seems to some) and embraced sincere piety. For he always served his idols but thought it was enough to leave the supreme place to the God of Israel. But, as we know, God cannot admit an associate, for he is jealous of his own glory.[1] Hence it was too weak for Darius to avow that the God whom Daniel worshipped was excellent above all gods; for when God reigns, all idols must of necessity be reduced to nothing — as it says also in the Psalm, 'God reigns, let all the gods of the heathen perish.'[2] Darius did not get so far as to devote himself to the true and only God; yet he was compelled to give the highest honour to the God of Israel, while always remaining submerged in his accustomed superstitions.

1. Mg., Is. 42:8.
2. Cf. Ps. 97:1, 7.

Afterwards he adds, *'Your God, whom you serve continually, was he not able to free you from the lions?'* Here he speaks doubtfully, as unbelievers do who think they are hopeful but really have no stability or firmness in their minds. It is an invocation from nature, as I may say; that is, some secret instinct impels men to flee naturally to God. But because scarcely one in a hundred relies on God's Word, they all call on God at hazard. They want to experience whether God is willing to help them and to succour their necessities; yet, as I said, there is no firm conviction in their hearts.

Such was the attitude of King Darius: *'Was your God not able to free you?'* he says, as if one could doubt the power of God. If he had said, 'Has your God freed you?' it would have been tolerable. For God is not bound by any rule that he must always rescue his people from death, as is well known. It lies in his choice. When, therefore, he yields his people to the will of the ungodly, his power is not diminished, for it depends simply on his will whether he shall save. But his power certainly ought not to be called in question. Hence we see that Darius was never truly converted; he knew nothing clearly about the true and only God but was overcome by blind fear which, whether he would or not, compelled him to ascribe the highest honour to the God of Israel. But this was not a free confession but forced.

He goes on now:

21 *Then Daniel spoke with the king, 'O King, live for ever.*
22 *My God sent his angel and shut the mouths of the lions, and they did not hurt me; because before him innocence* [or, "integrity"] *was found in me; and also before you, O King, I have committed no wrong.'*

Here Daniel replies modestly and pleasantly to the king at whose command he had been thrown into the den. He might justifiably have been angry and expostulated with him for deserting him so wickedly. For King Darius had found him a faithful servant, whose work had been useful to him. When he saw he was oppressed with unjust slanders, he did not oppose them so wholeheartedly as he should have done; in the end he was even broken down by the threats of his nobles and ordered Daniel to be thrown into the pit. So Daniel could, as I said, have complained of the king's cruelty and faithlessness. He did not do so, but hid the injury, for it was enough that by his liberation God's glory had been brilliantly celebrated. For the holy prophet strove for nothing else. He even prayed for the king's welfare. And although he used a common formula, yet it comes from his heart when he says, *'O King, live for ever'*; that is, 'May God prolong your life and bless you continually.' Many salute their kings in this way as an empty form — and even their associates. But there is no doubt at all that Daniel from his heart wished the king both long life and happiness.

Afterwards he adds, *'My God'*, he says, *'sent his angel and shut the mouth of the lions.'* Here we see that Daniel plainly ascribes the office of helping to angels in such a way that all the power rested with God. He says that he was saved by the hand and work of an angel; but he represents the angel the minister of his salvation, not its author. So *'It is God'*, he says, *'who sent an angel.'* We have frequently seen that the Chaldaeans spoke confusedly when they mentioned God. For they called him 'the holy gods'. But here Daniel solidly gives God alone his own glory. Nor does he here put forward a host of gods, according to the opinion always prevalent among the heathen. Therefore in the first place he declares the unity of God; then he adds that angels are at hand to help God's servants — but to do this inasmuch as it is a task laid upon them. Thus the whole praise of salvation rests with God alone; for the angels do not bring help to whomever they wish to help, nor are they moved by their own will; they only obey the rule of God.

We must also note what follows: *'God shut the mouth of the lions.'* For by these words the prophet teaches that lions and the most savage beasts are in the hand of God and are restrained by his secret curb; so that they may not attack nor be any way harmful, except so far as God permits. Let us know, then, that savage beasts are only harmful to us because God wishes to humble our pride. But let us also know that there is no beast so savage as to hurt us by claws or by teeth, except so far as God loosens their bridle.

This doctrine is extremely useful to know, for we tremble at the slightest danger, even at the rustle of a falling leaf. But because we must needs behold many dangers from different quarters (for on all sides we are surrounded by a hundred deaths), we shall be harassed by most wretched anxiety unless we remember that, not only is our life guarded by God, but that nothing is harmful to us which he himself does not direct by his choice and command. This should be extended even to the devils and to wicked and vicious men. For we know that the devil is always busied about our destruction and is like a roaring lion. For he runs about and seeks prey to devour, as says Peter in his First Epistle.[3] We see also how all the ungodly plot our deaths every moment and how their fury burns against us. But God, who can shut the mouths of lions, can likewise also bridle the devil and all the wicked, so that they shall not harm us apart from his permission. Even experience teaches us that both the devil and all the ungodly are restrained by him. For at every moment we should perish if his power were not interposed to repel the numberless injuries which hang over us. Therefore let us know that it is by the special benefit of God that even for one day we remain safe in the midst of the ferocity and rage of our enemies.

But Daniel says that the lions had done him no harm or injury because *'before God righteousness had been found in him'*. By which words he signifies

3. Mg., 1 Pet. 5:8.

that he had been preserved because God wished to assert his glory and the worship that he commanded by his Law. For here the prophet is not exalting his righteousness boastfully, but rather showing that he had been freed because God wanted to testify by certain and clear proof that he approved the worship for which Daniel had fought to the death. So we see that Daniel referred everything to that approval of God's service. The sum is that he had been the defender of a godly and holy cause and prepared to suffer death, not for some stupid idea, not on a rash impulse, not from confused zeal, but because he was convinced he was worshipping the living God. He says, then, that he was preserved because he was the defender of a godly and holy cause. That is the sum.

From this we may readily infer how dull are the papists who from this place and its like try to construct the righteousness of works and merits. 'Oh, Daniel was saved because righteousness before God was found in him. Therefore God repays anyone on account of the merits of works.' But first Daniel's purpose must be considered. For, as I have said already, he was not boasting of his merits but wanted the salvation which God gave him to be testimony to a true and pure worship, so that King Darius might be put to shame and all the superstitious shown to be impious. Above all, he wanted to protest about that sacrilegious edict; for Darius had arrogated to himself such supreme power as to abolish, so far as he could, all deity. So, to warn Darius, the prophet says that his cause was just.

To make the explanation easier, let it be noted that there is a difference between eternal salvation and special liberations. God frees us from eternal death and adopts us to the hope of eternal life, not because he finds some righteousness in us but because he freely elects us. Therefore he perfects his work in us without any respect of works. So far as eternal salvation is concerned, therefore, there can be no question of righteousness; for when God examines us, he finds nothing in us but matter for condemnation. But so far as particular liberations go, there God can look to a man's righteousness — not that that is our own property, but whom he governs by his Spirit to be obedient to his calling, to them he also reaches out his hand; and if they are in peril on account of trying to offer him obedience, he frees them. This is just as if one were saying that God favoured good causes. But this has nothing to do with merits. Hence, so far as this verse is concerned, the papists are too inept and childish when they elicit merits from it. Daniel meant nothing more than to assert the pure service of the one God; as if he were saying that God had not only had a care for him personally, but that there had been another reason for his liberation, that God had wanted to show by the event and by the trial that his cause was righteous.

He adds, '*And also before you, O King, I committed no crime.*' Certainly the prophet had violated the king's edict. Why then does he not honestly admit this? More, why does he insist that he has not sinned against the king? Simply, in that he had conducted himself faithfully in all his just duties, he could clear himself from the calumny, with which he knew he had been laden, that he had despised the king's authority. For Daniel was not so bound to the King of the Persians as that God could not claim for himself what could not be taken away from him. We know that earthly empires are established by God, but on the condition that he detracts nothing from himself but is alone supreme, and all rulers and the great in the world are forced into rank, subjected to his glory. Since, then, Daniel could not obey the king's edict without denying God, as we saw earlier, he was not sinning against the king when he steadfastly continued in his accustomed pious practice of praying to God three times a day.

And for this to be clearer we should remember Peter's words, 'Fear God, honour the king.'[4] These two things are interconnected and cannot be separated from one another. Hence, the fear of God must come first, if kings are to keep their authority. For if anyone overlooks God and begins at reverence for earthly princes, he is putting it back to front, making a perversion of the whole order of nature. So in the first place, let God be feared; earthly princes will keep their authority, yet in such a way that God is supreme, as I have already said.

Daniel therefore rightly defends himself here by saying that *'he had committed no fault against the king'* — precisely because he was compelled to obey the rule of God he disregarded what the king had commanded to the contrary. For earthly princes abdicate their power when they rise up against God — worse, they are unworthy to be accounted in the number of men. We ought rather to spit in their faces than obey them when they are so shameless as to want even to despoil God of his right and as it were occupy his throne, as if they could drag him out of heaven. So now we grasp the meaning of this passage.

He goes on:

23 *Then the king was very cheerful in himself* [or, 'about him']. *He ordered Daniel to be taken out of the cave. And Daniel was taken out of the cave; and no corruption* [or, 'injury'] *was found on him; because he believed* [or, 'trusted'] *in his God.*

Daniel confirms what he had before related about King Darius's feelings. Just as he had given way to anxiety in the palace, abstained from food and drink, and renounced all pleasures and delights, so now he rejoiced when he heard that the holy servant of God had been wonderfully saved from death.

Afterwards he adds, *And by the king's command Daniel was taken from*

4. Mg., 1 Pet. 2:17.

the cave; and no corruption was found on him. This cannot be ascribed to fortune. Therefore God was declaring his illustrious power when Daniel escaped safely, unharmed by the lions. He would have been torn to pieces had God not shut the lions' mouths. But it served not a little to magnify the miracle that no wound, no graze, was found on his body. That the lions had spared him came to pass by the secret help of God. And this also was more clearly known when his accusers were thrown into the cave and at once torn and devoured by the lions, as he adds a little after.

The reason which is given must be noted: *he was saved because he trusted in his God.* For it often happens that someone defending a good cause fares ill and is unsuccessful, because he has undertaken what was otherwise praiseworthy, trusting in his own plans and wisdom and energy. It is not surprising, then, if success is often denied to those who undertake to defend good causes, as appears in all the irreligious. For the histories of all periods bear witness that even those cherishing a just cause often fail. But this happens from their perverse self-confidence, in that their purpose was not to serve God; instead they looked for the praise and applause of the world. Ambition carried them away and they were satisfied with their own counsels. Hence came that saying of Brutus, 'Virtue is worthless.'[5] He thought he had been treated badly when he fought to preserve the liberty of the Roman people. He did not regard the gods as propitious but as unfeeling. As if God had to come to the help of one who had never hoped in him, never prayed to him! For we know how proud a spirit that man had. I put forward one example; but if we carefully weigh what motivates all the irreligious when they strenuously fight for good causes, we shall always find that ambition prevails. No wonder then if God leaves them in the crisis, for they are unworthy to experience his help.

Daniel declares that he had been kept safe *because he trusted in his God.* And this is the apostle's point in the eleventh chapter of Hebrews, when he says that by faith some were rescued, or saved, from the mouth of lions.[6] Thus he assigns the cause why Daniel escaped safely, and recalls us to faith. But here we must remember what the word 'believe' means and embraces. For the prophet is not simply teaching that he was preserved because he believed the God of Israel to be the true and only God, maker of heaven and earth, but because he committed his life to him, because he rested on his grace, because he was convinced that there would be a happy outcome if he served him. He says *he trusted in God* because Daniel was convinced that his life was in God's hand and that his hope in him was not in vain; and he faced danger bravely and intrepidly for the true worship of God.

We see then that the word 'believe' should not be taken so weakly as

5. Dio Cassius, *Roman History* 47:49.
6. Mg., Heb. 11:33.

267

the papists imagine — with their resultant ideas of 'implicit faith', and of 'dead faith' or 'unformed faith'. For they think faith is nothing but a confused apprehension of the Deity. When we grasp that there is a God, the papists think it is faith. But the Holy Spirit teaches us something very different. For we must remember what the apostle says, that we do not truly believe God unless we are convinced that he is the rewarder of all that seek him.[7] Therefore faith includes the conviction that God will not frustrate his worshippers.

Now we must bear in mind the way in which God is to be sought. God is not sought in foolish pride, as if by our merits we could put him under obligation to us. He is sought by faith; he is sought by humility; he is sought by invocation. When we are convinced that God is the rewarder of all that seek him and we know how he is to be sought, this is true faith. So Daniel did not doubt that God would rescue him because he did not doubt the teaching of godliness which he had learned from boyhood and in reliance on which he had always called upon God. This then was the cause of his liberation.

Meanwhile, it is also certain that Daniel did not believe God as if the outcome had already been told him. Rather he yielded his life to God because he was prepared to die. Before he had been cast into the cave and exposed to the lions Daniel could not know whether God wished to free him, as also we saw before with his friends: 'If God will, he will rescue us; but if not, we are prepared to worship him and not to obey your edict.'[8] And if Daniel had been told about the outcome, his constancy would not have been very praiseworthy. But because he was willing to encounter death fearlessly for the worship of his God and could deny himself and renounce the world, it was a genuine and serious testing of his faith and constancy. *He trusted in God,* not because he was looking for such a miracle, but because he knew he would be blessed if he stood firm in the pure worship of God. As Paul says, 'Christ is gain to me in living and in dying.'[9] So Daniel rested on God's help; but he shut his eyes to the outcome and was not over-anxious about his life. But because his mind was raised to the hope of a better life, even if he had to die a hundred deaths he would not cease to trust. For our faith stretches beyond the borders of this fleeting and corruptible life — as is well known to all the godly.

Afterwards there follows what I have already touched on:

24 *And the king commanded and they brought those men who had prepared* ['stirred up', 'clamoured'] *accusation* ['qui avoient dressé ceste calomnie']a *against him, that is, Daniel; and into the den* ['cave'] *of lions they cast them,*

---

7. Mg., Heb. 11:6.
8. Dn. 3:17-18.
9. Mg., Phil. 1:21.
a. qui . . . calomnie: 'who had drawn up this slander'.

their children, and their wives; and they had not got to the bottom [or, 'pave-
ment'] *of the cave when the lions dominated* [that is, 'prevailed'] *over them,
and broke all their bones.*

In this circumstance God's power in preserving Daniel shines more
clearly, in that those who had wickedly accused him were torn to pieces at
once by the lions. For if anyone should say that the lions were full, or that
there was some other reason why they did not devour Daniel, why, when he
was taken out, should those beasts be impelled by such rage as to tear and
devour not just one man but a great crowd? And none of the many nobles
escaped. What is more, their wives were brought, their children even. There
were hardly enough lions for such a shop-ful of meat. And yet every single
one perished. How did Daniel alone escape? We assuredly see that God
intended by this comparison to declare his power, lest any should object that
the lions left Daniel alone because they were full fed and had no appetite for
prey. For they would have been satisfied with three or four men. But they
devour men and women and children. From this it is clear that the mouths of
the lions had been curbed by God when Daniel was kept safe all night, but
these perished immediately they were thrown into the cave. For again we see
the beasts impelled to such a sudden rage that they did not wait until they had
reached the bottom but mauled them on the way down.

The rest we will leave until tomorrow.

*Grant, almighty God, since we have been created by you and
placed in this world and also nourished by your liberality to the
end that our lives may be consecrated to you, grant, I say, that we
may be prepared to live and to die for you, and not seek anything
else than to maintain the pure and sincere service of your Godhead; then, let us so rest on your help that we do not hesitate to
press through all dangers and to encounter death without delay
whenever it shall seem good to you; relying not only on your
enduring promise but on the many proofs which you have given in
the past, so that we may know that your power is alive today and
that you will be our liberator in whatever way, whether we live or
whether we die; so that nevertheless we may be blessed by going
on trusting in your name and witnessing a true confession, until
at last we are gathered into your heavenly kingdom, which you
have won for us by the blood of your only-begotten Son. Amen.*

Lecture 31

At the end of yesterday's lecture, Daniel's enemies, who had malignantly, enviously, and cruelly accused him, were, as soon as they were cast into the cave of lions, torn to pieces, along with their wives and children. From this, as was said, the miracle comes out the more clearly. Let us therefore again learn that lions are so ruled by God's hand that they cannot exercise their savagery everywhere or against everybody, but only when God arms them. For as it is said in Psalm 91, 'You shall walk upon the lion and the basilisk, and shall tread down the lion and the dragon.'[1] But on the other hand God warns unbelievers, in a prophet, 'Lions shall come against you if you leave your house.'[2] We see then that God restrains the savagery of lions as often as it seems good to him; but he excites them to rage when he wishes to punish men.

But we should not anxiously discuss whether it was a just punishment that the wives and children were cast into the cave. It seems a stable rule of equity that punishment should not be transferred to the innocent, especially when it is a matter of life or death. For although in all ages it has been accepted in well-ordered cities that many punishments involve children along with their parents, as in the confiscation of goods, when it is a question of violence and in the crime of lèse majesté, and moreover in criminal judgments, the infamy of the parents redounds to the children; yet it is far harsher to kill the children along with the parents when they could not be guilty of the same crime. But although this was not so usual, yet we should not condemn it out of hand. We see how God orders whole families to be exterminated from the earth as a sign

1. Mg., Ps. 91:13.
2. Mg., Am. 5:19.

270

of his detestation. But God is a just judge and always keeps moderation in his severity. Therefore this example cannot be condemned absolutely. We ought to leave it undecided. We know that Oriental kings practised a frightful and barbarous rule, or rather tyranny, over their peoples. So no-one need weary himself much over this question. King Darius was grieved that he had been so deceived. He therefore exacted punishment on the wicked slanderers, not only because they had oppressed Daniel unfairly, but because he himself was also affected by the injury. He wished to avenge himself rather than Daniel; and not satisfied with punishment in kind, he even carried off their children to the same execution.

He goes on:

25 *Then King Darius wrote to all the peoples and nations and languages which live in all the earth, 'May your peace be multiplied.*
26 *A decree has been set by me in all the dominion* [or, "the whole dominion"] *of my kingdom, that they may be fearing and trembling* [that is, "that they may fear and tremble"] *from the sight of the God of Daniel* [that is, "before the God of Daniel"]; *for he* [is] *the living God and remains for ever, and his kingdom shall not be destroyed and his dominion* [or, "power"] *even to the end;*
27 *Rescuing and saving and giving signs and miracles* ["wonderful works", as some translate it] *in heaven and on earth; who saved Daniel from the hand of the lions.'*

Here Daniel appends an edict of the king which he wished to proclaim. In this edict it was declared that he was so moved by Daniel's liberation that he ascribed supreme glory to the God of Israel. Yet I do not think that this proves the solid piety of the king, in the way that some interpreters here immoderately exalt him, as if he openly repented and embraced the pure religion prescribed in the Law of Moses. No such thing can be gathered from the words of the edict. And the facts themselves declare that his realm was never purged of superstitions. So King Darius allowed his subjects to worship idols and he did not cease to besmirch himself in the same way. But he wanted to put the God of Israel in the highest place, as if he could mix water and fire. And on this we have already spoken.

Irreligious men think they have done their duty by the true God if they do not utterly despise him but give him some place. In particular, when they set him above all the idols, they reckon that God will be satisfied. But this is useless; because, unless all superstitions are abolished, God will not at all keep his rights; for he does not allow associates. Hence, this place does not demonstrate a true and serious piety in King Darius. All that it is right to infer is that he was moved by the miracle to celebrate the glory and fame of the God of Israel through all his dependent regions. In short, just as King Darius was moved in this specific way, so he did not progress beyond this specific feeling. He did not acknowledge the power and goodness of God in every respect, but fastened on to that specimen that was set before his eyes. Therefore, he could not have a comprehensive knowledge of the God of Israel and devote himself to true and sincere piety. But, as I have already said, he wanted him to stand among other gods and indeed to stand out, yet so that he was not alone. But God repudiates this half-worship. So there is no reason why King Darius should be so highly praised.

Nevertheless, by his example he will condemn all those who today profess to be 'Catholic', or 'Christian', kings and 'Defenders of the Faith',[3] and yet not only oppress true godliness but even, so far as they can, undermine the whole service of God and would willingly extinguish his name from the world. They exert tyranny against all the godly; they establish impious superstitions by their cruelty. Darius will be the proper judge for them, and the edict that Daniel quotes will suffice to condemn them all.

Now he says *the edict was written to all the peoples and nations and tongues which lived in the whole earth*. We see that Darius not only wished to make God's power known to neighbouring peoples but took care to publish it far and wide. Therefore he wrote not only through Asia and Chaldaea but even to the Medes and Persians. He had never ruled in Persia, but his son-in-law made him an associate on the throne and his authority was valid there as well. And this is what is to be understood by *the whole earth*. It is not talking of the whole inhabited world but of the monarchy which covered nearly the whole of the East. For at that time the Medes and Persians ruled from the sea right to Egypt. Since their empire was so wide, Daniel has good cause to say that the edict was published through *the whole earth*.

'Peace be multiplied to you.' We know that kings mollify their subjects like this and use flattering prefaces to get their own way more easily — and also to keep their subjects more obedient. And it costs them nothing to wish their subjects peace. Yet, as I have already said, they often use it as a bait to catch their goodwill, so that the subjects may be ready to bear their yoke. By the word 'peace', as is well known, is meant a prosperous condition; as if he were saying, 'May you be well and happy.'

Afterwards he adds that *'the decree was set from his presence'*; that is, he commanded all his subjects on the strength of his authority. For this is a forceful expression. So, *'the edict has been set by me'* — that is, 'if my authority and power prevails among you, obey me in this matter'.

'That they may be all', he says, *'trembling'*; or, *'that all may tremble'*; *'and may fear before the God of Daniel.'* By 'fear' and 'trembling' he meant

3. See p. 4, n. 3.

nothing but 'reverence'. But he spoke like all the heathen do who dread the name of God. Yet he seems to want to express that the power of the God of Israel had been plainly visible, a power which really ought to affect everyone, so that they serve him reverently and with trembling and fear.

This way of speaking is seen to be taken from a right principle, since legitimate worship is never paid to God except when men are humbled. God often calls himself terrible, not because he wants to compel his servants by fear, but because, as was said, men's minds are never composed to reverence unless they earnestly understand and grasp the power of God, so that they are fearful of his judgment. But if fear alone is active in their minds, it cannot form them into godliness; for we must remember the saying in the Psalm, 'With you is propitiation, that you may be feared.'[4] God therefore cannot rightly be worshipped or feared unless we are convinced he is open to our requests, more, unless we are certain that he is propitious to us. Nevertheless, it is necessary for him who will humble the pride of his flesh to begin with fear and trembling. This is the meaning of the words used here *that all may fear and tremble before the God of Israel'*.

Moreover, the king calls him *'the God of Daniel'* — not one that Daniel had invented for himself, but one whose servant he was. We may quite rightly call Jupiter the god of the Greeks because he is the deification of their foolishness, and from this obtains fame and celebrity in the rest of the world. Nevertheless, Jupiter and Minerva and all that host of false gods take their name from their origin. There is another reason for King Darius calling him whom Daniel worshipped *'the God of Daniel'*. He is also called 'the God of Abraham', not because he takes his authority as it were on sufferance from Abraham, but because he revealed himself to Abraham.

Let us explain this more clearly. Why was he called 'the God of Daniel' rather than 'the God of the Babylonians?' Precisely because Daniel, as he had learned the Law of Moses, purely worshipped the God who had made his covenant with Abraham and the holy fathers and who had adopted the Israelites to be his own. This, then, depended on the worship prescribed in the Law, but the worship depended on the covenant. Hence, the name of Daniel is not put here as if he had been free to invent or imagine a god, but because he worshipped the God who had revealed himself in his Word. In short, this expression ought to be resolved into this, that all may fear the God who made his covenant with Abraham and his seed and who chose that people peculiar to himself, who taught the way of true and legitimate service and showed it in his Law, and whom Daniel worshipped. So now we grasp what this means.

Therefore, let us learn to distinguish the true God from all idols and inventions of men if we want our worship to be approved. For many think

4. Mg., Ps. 130:4.

they worship God, yet only wander about in all sorts of errors and are not attached to the one true God. But it is perverse, nothing but a profanation of true piety, to worship God so confusedly. We must hold to the distinction that I made and keep our minds always enclosed within the confines of the Word, lest we wander from the true God — that is, if we really want to keep him and to follow the religion which pleases him. I say that we must keep within the confines of the Word and not turn away from it in any direction. For we shall at once encounter innumerable deceptions of the devil unless we keep ourselves, so to say, bound to the Word.

As for Darius, he of course acknowledged him to be the supreme God; but, as I have already said, he did not give up the fictitious and perverted cults to which he was accustomed. But such a mixture is intolerable before God.

He adds that *'he is living and remains for ever'*. He certainly here seems to reduce all false gods to nothing. But it has already been said, and the event itself shows clearly enough, that the heathen lift up their minds to the supreme God in such a way that they fade away at once. If they steadfastly acknowledged the true God they would at once have done with all inventions. But they think it enough for God to get the highest place. Meanwhile they add lesser gods to him, so that he is hidden in a crowd, so to say, even if they ascribe him a certain eminence. Such was the reason and such the purpose of Darius that he held no sincere or pure view of the unique essence of God but thought the highest power lay with the God of Israel, while other nations might serve their own gods. Thus we see that he did not leave the superstitions he had imbibed from childhood. And therefore there is no reason to praise his piety, except in this 'specific act', as they call it. Yet God extorted from his lips the confession in which his nature is described to us.

He calls him *'the living God'*, not only because he has life in himself, but from himself, and because he is also the fount and origin of life. The adjective should therefore be taken actively; that God not only lives but has life from himself; next, he is vivifying, that is, there is no life outside him and apart from him.

Afterwards he adds that *'he remains in perpetuity'*. Thus he distinguishes him from all creatures, in which there is nothing firm or stable. For we know that not only is everything under heaven liable to manifold changes, but even heaven itself. Therefore God differs from all creatures in that he suffers no change but perpetually remains like himself.

He adds that *'his kingdom is not destroyed and his dominion is unto the end'*. Here he more clearly expresses what he had said before about the firm status of God. God not only abides in his essential being, but also exercises his power in the whole world and, because he governs the world by his power, upholds all things. For if he had said only that God abides perpetually, the thought could have crept into our minds (wicked and restricted that we are) that God in his essential being is not liable to change — but without our grasping that his power is everywhere diffused. So this explanation is noteworthy, when Darius expressly says that 'God's kingdom is not destroyed and his dominion is unto the end.'

In the second place he calls God the liberator. Those who fasten on this edict as a shining testimony of piety say that Darius was speaking in a gospel sort of way and that he was a herald of God's mercy. But, as has already been said, Darius never embraced the comprehensive teaching of Scripture that God mercifully cherishes his own and helps them, because he is merciful and deems them worthy of his fatherly favour. King Darius did not grasp the cause. He had seen Daniel's deliverance, a specific example of God's grace. Thus Darius feels only partially that God is propitious to his servants and is ready to save and deliver them.

But this would be weak unless at the same time the cause is added: *'therefore God is the liberator',* because he has deigned to elect his servants, and because he has testified that he would be their Father; because he is open to prayer; because he pardons when they sin. Unless the hope of liberation is founded on the free adoption and mercy of God, it will be a certain partial knowledge and inefficacious. Darius does not here speak as if he had been taught truly and rightly about God's mercy, but only says that he is the liberator of his own. He rightly makes the specific inference that God is liberator *'in that he saved Daniel from the hand of the lions',* that is, 'from the power and rage of the lions'. Darius reasons correctly, I say, when from one example he deduces the fuller doctrine that it is in God's power to save and rescue his own as often as he will. But yet, while acknowledging the visible power of God in one action, the principal cause or spring escapes him — that God embraced Daniel, just as the other sons of Abraham, and saved him by his fatherly favour.

Hence, for this doctrine to be useful to us and touch our minds efficaciously — that God is the liberator — we must in the first place decide that we are received into his grace under the terms that he pardons us and does not deal with us as we deserve, but treats us gently like children, according to his immeasurable kindness. This, then, we must remember.

Finally, he says that *'he gives signs and wonders in heaven and on earth'.* This should be referred to his rule and dominion, which was mentioned earlier. But Darius goes on dwelling on the present spectacle. He had seen that Daniel had dwelt safely with the lions; he had seen all the others torn to pieces; these were manifest tokens of God's power. Rightly, therefore, he says that *'he gives miracles and signs'.* But there is no doubt at all that Darius had then also been told of the other signs which had been done before he had obtained the monarchy. Without doubt he had heard of all that had happened to King Nebuchadnezzar and to King Belshazzar, whom Darius himself had killed to occupy his kingdom. So he collects many testimonies of God's power, along

275

with the way he had shown his glory in the act of rescuing Daniel. In sum, if Darius had renounced his superstitions, it would have been a pure and open confession and completely godly. Because he did not cease to serve his false gods but clung on always to his accustomed pollutions, his piety cannot be praised; nor can a true and earnest conversion be inferred from his edict. This is the sum.

Now he goes on:

28 *But Daniel himself prospered in the reign of Darius and in the reign of Cyrus of Persia.*

Or 'he crossed over': for צלח, *zalah,* properly means 'to cross over', and the sense is metaphorical when it is taken for 'prospering'. However that may be, I do not doubt that here there is a tacit antithesis between the kingdom of the Persians and the Chaldaean monarchy; that is, to speak more briefly and clearly, between a twofold condition of Daniel. For Daniel had sometimes declined under Nebuchadnezzar, as was said; later, in the end, when the destruction of the monarchy was imminent, he again came into prominence; but during nearly the whole of the Chaldaean reign he was obscure and despised. Of course, everyone had heard he was a remarkable and great prophet, but he was rejected from the court; and when for some time he had sat at the king's gate and had enjoyed high honours, he was suddenly dismissed. So as long as the Chaldaean monarchy lasted Daniel was not in great esteem or honour. Under the monarchy of the Persians and Medes, however, he prospered; that is, he held high rank continually. Cyrus and Darius were not so negligent as to forget at once how wonderfully God had worked by his hand.

I like the term 'crossed over', because it indicates, as I said, a continuing career of honour. Not only had King Darius exalted him, but Cyrus also, when he had heard of his fame, kept him in his presence among his nobles. And it is clear enough that he left Babylon and went elsewhere. Yet it is probable that he was not long with the Medes. For a little later, Darius, or Cyaxares, died, and, since he had no male heir, the whole power passed to Cyrus alone (who was also his nephew, through his sister, and also his son-in-law, because he had married his daughter). There is no doubt that Daniel here commemorates the favour and kindness of God towards him, for it was not a usual comfort for exiles to obtain high favour among foreign and barbarous peoples, and to enjoy the greatest degree of honour, with everyone reverencing him. God therefore softened the sadness of exile with this comfort.

Again, Daniel is thinking not only of himself personally but of the purpose of his high rank. For God intended his own name to be published and celebrated through all those regions where Daniel was notable. For none could cast eyes on him without thinking of the glory and power of the God of Israel. This is what Daniel wanted to signify.

On the other hand, there can be no doubt that the loss of his fatherland was a heavy burden and bitter to him — not as it usually is to others, but because the land of Canaan was the peculiar inheritance of the people of God. When, therefore, Daniel was stolen away and taken far off, that is, to Media, and finally to Persia, so that there was no hope of return, without doubt he mourned continually. For he preferred that pledge of God's grace and fatherly adoption, the land of Canaan, to all the heights of splendour among the heathen. Without doubt there was engraven on his heart what had once been written by David: 'I would rather be in the courts of the Lord than among the highest wealth of the wicked'; and, 'I would rather be the lowest in the house of God than live in the tents of the ungodly.'⁵ This Daniel had learned.

And it was no empty praise when Ezekiel called him one of the three most holy men who had lived from the beginning of the world.⁶ It was a very great thing, when he was still a youth, or even in middle age, to be joined with Job and Noah, as the third in a rare, an almost incredible, sanctity. Since he was such a man, we cannot doubt that he was affected with the deepest sorrow when he saw himself destined to eternal exile, with no hope of returning and worshipping God in his temple and offering sacrifices with the others. But yet he was not ungrateful to God and wished to testify that he was aware of his uncommon benevolence that, when he was an exile, torn from his native land, even treated contemptuously among the captives, he was nevertheless also treated with honour among the Medes and Persians. This therefore was his straightforward meaning.

It is certain that, after the death of Darius, as I have just said, Cyrus succeeded to the whole monarchy; and we shall see afterwards in its place that Daniel lived with Cyrus, who reigned nearly thirty years. Thus a long time elapsed between his death and the death of Darius. It did not happen without the wonderful counsel of God that a change of kingdoms did not upset Daniel's state, as often happens. (For a fresh sovereignty, as we know, is like a complete changing round of the world.) But Daniel always kept his rank, so that God's goodness might be visible in him, and that wherever he went he might bear a testimony in himself of the grace of God.

I will not go any further. Tomorrow we will embark on the prophesying.

Grant, almighty God, since you wish us, surrounded as we are by the many errors of men, to bear witness to your power, that today we may not be blind in the great light which is shown to us by the

5. Mg., Ps. 84:11, i.e., 84:10.
6. Mg., 14:14, i.e., Ezk. 14:12-20.

Sun of righteousness, Christ your Son; and that also we may not be ashamed to profit from the words of a heathen, untrained in your Law but taught by only one miracle to celebrate your name magnificently; therefore, that we may learn from his example to acknowledge you not only as the true supreme God but also as unique. And even as you have bound us to yourself by sealing your covenant with the blood of your only-begotten Son, grant that we may cleave to you with a true faith and so renounce all the clouds of errors that we may always be intent on the light to which you invite us and by which you lead us; until we arrive at last at the sight of your glory and majesty, so that, conformed to you, we may enjoy at last the substance of that glory which now we see only in part. Amen.

Index of Subjects

Index of Names

Index of Biblical References

Index of Words

Hebrew and Aramaic Words

298

Hebrew and Aramaic Transliterations

Greek Words

Latin Words

INDEX OF WORDS